Patterns of

ANTI-DEMOCRATIC THOUGHT

THE MACMILLAN COMPANY
NEW YORK · BOSTON · CHICAGO · DALLAS
ATLANTA · SAN FRANCISCO
MACMILLAN AND CO., Limited
LONDON · BOMBAY · CALCUTTA · MADRAS
MELBOURNE
THE MACMILLAN COMPANY
OF CANADA, Limited
TORONTO

Patterns of
ANTI-DEMOCRATIC
THOUGHT

*An Analysis and a Criticism, with Special Reference to
the American Political Mind in Recent Times*

DAVID SPITZ

*Department of Political Science
Ohio State University*

New York: The Macmillan Company

1949

For permission to quote passages from their respective publications I am grateful to the following authors, editors, publishers, and literary executors:

George Allen & Unwin, Ltd.: Salvador de Madariaga, *Anarchy or Hierarchy* (1937).
Appleton-Century-Crofts, Inc.: Edward M. Sait, *Political Institutions: A Preface* (1938).
B. H. Blackwell, Ltd.: Karl Pearson, *Nature and Nurture* (copyright Dulau and Co. 1910).
Dr. Ernst P. Boas: Franz Boas, *The Genetic Basis for Democracy* (1939).
The Clarendon Press, Oxford: Ernest Barker, *Nietzsche and Treitschke* (1914); G. W. F. Hegel, *Philosophy of Right,* transl. T. M. Knox (1945).
Columbia University Press: Otto Klineberg, *Negro Intelligence and Selective Migration* (1935).
The John Day Company: James Burnham, *The Managerial Revolution* (1941) and *The Machiavellians* (1943).
Mr. Lawrence Dennis: *The Coming American Fascism* (copyright Harper & Brothers, 1936) and *The Dynamics of War and Revolution* (copyright The Weekly Foreign Letter, 1940).
Dodd, Mead & Company: Houston Stewart Chamberlain, *The Foundations of the Nineteenth Century* (copyright The John Lane Co., 1910).
Victor Gollancz, Ltd.: Aurel Kolnai, *The War Against the West* (1938).
Harcourt, Brace & Company: Vilfredo Pareto, *The Mind and Society* (1935); Vernon L. Parrington, *Main Currents in American Thought* (1927 and 1930).
Harper & Brothers: Lawrence Dennis, *The Coming American Fascism* (1936); Dorothy Fosdick, *What Is Liberty?* (1939); Melville J. Herskovits, *The Myth of the Negro Past* (1941); William R. Inge, *Labels and Libels* (1929); Albert Jay Nock, *Memoirs of a Superfluous Man* (1943).
Harvard University Press: William Haber, *Industrial Relations in the Building Industry* (1930).
Henry Holt & Company: Otto Klineberg, *Social Psychology* (1940); Robert R. LaMonte and H. L. Mencken, *Men Versus the Man* (1910).
Houghton Mifflin Company: Irving Babbitt, *Democracy and Leadership* (1924) and *The New Laokoon* (1910).
Alfred A. Knopf, Inc.: H. L. Mencken, *Notes on Democracy* (1926).
Little, Brown & Company: Ludwig Bauer, *Leopold the Unloved* (1935).
Louisiana State University Press: R. M. MacIver, *Leviathan and the People* (1939).
The Macmillan Company: Frank H. Hankins, *An Introduction to the Study of Society* (1928); Walter Lippmann, *The Phantom Public* (copyright Harcourt, Brace & Co., 1925); R. M. MacIver, *The Web of Government* (1947); Salvador de Madariaga, *Anarchy or Hierarchy* (1937); William B. Munro, *The Invisible Government* (1928); Paul Popenoe and R. H. Johnson, *Applied Eugenics* (1920).
Macmillan & Company, Ltd.: Francis Galton, *Inquiries into Human Faculty and Its Development* (1883); R. M. MacIver, *Community* (2nd ed., 1920); A. C. Pigou, *The Economics of Welfare* (1920).
Marshall Jones Company: Ralph Adams Cram, *Convictions and Controversies* (1935) and *Towards the Great Peace* (1922).
Modern Review: Rudolf Hilferding, "State Capitalism or Totalitarian State Economy," I (1947), 266–271.
W. W. Norton & Company, Inc.: H. S. Jennings, *The Biological Basis of Human Nature* (1930).
Mr. Frederick Osborn: Gladys C. Schwesinger, *Heredity and Environment* (copyright The Macmillan Company, 1933).
Rinehart & Company, Inc.: R. M. MacIver, *Society: A Textbook of Sociology* (1937); Joel Seidman, *The Needle Trades* (1942).
Charles Scribner's Sons: Madison Grant, *The Passing of the Great Race* (4th ed., 1929); George Santayana, *Dialogues in Limbo* (1926) and *Reason in Society* (Vol. II of *The Life of Reason,* 2nd ed., 1936); Lothrop Stoddard, *The Rising Tide of Color Against White World-Supremacy* (1920).
University of Pennsylvania Press: A. D. Lindsay, *The Essentials of Democracy* (1929).
Vanguard Press, Inc.: Ralph Barton Perry, *Puritanism and Democracy* (1944).
Yale University Press: Raymond Dodge and Eugen Kahn, *The Craving for Superiority* (1931).

To my parents

Geza and Irma Spitz

*for their understanding
and selfless devotion*

I shall be asked if I am a prince or a legislator, to write on politics. I answer that I am neither, and that is why I do so. If I were a prince or a legislator, I should not waste time in saying what wants doing; I should do it, or hold my peace.

—ROUSSEAU

Foreword

From the tragic experiences of our own and earlier times men have learned a simple yet crucial truth: that tyranny is the handmaiden of power divorced from responsibility. It is the meaning and the value of democracy that it links power with responsibility and thus enforces limits on the exercise of coercive authority, so that the conditions of freedom rather than of tyranny are assured.

Yet in the history of ideas—as well, indeed, as in the history of political institutions—men have long sought to dissolve that union. From a variety of motives and for a variety of ideas and ideals, they have argued for some form of subjection of the many to the few. Their arguments—and the "facts" and philosophies involved in their arguments—are the subject matter of this book.

It is a subject that both merits and demands exploration. So long as men advance a theory of politics that seeks to justify the enslavement or the subordination of the masses of mankind, so long ought the intelligence and sensibilities of free men rebel; for those who cherish freedom know they dare deny it to none lest it be denied to themselves. And so long as there are those who plead special privilege as a matter of "right," who claim power without accountability to those over whom that power is to be exercised, just so long must other men investigate their credentials to that claim.

This book, then, begins with a faith in democracy, with a conviction that freedom is the province of all men, not simply the prerogative of a chosen few. And it seeks, in terms of that philosophy, to inquire into the nature and validity of the arguments leveled against that faith.

A few methodological notes may be in order. This book is an inquiry into the theory of *political* government. Throughout, therefore, the word "democracy" is employed only in a political sense, not as a social, economic, or other institutional concept.

Since this book is concerned only with the *arguments* that deny or repudiate democracy, no attempt will be made to treat individuals or organizations as such. Though both are necessarily involved, they enter only as they illustrate the particular doctrine under examination. Communism, for example, is not approached as a systematic

vii

body of anti-democratic theory; its central aspects, however, are dealt with as part of the more general attack on democracy in Chapters 2 and 9. For purposes of simplification, each major chapter is divided into four sections. Sections I and II endeavor to answer the question: What is the precise nature of the anti-democratic argument? Sections III and IV attempt to answer the question: Is it valid? Though the emphasis throughout is on contemporary and recent American thought, it should be understood—as the first section of each chapter, indeed, tries to make clear—that the arguments treated here are representative of a broader and age-old attitude.

Many of the things said in this book have been said before. They need to be said again. Though the reaffirmation of great truths will not in itself ensure freedom, a neglect of those truths will foster tyranny. An awareness of those truths may reinforce allegiance to man's greatest heritage—democracy and freedom.

DAVID SPITZ

Columbus, Ohio
August 9, 1948

Acknowledgments

No words of acknowledgment can adequately convey the sense of my indebtedness to Professor R. M. MacIver of Columbia University, who has not only guided me at every stage in the development of this study but has provided that intellectual challenge which compels a re-examination of fundamental presuppositions. Perhaps he will understand when I say that to have worked with him has been an immensely rewarding experience.

I am hardly the less indebted to my friend, Morris Watnick, whose broad knowledge and exacting criticism have been of immeasurable assistance. Professor Arthur W. Macmahon of Columbia University, Professor Harry N. Rivlin of Queens College, Dr. Charles A. Welsh, formerly of the Antitrust Division of the Department of Justice, and Professor George Catlin, sometime of Cornell University, have read the manuscript in whole or in part, and I am grateful to them for their several suggestions. Among those friends who have talked and read the subject with me for hours on end, I want especially to thank Rubin Maloff, Thomas Larson, Howard Rosen, Joel Weinberg, and my brother Herbert Spitz. No mention of acknowledgments would be complete without the inclusion of my revered teacher, the late Professor Morris R. Cohen, who taught me to appreciate the refinements of logical analysis, even in the face of the broad sweep of philosophic systems. I want to thank, too, for their typing of the final draft, Mrs. Alice Dunlap and Miss Betty Le Sueur, and, for needed research facilities, the librarians of the Library of Congress. It seems hardly necessary to add that none of the foregoing is in any wise responsible for errors of omission or commission; these are mine alone.

What this book owes to my wife, only those who have known us can fully understand. Her great tolerance and warm friendship did much to sustain us during the many months when the doctrines of anti-democratic thought tyrannized our lives.

Contents

8

The Concept of Natural Aristocracy 191

9

Authority and the Restrictive Way of Life 219

l

Part One

INTRODUCTORY

1

The Nature and Categories of Anti-Democratic Thought

I

THE NATURE OF ANTI-DEMOCRATIC THOUGHT: DEFINITIONS

Language is a medium of intellectual exchange; it is also a method of concealment, an artifice men employ to deceive others as well as themselves. We speak, for example, of justice, but we mean retribution or, if we are not to give but to receive, mercy. We insist on the governance of reason, but the appeal is peculiarly to *our*, not *your*, reason. We resort to the sacred name of freedom, but by freedom we generally—and indeed necessarily—mean a liberty for ourselves to do this and a restraint on another's liberty to do that. The same word, as Voltaire observed, does not always signify the same thing.

What is true of language in general is true of democracy in particular. Few words in our political lexicon have so challenged the logic and the ingenuity of men, and few have proved so provocative and protean. Even a passing glance at the variety of doctrines enunciated in our contemporary literature would reveal that there are almost as many definitions of democracy as there are political thinkers, and that this diversity of views concerns many of the things that democracy is *not* as well as everything that democracy conceivably might be. In fact, so extreme have been some of the theorists in this former category that one is left at times with the remarkable paradox that there is no necessary contradiction between democracy and dictatorship at all, that democracy, "far from being opposed to Dictatorship, is a mode of Dictatorship," [1] and that there can be a "totalitarian democracy" [2] just as there can be a "democratic dictatorship." [3]

With such semantic exertions it is, of course, difficult to argue. They involve a kind of convoluted yet rigid adherence to a faith which one can disbelieve, but not easily debate. Yet if democracy and dictatorship are to have any real and distinct meanings of their own, there must, it is plain, be some few essential criteria that will enable us clearly to distinguish the one from the other. There must be some sharply defined qualities uniquely characteristic of democracy that are not present, at least not in the same way, in dictatorship and other kinds of oligarchical governments. These alone are the working elements that need concern us, for these alone will point the way to an understanding of democracy and anti-democratic thought. [4]

Analyzed from this standpoint, the democratic state is seen to contain at least two central ingredients that crucially set it apart from all other forms of state. One is the free play of conflicting opinions. The other is the constitutional responsibility of the rulers to the ruled. Why this is so we shall endeavor to make clear in the course of our exposition throughout this book. Here it is necessary only to point out that democracy, alone of the forms of state, completely and ineluctably depends on the unrestrained organization of opposing views, that democracy, alone of the systems or modes of government, makes conflict in ideas the very basis of the state. Through this primary liberty of opinion those who temporarily sit on the thrones of power are held accountable to those over whom that power is exercised, and men, free to speak their individual minds and to organize the more effectively to express their divergent beliefs, share equally as citizens in the formulation of the general conditions under which they are to live.

Several important corollaries follow from this recognition. It means, in the first place, that democracy is not to be identified with a particular way of governing, whether by the mass, the mob, or the majority, but that it is "primarily a way of determining who shall govern and, broadly, to what ends." [5] It means, secondly, that those who are vested with the power of determination must be not the one or the few but at least the many. It means, further, that as a practical instrument for determining the will of the many, the majority decision must prevail. And it means that minorities shall at all times remain free to oppose, to organize, and eventually—when sufficient support is commanded—to become in turn the dominant majority. Majority rule, that is to say, is the inescapable necessity of the democratic state, but it is always a fluctuating and temporary, never a fixed, majority; always minorities must be free to pursue their contrary ways and to strive unhampered for the control of political power. These together are the unique as they are the fundamental components of democracy. Corresponding practices and attitudes exist in no other form of state.

Regarded in these terms, the doctrines of anti-democratic thought are, simply, those ideas which deny the possibility or challenge the desirability of democracy: the first by insisting that the free play of conflicting opinions *cannot* have any fundamental impact on the policy and composition of government; the second by urging that the free play of conflicting opinions *should not* have any fundamental impact on the policy and composition of government. Anti-democratic theories would, further, and in consequence, argue that rulers could not or should not be rendered responsible to those over whom they rule: that the few rather than the many must or should command the instruments of political power, that minorities rather than majorities must or should prevail.

These crucial aspects of oligarchical thought underscore a further and no less significant point of contrast, one that pertains to the scope, as distinguished from the locus, of political power. This is the fact that democracy is necessarily a limited state; oligarchy may be a totalitarian one. Men, despite the authority of Hegel, dwell without as well as within the state. They pursue activities outside the jurisdiction of the political sphere alone. They think and they live as social, not merely as political, beings. Democracy, because it limits the range of government intervention, because it largely excludes from the purview of the state the control of the area of opinion, indeed the area of culture itself, constitutionally sanctions and confirms this appreciation of extra-political realities; it makes the distinction between state and community plain and emphatic. Oligarchy, on the other hand, may or may not observe this distinction. Where it does not, as is always the case in totalitarian dictatorships, for example, opinion and the entire realm of culture are absorbed within the dragnet of the all-inclusive state. Men are not free to hold and to express conflicting ideas. Ideas are not free to mold and to correct the policies of government. Where oligarchy does observe this distinction between state and society, as it did in the enlightened absolutisms of the eighteenth century, for instance, opinion is free but at the same time indeterminative; it does not set the ends or select the personnel of government. Where either of these conditions prevails, there democracy does not exist.[6]

Thus we see from another standpoint the vital difference between the democratic and the oligarchic conceptions. In the one case opinion is free; in the other it may be controlled. In democracy this free opinion makes and unmakes governments, influences and shapes the broad channels of public policy. In oligarchy, whether opinion be free or restricted, it is indeterminative as a primary force in the political process. It may be invoked formally to sustain the party or group in power; it does not direct or immediately influence them. Democracy, and democracy alone, depends for its survival on the free operation of opposing views. Oligarchy recognizes but one view, that of the rulers. Here is the crucial demarcation of democratic from oligarchical thought. Here is the matrix of all anti-democratic ideas.

II

THE CATEGORIES OF ANTI-DEMOCRATIC THOUGHT

From this core of opposition to the free play of conflicting opinions many and diverse patterns have been spun. The argument of Plato, for example, is not that of Machiavelli, nor is either in every respect the argument of Mosca or Michels. The constructs of the Puritan theocracy are not those of the "Nordic aristocracy"; the theory of the best is not that of the *Führerprinzip*. Men differ in the doctrines they espouse, and often appreciably. Men may also agree. The mind of Burnham, for example, repeats in some wise the scriptures of Marx. The mind of Dennis pursues closely the instructions of Pareto, and of Thrasymachus the Greek Sophist before him. There is continuity as well as difference in the intricacies of the human mind. No one generality can encompass the many facets of its expression.

Further complications confront the classifier. Categories overlap. The same man, Santayana for instance, may hold several doctrines. To treat men, in consequence, is to compel repetition of ideas; no one man, moreover, can be held adequately to represent several views. To treat doctrines, on the other hand, is to make impossible a fair and rounded estimate of a person's thought; it is also artificially to separate concepts that may closely be allied. Yet our central interest, it is clear, is not in the individual but in his ideas. A theorist survives by virtue of the doctrines he begets; his progeny, not his personal qualities, invite the attention of mankind. We shall not attempt here, accordingly, to evaluate a man as a total philosopher; we shall be concerned with him only as he is the representative of an idea, only, that is, as he effectively embodies a particular doctrine of anti-democratic thought. And in the delineation of our categories we must consider not merely the distinctions that make them meaningful, but the agreements that cause them to overlap.

With these several factors in mind, the doctrines of anti-democratic thought may be classified, broadly, according to the scheme of the table below. We note first the general demarcation of all anti-democratic theories into two major headings: (*a*) the impossibility of democracy, and (*b*) the undesirability of democracy. Under the first of these headings we include all those doctrines that hold democracy to be impossible of attainment because, whether we will it or no, political power always resides in the hands of a few, a ruling class. This ruling class does not, in this interpretation, rest on the acquiescence of the people; it does not move with the changing tides of opinion. It rules, and rules irresponsibly, in accordance with the necessary dictates of unalterable imperatives. This, say the theorists of this school, is the way political power has always been determined; it is the way it is determined today; so, they conclude, it is the way—and the only way—that political power will be determined in the future.

Of the several expressions of this doctrine two are pre-eminent and merit particular attention. One is the theory of the ruling class as organizational necessity. In this view, perhaps best exemplified in recent American thought by James Burnham, democracy is held

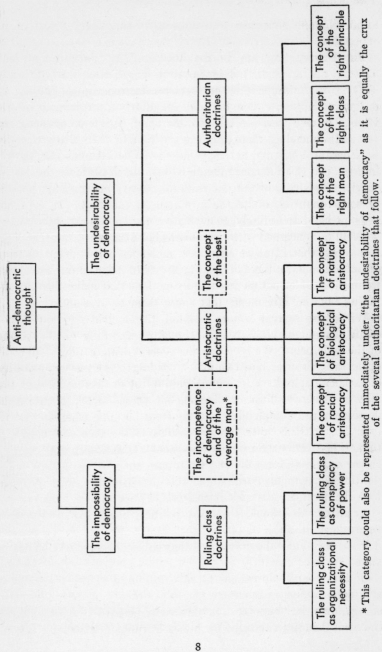

* This category could also be represented immediately under "the undesirability of democracy" as it is equally the crux of the several authoritarian doctrines that follow.

8

to be impossible because of certain organizational imperatives inherent in the social structure. Every society, it is noted, is organized in a particular way, and in the process of organization some one factor or characteristic becomes central. Those who control this key factor (for Burnham it is the economic factor) control the organization, and those who control the organization are held to be the masters of that society. It is not, therefore, by virtue of being the best that the ruling class comes to power; nor is it in consequence of the aspirations and activities of men. The command of power, according to this interpretation, is always determined by the nature of the social organization; it is the necessary concomitant of key functional control.

The second and somewhat more diversified argument against the possibility of democracy is the theory of the ruling class as conspiracy of power. In this construction, of which Lawrence Dennis is an able exponent, it is not the organization of the social order but the quality of men that is the decisive factor. Those who rule are not so much a class as they are a clique, a group of power-holding or power-seeking men who conjoin force with ambition, deceit with the will-to-dominate. They are not men who sit idly or patiently by in the hope or expectation that their unique qualities will be recognized and rewarded. Instead they ruthlessly employ those qualities in an irresistible drive for power that will give them control of the state and therewith the benefits of that control. That this category is in no sense completely divorced from the preceding theory of organizational necessity is evidenced by the simple consideration that those who control the key factor in the economy may also be those who strive for political power, just as those who conspire for political mastery may seek to control the economic factor as well. But this we must leave for later treatment.

Under our second major heading, the undesirability of democracy, we include all those doctrines that accept the possibility of the democratic state but reject as undesirable its operation and its consequences. The argument is not that public opinion cannot but that public opinion should not exert a determining influence on the policy and composition of government, that the few should rule irresponsible to the many. In the aristocratic conception these few are the best, that superior minority available and competent to rule, as compared with the inferior mass or majority, perhaps equally available but far less competent to decide matters of state. The peculiar problems involved in this theory or concept of the best are primarily two: how are the best defined? and how are the best selected? Before inquiring into the nature and validity of the replies to these questions, however, it is important to emphasize the central doctrine on which both the aristocratic and authoritarian theories rest. This is the alleged incompetence of democracy and of the average man.

Democracy, according to the theorists of this view—of which Ralph Adams Cram is an adequate representative—is the rule of the average man; and the average man, it is held, is plainly an irrational and incompetent man. He is, indeed almost by definition, a mediocrity, and as such cannot be expected to judge wisely of the numerous and complex affairs of state. To entrust to this average man, in consequence, the great and small everyday issues of government, is to ensure irrationality and incompetence of decision. Only where the determination of policy is restricted to wise and competent rulers, it is argued, can the greatness and well-being of the state be secured. Where it is not, where, as in democracy, the mediocrity of the many overthrows the superior leadership of the few, inefficiency and incoherence inescapably follow. This, the theorists of this interpretation insist, is the nature and the result of democracy. It is the denial of wisdom and the institutionalization of decline. This indictment of democracy has a unique claim to prominence not merely because it is fundamental to other anti-democratic doctrines which build upon it, but also, as we shall see, because it is advanced in lesser or greater degree, and without a full awareness or acceptance of the aristocratic or authoritarian corollaries, by friendly as well as hostile critics of democracy.

Of the many specific formulations of the aristocratic doctrine three warrant delineation and extended analysis. One is the theory of racial aristocracy, a concept given effective and representative articulation in the writings of its leading American exponent, Madison Grant. Here democracy is condemned because it ignores what are held to be certain basic inequalities inherent in racial differences among men, thereby denying to the racially superior their rightful role as leaders of the state. The physical factors that visibly distinguish the races of mankind are not, in this view, the only criteria of difference. Races vary also, it is argued, in mental capacity and social astuteness. The white race is declared to be superior to the colored races, and within the white race there are said to be several grades or levels of superiority. Of these, according to the theorists of racial aristocracy, the "Nordic race" is incomparably the best. What the right state should do, in consequence, is to formalize these differences into the fabric of the political system, thus placing the Nordics alone in positions of power. Democracy's failure to do this is, for the theorists of this school, the guarantee of its own destruction.

Somewhat similar to this view is the theory of biological aristocracy, a concept expounded, for example, by E. M. Sait. In this interpretation it is the differences within rather than between races that are the truly crucial consideration. The racial theory may or may not be accepted, but the principle that inequalities of intellect and ability among men derive from familial inheritance alone, is. Individual intelligence and capacities, it is held, are innate and cannot be acquired. They are transmitted biologically from parent to child, thus securing a continuity of superior intelligence, as well of course as a continuity of mental inferiority. Through the unrestricted operation of the social ladder in a democracy, the argument runs, the best rise to the top (i.e., of the social, not the political, ladder) and the worse congregate at the bottom. Since the best are few and the worse many, and since like mates with like to produce like, in time, these theorists say, democracy finds itself with two disparate classes: one a biological and therefore true aristocracy, the other a degenerate and incompetent mass. If the state is to survive, accordingly, political power must be concentrated in the hands of the superior few and control denied to the many. The refusal of democracy to heed this injunction is, in this construction, sufficient ground for its repudiation.

The third of the aristocratic formulations is the theory of natural aristocracy, a concept elaborately developed by Plato in the *Republic* and given new and incisive restatement in recent American thought by a variety of able theorists, for instance George Santayana. According to this view, the inequalities that patently exist among men are not to be ascribed primarily to racial or biological factors (though these too may be admitted), but to natural differences that are there simply because they are there. There is no mystery about such inequalities; they exist everywhere in nature; they are in fact, it is said, inherent in the very composition of things. Consider, say the expounders of this doctrine, the universe about us. It is an ordered and hierarchical scheme of things reflecting the natural gradations of position, of degree. And just as there are inequality and hierarchy in nature, so, these theorists argue, there are inequality and hierarchy in man. What democracy does, however, is to treat as equals men who are unequal, thereby denying the fundamental natural principle of degree. In consequence, it is asserted, the social order collapses, the commonplace, inferior man ascends to positions of power when he should remain instead at his proper level, and the unity of the state is destroyed. Once again, therefore, democracy is held to be an undesirable form of state.

The last of the anti-democratic theories that will command our attention here is the doctrine of authoritarianism. On the one hand this is merely the reverse of the aristocratic shield, insisting as it does that the state maintain by authority the right of the best to rule. On the other hand it is a doctrine in its own right, offering as central objection to democracy the argument that democratic government fails to maintain the order and the authority necessary to the operation and survival of the state. To secure and maintain this authority various alternatives have been evolved. One is the recourse to the right man, the leader, he who not only knows what is right but is strong enough to assure it. Another is the authoritarian appeal to the right class, in one construction made up of those elements generally included under the rubric of "the right," in another of those elements generally identified as "the left." A third resort is the appeal to the right principle, the absolute of Hegel, for example, or the theocracy of the early Puritans. None of these alternatives, it is plain, are totally exclusive, yet each has a distinct emphasis of its own. In each case, moreover, the plea is essentially the same—for some form of absolute oligarchical rule. In each case the supremacy of public opinion is denied.

The ends for which this authoritarian control is to be employed vary, of course, with the particular theorist and the aspect stressed. For Irving Babbitt, who embodies in a curious way many of the manifestations of this line of thought, the end is frugal: it is the restrictive way of life. For others the pattern is expansive, or partially the one and partially the other. And for some, indeed, as the author of the *Revolution of Nihilism* suggests,[7] the pattern may be nonexistent or not clearly defined at all. For all these theorists of authoritarianism, however, the refusal of democracy to make absolute and universal their particular pattern of existence, the refusal to recognize in constitutional form their particular concept of the right leadership, the refusal, further, to remove from the many the right to participate in the political process and so to determine the broad ends of government—these are the decisive considerations that lead them to reject the democratic form of state.

Here, then, are the several doctrines of anti-democratic thought. They all unite in the general repudiation of democracy. They all agree on the inevitability or desirability of irresponsible minority rule. They all oppose the democratic tenet that free conflict in ideas should determine policy and select key personnel. Yet each differs from the other in the central reason on which that rejection of democracy is based. Each offers a different minority, a different will, that is or should be enthroned. These are the problems—the differences as well as the agreements—that will engage us for the rest of this book.

Part Two

THE IMPOSSIBILITY OF DEMOCRACY

2

The Ruling Class as Organizational Necessity

The government of man over man, of ruler over ruled, is, in the democratic view, a function of consent: he who wields power does so not merely at the tolerance but with the active participation, indeed even the guidance, of those over whom that power is wielded. For those who look upon democracy as an impossible attainment, however, government is only incidentally or not at all a product of consent. It is, as with Burnham, the resultant of organizational imperatives completely and inexorably outside the control of the masses of mankind. Or it is, as with Dennis, solely a matter of force, of power seized and maintained by those who are both capable and desirous of doing so.

In both these constructions there is an attempt to describe what is or what must be, not what ought to be. This is in line with the familiar Machiavellian prescription that "how one lives is so far distant from how one ought to live that he who neglects what is done for what ought to be done, sooner effects his ruin than his preservation." [1] With close adherence to this principle, and with a systematic regard to the politics of their time, these men—and others— have sought to depict not the intentions but the reality of their age. This reality they hold to be the impossibility of democracy and the inevitability of oligarchy.

In this respect they differ profoundly from those critics of democracy who accept the possibility of the democratic system but reject as undesirable the operation and the consequences of that system.

They differ, too, from one another in that they attribute to their oligarchies both a different nature and a different manner of attaining to power. In the one case (Dennis), the theory rests upon the power-lust, the impulse of man. In the other case (Burnham), it stems from the necessary organization of man; it is, so to say, a concept of structural imperatives—a study, in Mosca's phrase, of "anatomical differences"—and as such dependent neither upon the existence of particular individuals (with their psychological drive for mastery) nor on the moral compulsions of a cause, though both, to be sure, are inescapably involved.

In a succeeding chapter we shall endeavor to deal with the power or force theory of the state. Here we are concerned only with the organizational indictment.

I

THE ORGANIZATIONAL FACTOR IN OLIGARCHICAL THOUGHT

This theory holds, as with Michels, that society cannot exist without a dominant or political or ruling class, that the ruling class is the only factor of sufficiently durable efficacy in the history of human development. All societies, he notes, must organize, and in the process of organization a society is divided into "a minority of directors and a majority of directed." This simple truth about the nature of all organization is extended, by Michels, into a principle of perpetual oligarchy through the addition of technical and psychological factors that are held to free the minority from control by the majority. In fact, Michels argues, it is the minority which controls the majority and imposes on it a legal order that is the outcome of the exigencies of its domination. As it is with the governments of social groups, he affirms, so it is with the governments of states: they are never more than the organization of a minority and are never representative of the majority. Even when, in exceptional circumstances, the majority manages to deprive the leadership of power, it does not thereby obtain self-government; for, says Michels, a new organized minority comes forward and raises itself to the rank of a governing class. The majority must, in consequence, always submit to the domination of a small minority; it must always constitute the pedestal of an oligarchy. This, according to Michels, is inevitable; it is an "iron law." [2]

Michels documented his thesis with a wealth of illustrative material drawn from the experience of the German trade unions and the Social Democratic parties, in a synthesis of fact with logic that makes his work one of the seminal volumes in the vast literature of anti-democratic thought. But no less significant are the contributions of Mosca and Pareto who, while they agreed with Michels that democracy is organizationally impossible, differed from him in the emphasis placed on the specific structural attribute that was held to make it so. Thus, where Michels saw the inevitability of oligarchy inherent in *group* organization and in the psychological conditions under which power is obtainable, Mosca found his ruling class primarily in the structural imperatives of *political* organization and in the psychological laws of political behavior,[3] while Pareto discovered his governing elite emerging as the inescapable consequence of *social* organization.[4]

There was, curiously enough, still room for a thorough exploration and development of the same thesis based on the *economic* organization of society, a void left unfilled despite the brilliant criticism with which Marx had assailed the postulates of the capitalist order. For in arguing, as he did, the impossibility of democracy so long as private property in the means of production continued, he argued not against democracy but against what he conceived to be the hindrances to democracy. In delineating the significance of the economic factor, however, and in insisting on its dominance in the development of human history, he set forth in incisive form the elements which anti-democratic theorists were later to employ as the doctrinal foundations of their thought.[5]

These several concepts of structural determinism—social, political, economic—have been given effective restatement by American as well as by European writers on democracy, though frequently in partial and somewhat varied a form. A good example of this is Bentley's penetrating study *The Process of Government,* which suggests in striking fashion the social approach of the organizational theorists but differs greatly in its hypothesis of multi-group struggle from, say, Michels' concept of a single dominant group.

According to Bentley, a proper interpretation of political rule must lay chief emphasis on the nature of the social organization, for, he holds, government can only be understood in terms of the functioning of group pressures within that structural arrangement. It is not in the ideas and ideals of men, he argues, that we find the causes of social action; it is rather in the pressures that groups exert in the service of those ideas and ideals. To understand democracy we must disregard the theory of "government by the people"; that phrase, he insists, is merely "a slogan and rallying cry for some particular groups at special stages of their activity." Democracy, instead, must always be considered "in terms of the various group pressures that form its substance," in terms of the functioning, blocking, and adjusting of group interests.[6]

The failure of Bentley effectively to distinguish pressures from interests, indeed his final reduction of pressures to interests after having begun by denying that interests could serve as an adequate explanation of social phenomena, seriously mars the validity of his general thesis.[7] More important in the immediate context, however, is his recognition that the dominance of a particular group or combination of groups is always a matter of shifting and therefore temporary alignments and not the result of a fixed and determinate situation. In no sense, consequently, is his a theory of inevitable oligarchy, as his extended attempt to reconcile democracy with structural imperatives makes clear.[8]

For Frank R. Kent, on the other hand, who views the organizational theory from the political rather than the social or economic side, domination is localized in a specific political oligarchy, the party bosses. As with all the theorists of structural determinism, Kent approaches his subject with the self-professed objectivity of the scientific observer. "There is no use talking," he says, "about things as they ought to be or as we would like to have them. The thing to do is to look squarely at them as they are." And if we do this we inescapably come to the conclusion that political organization is essential and inevitable to human society, that for the organization to run there must be a machine, and for the machine to run there must be a boss, whether the boss be a person or an oligarchic group. The several local bosses together, Kent argues, form a political ruling class that is "in practical control of the country. They are the real rulers of America." [9]

But while Kent asserts the inevitability of the boss, a careful reading of his volume reveals that he has done little more than this, that he has presented not another "iron law" but what may be termed an attitude of provisional pessimism. He perceives that political officials and even bosses may be made responsive and indeed responsible to the people through the latter's active participation in the electoral process, and he notes the dominance in certain situations of the economic over the political boss.[10] What he fails to perceive, however, is that political bosses may disagree among themselves and thus disrupt the compactness of the oligarchy, that political bosses may not only be dominated in some cases by economic bosses but also by popular leaders such as Wilson and Franklin Roosevelt, and that political bosses decline in influence as the electorate is more widely educated and increasingly alert, as the classified civil service is extended, as the foreign-born are steadily "Americanized." He errs, too, in resting the problem of popular expression and control on elections alone, for this, while essential, takes no account of other forms through which democratic "will" may be expressed.[11] For these and other considerations, Kent's doctrine of a political oligarchy as the inexorable ruler of society cannot stand; though it is to be recognized that in his vivid redirection of political thought to the perversion of democracy embodied in boss-rule, and in his re-emphasis on the structural and psychological conditions which make that rule possible, Kent has made a valuable contribution to our political literature.

A more trenchant and less friendly criticism of democracy in organizational terms is contained in the economic analyses of William K. Wallace and James Burnham. But while Wallace separated politics from economics and perceived in the structural imperatives of the new technology our necessary passage from the one to the other, from "political organization" to "industrial organization,"[12] Burnham fused the two and perceived in the same economic compulsions our transition to a unitary political-economic society, in which, however, the economic would absorb the political.[13] Both envisioned in the new industrial society "Caesarism as its rule," and both embodied this Caesarism in the persons of those who controlled or would control the industrial process: for Wallace, the "engineers and technical experts" were to become "its spiritual ministrants"; [14] for Burnham, the managers alone would rule.

In the incisiveness with which Burnham synthesized the available arguments, and in the eloquence with which he pleaded his cause, his work commends itself as perhaps the ablest American statement of the organizational school; so it is, consequently, to his major tract, *The Managerial Revolution*, that we now turn for an extended analysis.[15]

II

THE ECONOMIC-POLITICAL OLIGARCHY OF JAMES BURNHAM

The essence of Burnham's work is a synthesis of Marx and Machajski. It combines the Marxian postulate that capitalism as a social system renders democracy impossible because of the economic inequalities inherent in that system, with Machajski's thesis that such inequalities are inherent in all systems and are, therefore, a permanent feature of social organization.[16] In placing emphasis on the economic factor as the fundamental force in human history and in offering a theory of social classes which purports to identify the few who control that economic force, Marx had adumbrated for Burnham the structural outlines of his managerial theory. In calling attention to the significance of the mental worker, the intellectual or technician, as a social class distinct from the Marxian division into capitalist and proletariat, and in stressing the emergence of this third class as the permanent ruling force in history, Machajski had crystallized and consolidated the pattern. Burnham's achievement, then, was to extend, with Machajski, the Marxian doctrines of the economic interpretation of history and the class struggle into eternal law, to join with these Machajski's further concept of the technical or intellectual class, and to apply the emerging theory to contemporary affairs.

In the elaboration of this theory Burnham effectively employed Nomad's restatement of Machajski as well as the perceptive arguments of Lucien Laurat and other European and American theorists who had graphically portrayed the bureaucrat, technician, manager,

as the potential or actual dominating force in the modern world—
though not all of whom, of course, had arrived at the same conclusions to which Burnham was led.[17] He was aided, too, by the several
writings of Veblen,[18] Hilferding,[19] and Berle and Means,[20] who had
strikingly noted the shift in the distribution of economic power
brought about by the changing structural patterns of industry—
though here again without concurring in the specific inferences Burnham drew. And from the volumes of his Italian and Swiss mentors
—Mosca, Pareto, and Michels—Burnham obtained a keen understanding of the basic critiques to be leveled against democracy.
The result is an argument penetrating in its analysis and cogent
in its simple plausibility, though somewhat impaired, as we shall
see, by its omniscient pretensions and schematic oversimplifications.

We must begin, says Burnham, not "with whether the facts indicated by this theory are 'good' or 'bad,' just or unjust, desirable or
undesirable—but simply with whether the theory is true or false
on the basis of the evidence now at our disposal." We must attempt
not prescription but description, for only on the basis of adequate
knowledge can we hope to discover the truth about the world. Our
approach must be "scientific in its aim." [21] If we begin, in this
manner, with the study of history, we observe therein the operation
of certain basic laws or patterns of social organization and behavior.
Central to these laws is the theory or principle of the ruling class,
that the few always dominate the many. Indeed, Burnham insists,
the existence of such a minority ruling class is

"a universal feature of all organized societies of which we have any
record. It holds no matter what the social and political forms—
whether the society is feudal or capitalist or slave or collectivist,
monarchical or oligarchical or democratic, no matter what the constitutions and laws, no matter what the professions and beliefs.
. . . We are fully entitled to conclude that this not only has been
and is always the case, but that also it always will be. That it will
be, follows . . . from the univocal experience of the past: since,
under all conditions, it has always been true of political organization, it must be presumed that it is a constant attribute of political
life and will continue to hold for the future." [22]

This domination or rule, history further shows, is secured through control of a single factor, the instruments of economic production. In Burnham's words:

"The instruments of economic production are, simply, the means whereby men live. In any society, the group of persons controlling these means is by that very fact socially dominant. . . . Where there is such a controlling group in society, a group which, as against the rest of society, has a greater measure of control over the access to the instruments of production and a preferential treatment in the distribution of the products of those instruments, we may speak of this group as the socially dominant or ruling class in that society. It is hard, indeed, to see what else could be meant by 'dominant' or 'ruling' class. Such a group has the power and privilege and wealth in the society, as against the remainder of society." [23]

This ruling class comes to power, moreover, not through the intentions or activities of men but, according to Burnham, through the technical imperatives of the social structure. All societies, that is to say, are organized, and in the process of organization some men rule while others are ruled. Those who rule do so not by virtue of their superior force or by the employment of deceit but by the function they perform in that organization. And since the economic process is paramount, those whose function it is to manage or control the economic process manage or control the society itself. Thus, Burnham argues, in the Middle Ages society was organized in such a way that the feudal lords, who controlled access to the instruments of production through ownership of the land, were the ruling class, possessed of supreme power and privilege; later society was organized differently, in such a way that the bourgeoisie, the industrial and finance capitalists who controlled access to the instruments of production through the ownership of private property, were the ruling class; in a comparatively short time, he concludes, when the managerial revolution will have been fully accomplished, society will be organized in a new and different way, so that the managers, who, in his interpretation, control access to the instruments of production through control of the state—the collective owner of those instruments—will constitute the ruling class. [24]

It is, then, Burnham holds, the way in which society is organized, the structure of the economy, that determines who rules. This, and this alone, is where we are to look for the source and the explanation of power; for those who control the economic institutions of society control, *ipso facto,* the political institutions of that society.[25]

What are the consequences of this for democracy? Does it make democracy impossible, or merely difficult? Does it mean that democracy, if it is to survive, can do so only in altered form, or does it imply that democracy, far from surviving, has never yet come to be? Here Burnham does not make his position quite plain.

It would appear from the terms of his argument that democracy is, in fact, a principle incapable of realization, for it is in conflict with the existence of a ruling class. And since the theory of the ruling class is not merely a theory but a law of history—eternal and inevitable—it must permanently exclude democracy as a working principle of politics. Burnham appears to affirm this view when he argues that the totalitarianism of managerial society means the concentration of political rule in the form of dictatorship. But elsewhere he assumes the possibility that the managerial society may become democratic and institute its own type of democracy, a "controlled democracy" compatible with managerial social structure and with class rule. In his expository phrase: "Democracy, within a class society, must be so limited as not to interfere with the basic social relations whereby the ruling class maintains its position of power and privilege." However, he continues, even this partial or limited democracy is not assured; for the economic structure of managerial society, in removing the institutional bases for opposition groups, raises serious obstacles to democracy, obstacles which are strengthened by the transfer of sovereignty from democratic parliaments to managerial administrative agencies.[26]

Here, in Burnham's view, is the decisive factual refutation of what he calls "the abstract, empty, sentimental rhetoric of democratic idealism." [27] Under democracy, he argues, sovereignty has been localized in the parliaments, "the typical political institutions of the capitalists"; but sovereignty is leaving, indeed has already left, the area of parliament for that of the administrative boards, commissions, and bureaus. "Very little control over the state is actually, today, possessed by Congress." That control, instead, is in the bureaus, "the sovereign bodies of the unlimited state of managerial society." [28]

When we add to these considerations, moreover, the realization that no societies are governed by the people, or by a majority, that all societies, including those called democratic, are ruled by a minority, then it is clear, Burnham insists, that democracy as usually conceived is impossible. [29] In fact, Burnham in one place concludes,

"Democracy can never win. Democracy always loses, because the forces of democracy, in winning, cease to be democratic. Those who want democracy, therefore, must be willing to lose." [30]

III

ANALYSIS AND CRITICISM OF THE ORGANIZATIONAL THEORY

The validity of Burnham's argument, it will readily be noted, hinges on the validity of three assumptions and an inference. The assumptions are, first, that there are permanent and inexorable laws of history and of politics and that the principle of oligarchy—a ruling class irresponsible to the ruled—is such a law; second, that the ruling class is an economic class, exercising supreme power through its functional role in the economic process; and third, that the ruling class rules by virtue of structural or organizational necessity, by the relationships that ensue from the imperatives of the economic order. If these assumptions are true, the inference that democracy is impossible is unavoidable. An examination of these precepts is therefore in order.

A. THE RULING CLASS AS HISTORICAL LAW

The theory of the ruling class as historical law affirms, simply, that the few always govern the many. It has always been so in the past; it is so now; it will always be so. Burnham admits that we cannot find in history elaborate mathematical constructions having the precision of physical laws. "Nevertheless," he says, "sufficiently meaningful and accurate broad answers can be given." And among these answers, he argues, none is so clear as the eternal subjection of the many to the few, the inescapable reality of the ruling class. [31]

Now this, it should be observed, is at once a description of the past and a prognosis of the future. So far as it applies to the past, so far as it argues the pervasiveness of oligarchy in history, it is a thesis abundantly supported by the experience of mankind. Ruling classes have in one form or another prevailed throughout much of the course of human history, and the evidence of the totalitarian states, to cite but a single illustration, amply shows that intrenched minorities rule or have ruled in many of the states of the contemporary or recent world. But it is important, along with this, not to ignore or underestimate the profound differences that exist beween oligarchies. The oligarchy of Athens, for example, was not the oligarchy of Louis XIV, and both differed greatly from the oligarchy that ruled Nazi Germany. To formulate a general law that does not account for essential points of difference is to obscure the truth for the sake of an unduly simplified uniformity.

These distinctions having been noted, however, and the general validity of Burnham's thesis as historical description having been granted, there is yet a crucial consideration to be taken into account. This is the elementary truth that evidences of things past in no way establish the nature of the present. To say that there has always been a ruling class is not in itself a sufficient demonstration that it *must* persist into the present. The proof must lie rather in the actual analysis of contemporary societies; and here, it is instructive to note, Burnham fails to consider or adequately to evaluate a variety of experiences that offer serious challenge to his thesis. Despite his recognition that "democracy is a matter of degree, or more or less," [32] he largely ignores those forms of state which have, in the modern world, increasingly approximated to the democratic principle, forms such as those embodied in the governments of England, the United States, Switzerland, Australia, and others.

It is with respect to his argument as it applies to the future, however, that Burnham's hypothesis is most vulnerable. He assumes a monistic and mechanical theory of causation: that the automatic workings of a social arrangement produced a ruling class in the past and will continue to do so in the foreseeable future, quite apart from human volition or the element of contingency. This, of course, is the naïve mechanical determinism characteristic of the classical school of pre-1914 German Marxism and given ultimate expression in

Bukharin's *Historical Materialism*. Burnham accepts, to be sure, "the historical importance of what people want and feel and hope for," but, like Bukharin, he so qualifies and minimizes the significance of this factor as effectively to emasculate it. [33] For him, it is clear, it is not the ideas and ideals of men, not the interplay of choice and chance, that are historically effective. The crucial, indeed determinative, element is always the play of impersonal forces that direct, rather than are directed by, man.

Now the nature of these impersonal forces—be they economic, political, military, social, and the like—is not the important thing. What is important is the metaphysical assumption that the human factor is a mere passive or inconsequential agent in the distribution of political power. This is patently false. It is true, of course, that the nature of the social environment places limitations on human actions and human desires: men do not build airplanes in a jungle or fight modern wars with bows and arrows; nor do they reasonably expect to build feudal domains in a highly centralized industrial economy. But the response to given limitations is not determined by the limitations as such, any more than the materials we use to build our houses determine their design. There are rarely situations that do not permit of major alternative paths of development, and, where those alternatives exist, men, not the situation that presents those alternatives, decide. The Russian Revolution, for example, may have been inevitable, but its particular form and outcome depended upon the characters and ideas of its leading personalities no less than upon the nature of the social order. [34] The histories of France and of ancient Rome were affected, and affected profoundly, by Napoleon and Caesar; the history of the modern world is still in part the consequence of Engels and Marx. Men, and the ideas men hold, have made and can make history; they are not mere pawns moved by impersonal forces beyond their control. [35]

The further fallacy of Burnham's deterministic principle is its acceptance of a single law to the exclusion of the element of chance, again in strict conformity with the orthodox Marxist position that the imperatives of the economic order alone determine the course of history. But it was Plekhanov, theoretical head of the Russian Marxists at the turn of the century, who admitted that Frederick II was saved at Striegau by the irresolution of Buturlin, who acknowledged that if Suvorov had been in Buturlin's place Frederick would in all likelihood have been annihilated and "the history of Prussia might have taken a different course." [36] What if the Persian armies had been victorious at Marathon, at Salamis, at Plataea? What if Napoleon had not invaded Russia, or if, when he had reached Vilna, he had accepted Alexander's offer of peace? What if Lenin had been denied permission to cross from Switzerland through Germany to Russia? What if England had succumbed to Hitler's bombs? Would the course of history in all these cases have been the same? The evidence is overwhelmingly in the negative. [37] Chance *is* important in history, as innumerable historiographers as well as philosophers like Peirce, anthropologists like Boas, and novelists like Tolstoy have all made clear. [38]

These reflections help us to see the invalidity of Burnham's broad hypothesis that what has been must forever be. So sweeping a formulation not only assumes "a certain inherent and invariable constancy in the order of nature which no number of past observations can by themselves prove"; [39] it ignores, over and beyond this, the central consideration that history, unlike the mechanical phases of physics, is a discipline not subject to "iron laws." Men have long sought to make history a science, even indeed an absolute science that would fix with mathematical certainty the path that human society has got to follow, but all attempts to realize this hope of predictability have up to now failed. In the evaluative and selective reading that men apply to history, in the diversity and uniqueness of historical events, in the subjective determination of past and even present facts, history presents a multidimensional web that no one key can unravel. The ruling class may be a *tendency*; it is in no sense a mechanically determined *law*. [40]

To argue, therefore, as Burnham does, that in all states oligarchy rules and must rule, is to formulate from the accidental course of history a principle of necessity. It is to advance, in blatant disregard of the methods of logical inquiry, a heuristic proposition that can at best be documented but not proved; for no one absolute derived from the uniqueness or occasional pattern of historical events can explain the wealth and the diversity of human experience any more than it can anticipate the unimaginable variables that always lie ahead. History would have cruelly vitiated Burnham's thesis if it had been advanced in the age of Pericles to demonstrate that human slavery and human society are inseparable. The future, indeed, may well play havoc with his iron law of oligarchy so confidently advanced in our own day.

It is the strength of Burnham's argument that he does not rest his case on so demonstrably weak a historical position alone, but endeavors, in addition, to prove his thesis by a more elaborate demonstration in organizational terms.

B. THE RULING CLASS AS ECONOMIC CLASS

Burnham makes it quite clear that he conceives his ruling class solely as an economic class; those who control the means whereby men live are, he says, by that very fact dominant. In this Burnham pursues a conception familiar not only to Marx but to Aristotle, Harrington, Madison, and innumerable others. It is a conception supported not alone by the weight of an impressive authority but by the evident fact that, to survive no less than to secure many of the interests or satisfactions in life, economic means are essential. In Burnham's formula, however, the essential becomes, as with Marx, the decisive or central or fundamental element, thereby affirming a condition in which those who control the economic power of a society control by that very token the political power of that society, and thus the state itself—become, in a word, the ruling class.

This explanation of supreme power solely or dominantly in economic terms depends, as with Burnham, on the demonstration of three major propositions: first, that economic power is always concentrated in the hands of a particular economic group—for Burnham the managers are today that group; second, that this economic or managerial group is a socially integrated class resting on a community of economic function; and third, that control of economic power by this social class (the managers) *ipso facto* gives them control of political power. Let us consider each of these propositions in turn.

The managerial control of economic power. Under capitalism, Burnham holds, the control of economic power has been concentrated in the owners of the means of production. Today, however, because of the separation of ownership from control, *de facto* control of those means of production is moving, and in many cases has already moved, from the capitalists to the managers, from those who theoretically direct to those who actually direct the course of economic affairs. "The completion of this process," he observes, "means the elimination of the capitalists from control over the economy; that is, their disappearance as a ruling class." And the managers, "who are taking up the control as it slips from the capitalist grasp," thereby acquire the two rights which make them dominant: the rights of "control over the access to the instruments of production and a preferential treatment in the distribution of the products of those instruments." [41]

It will be seen that this argument is, in essence, a matter of the changing distribution of power. It builds, and builds only, on the shift from owners to managers. That there has been a shift in power from ownership control to managerial control, and that this shift has been of a very profound nature, are issues no longer open to question. [42] But that this shift from ownership control to managerial control has been the only pronounced change in the distribution of economic power, and that managerial control is a clearly defined indivisible function being exercised by a single compact group, the managers, are propositions impossible to sustain.

It is not merely that the very term "management" is susceptible of a variety of definitions and so lends itself to any number of ambiguous interpretations. [43] It is the fact that both "management" and "control" are web-like complexities that cannot intelligibly be reduced to a simple monistic analysis. We need only pause to consider, for example, the important role still played by boards of directors in, say, the manufacturing industries; or the continuing entrepreneurial activities and controls of men such as Kaiser and Ford; or the increasing influence of labor and government. Or we may consider, again, not merely the widening separation of ownership from management, but with this the new and even faster-growing separation of powers within management, with all that this implies in the way of increasing specialization of function. Then too there are the conflicts that prevail among managers of rival corporations in the same industry, with the consequent introduction of economic and political forces that render the realities of control both complex and unstable. [44] Or we may bear in mind, to cite but one further consideration, that the shift away from ownership control has lodged power not merely in the hands of the managers but in the hands of the finance-capitalists or investment-bankers as well, in those who, as Hilferding and Berle and Means and others have pointed out with reference to certain stages of economic development, have the actual power to appoint the boards of directors and to determine the selection of the head managers.

That these are central rather than incidental considerations Burnham himself admits when he writes (in typical exaggeration of an important truth) : "The big *bourgeoisie,* the finance-capitalists, are still the ruling class in the United States; the final control is still in their hands." [45] What we have, in consequence, in Burnham's interpretation, is a theory of managerial supremacy not as a thing of the past or present; it is not a description of what is or has been; it is primarily a prediction as to what will, indeed what must, be. He assumes not only that this shift from owners to managers has been the only pronounced change in the distribution of economic power, but that it can be the only such change.

This, of course, is greatly to simplify the picture. It is to minimize or ignore the many complexities of the real situation as it exists today in order to seize upon a single prominent trend. It is to make that trend both dominant and ineluctable by resorting once again to that historical automatism which leaves no room for the inducing of changes by the creative energies of mankind. And it is to neglect the fact that, in a highly specialized and delicately adjusted economy, control of a single specialized category in no way mechanically assures control of the entire scheme of specialization. Those who control one aspect or segment of the social mechanism may, that is to say, so employ their control as effectively to block the dominance of those who control another aspect. [46] We can perceive these truths the more readily, perhaps, if we examine in some detail the controls (actual and potential) exercised by some of the other elements in this total economic process, for example labor and government.

Let us begin with an elementary consideration, the degree to which managerial control has been limited in recent years by labor's assumption of certain "management prerogatives." Here we have, for instance, the cardinal problem of the restriction of output, a restriction almost inherent in the nature of any large industrial organization where certain accommodations must be made from the time orders are issued by management to the time those orders are actually effectuated by labor. This accommodation, what Mayo has termed the conflict between efficiency and sentiment, expresses itself even in those plants where the workers are unorganized; not merely in a restriction ensuing from a simple neglect of duties or a mere disinclination to effort but from a deliberate intent on the part of the workers to restrict certain productive practices in order to stabilize their earnings and to secure a more steady employment. [47]

This conscious withdrawal of efficiency is not, of course, unilateral. As Veblen made clear, it is also a practice systematically engaged in by businessmen in their endeavor to maximize profits. [48] And from this point of view, indeed, the problem of restriction is not so much a clash of power as it is of profits on the one hand and group welfare on the other; both labor and management pursue a policy of restriction to better their relative economic positions. But from the standpoint of power-relationships the restriction of output, when solidified by the organization of workers into large and powerful unions, can and does limit managerial control.

Through collective bargaining, by far the most important part or aspect of restriction, labor unions obtain a significant voice in the determination of production standards. This is evidenced, for example, in the controls exercised by the unions in the building trades, where not only are production and output restricted but stringent working rules are applied by the unions in order to protect the wages, hours, and working conditions of their members. In the words of one investigator:

"Such rules prohibit the employer from working at his trade; compel him to employ a foreman on every job, or one foreman for a certain number of journeymen; force him to employ skilled men on work which can be done with equal expedition and efficiency by unskilled labor; specify the number of men that must be employed on each job; prohibit the employer from dividing his work in the manner he sees fit and from doing work by machinery in the shop and force him to do it by hand on the job; impose restrictions on him as to how he shall pay for his work; prohibit piecework, lumping, or a bonus system; forbid him to install timing devices; and in some instances provide that he hire his men from the union office." [49]

The net consequence of these working rules, this same investigator concludes, has been to give labor an effective voice in controlling the job and in limiting the initiative of management by prescribing "to the employer under what conditions his work should be done and who should do it." [50]

The prevalence of such labor controls in other industries, particularly in the printing and needle trades and in the mining industry, attests to the inability of the managers decisively and everywhere to control many of the specialized factors in the productive process.[51] In fact, in the peculiarly disorganized and chaotic conditions that have prevailed in the garment industries, the unions have been compelled to assume so many of the ordinary functions of management that they are today unusually powerful and influential, even in some cases dominant, as compared with the great majority of the firms with which they deal. [52] Thus one of the two major unions in that field, the Amalgamated Clothing Workers of America, after the economic depression of the early twenties,

"developed a number of highly skilled officials, expert in production and management techniques in various departments of the industry, and through these men it was able to give a practical industrial engineering service to union employers who were experiencing difficulties in competition. At the same time the union insisted that management be efficient, and that incompetent supervisors be replaced. From that time on the union helped employers to produce more efficiently, so that union wage rates might be raised or maintained in the face of competition, and union manufacturers helped to keep or to increase their volume of business. . . . In certain instances the union largely assumed responsibility for organizing a new shop for an established firm in order to enable it to compete in a different price range." [53]

It may, however, with much validity, be pointed out that despite the assumption of these various controls by labor there has been no successful wholesale interference with the command of the major technological processes by management. But there have been interferences, many and important ones, else the pressure for the Taft-Hartley bill (which finally became law in 1947) could never have arisen. And while in some instances managerial control is clear, in others it is blurred: John L. Lewis, for example, would hardly consider himself the lackey of the mine operators. And if the unions have failed thus far to use their economic power to fullest advantage, if they have been content merely to extend the range or area of negative checks on the power of management and capital without at the same time pressing for greater participation in the actual determination of industrial policy, it is primarily because the unions still see the problem not as a philosophic issue but as an exercise in expediency. Whatever intrusions labor has made on the prerogatives of management have been necessitated by the demands of the moment rather than by any systematically conceived attempt to displace or to penetrate managerial control.[54] Should this broader appreciation come to dominate labor ideology, then the issue will cease to have the tangential impact it now largely assumes and emerge, as in England it has already emerged, as one of the truly profound social conflicts of the contemporary age. In a free society there is no inevitable reason why these things cannot come to be. Indeed, as we have seen, in some degree they already are.[55]

Of equal if not greater significance in this problem of the control of economic power is the steadily increasing role of government. No longer is it possible to say, as one might at times have said, that government is merely an adjunct of economic power, that the business of the state, from an economic standpoint, is merely to serve and to further the interests of a dominant economic group. This may have been true, or largely true, of particular governments—of those, for example, of McKinley and Coolidge and Hoover. But it is not true of all governments—witness Attlee in England and Franklin Roosevelt in the United States—for government as an instrument of power readily exceeds such servile limitations. Government today is not simply a mild regulator operating, as it were, from outside the economic process; it is very much an integral and significant part of that process itself.

Consider, for example, the work of the Antitrust Division of the

Department of Justice in regulating the relations of private enterprise to the market and combatting certain trade practices designed to effectuate monopolistic control of some portion of the economic order. Consider such policing agencies as the Federal Trade Commission and the National Labor Relations Board (prior to the enactment of the Taft-Hartley law, which, it is instructive to note, is a governmental rather than a managerial check on labor's power), the former prohibiting certain "unfair practices" in interstate commerce, the latter prohibiting certain "unfair practices" in the labor-management field. Consider, further, the achievement of the Packers and Stockyards Act of 1921 in curtailing the power of the major firms in the packing industry; and conjoin with this the federal regulation of public utilities, of currency and of credit, of foods and drugs, of airplane carriers, of communication, of securities. Directly through legislation and through government corporations such as the Tennessee Valley Authority, or indirectly through taxation, the issuance of charters, and administrative agencies such as the independent regulatory commissions, government has increasingly exercised a significant degree of control over the varying phases of our economic life.[56]

These considerations demonstrate that Burnham, in making central the monopolization that a particular factor in the process of production has come to have, and in arguing therefrom that control of that monopolized factor ensures control over all the factors in the process of production, has overlooked the fact that in a specialized firm or economy there are not one but many diverse controls which may operate to block others. The foregoing illustrations have pointed up the nature of these controls in the normal or routine pattern of the economic process. But there are, in addition, striking instances that show the effective way in which managerial power can be blocked or restricted in exceptional circumstances, when th' full power of labor or government is exercised.

A case in point is the checking of managerial power in the automobile industry in recent years. There, early in 1942, the government stepped in to prohibit the continued manufacture of civilian passenger cars and to compel the industry to convert fully to war production. Later, when the industry had returned to its regular peacetime pursuits, the labor unions succeeded, through a succession of strikes, in securing managerial compliance with a considerable number of their demands. This picture of labor interference through strikes—a form of power, oddly enough, brought into play only through the concerted withdrawal of another form of power—is further complicated when we take into account the dependence of one industry upon another, when we recall, for example, how the 1946 strike in steel compelled the closing of the automobile industry, and how much of the country's economy was paralyzed by the coal stoppage in the winter of that same year, a dispute in which not the managers but government and labor were the dominant forces.

It may of course be argued at this point that these interferences with managerial power are essentially only interferences by other managers, thereby leaving unimpaired the managerial control of the economic process. As Burnham repeatedly says, the managers are not only the "managers-in-industry"; they are also the "managers-in-government," and even, he in one place suggests, the leaders of labor.[57]

But this is a specious argument. In the first place, bureaucracy is not, as Burnham would have us believe, supreme; administrative heads are still subject to Congressional and Presidential direction and control; governmental action is not merely managerial action. Moreover, government is not simply a partner; it is also a regulator, an antagonist, of industry. In the second place, the leaders of labor, if they are to be embraced within the managerial category at all, are "managers" in a vastly different sense than are the "managers" of either government or industry. For one thing, they owe their allegiance to, and act in the interests of, a group other than the owners of a corporation or an industry. For another, they do not, today, determine the actual contours of total economic policy. Though labor leaders sometimes share in the formulation of that decision, their immediate role, from the standpoint of power, is to block, condition, or otherwise set limits to those (managers and capitalists and governmental officials alike) who make that determination. Theirs is a negative function predominantly. Thus we see that the logic of Burnham's argument produces "managers" who are structually antagonistic as well as complementary to one another: those who share in the control of the economic process are not merely managers; and those who manage do not always rule.[58]

It is plain then that, by concentrating his discussion on only one aspect of this changing distribution of economic power, Burnham has fallen prey to two of the most elementary errors of logical analysis: (*a*) the fallacy of exaggeration, of extending a partial truth to a false universal; and (*b*) the fallacy of oversimplification, of treating a multidimensional problem in monistic terms. No adequate analysis can omit the play of other essential elements, especially when we bear in mind not only the continuing exercise of capitalist controls but also, as we shall see later, the dominance in many situations of elements other than the managerial or even the economic alone.[59]

The managers as a social class. According to Burnham, the "managerial class" is a cohesive and integrated group made up of those men who share a common economic function, the managerial function. What they do (i.e., in the process of production), not what they may happen to think or want or feel, is, in his view, the crucial element that divides men into classes.[60]

In these terms, a manager is a member of the ruling (managerial) class not because he wills it—for what he wills is of minor consequence—but simply because he performs a particular job, that of managing. Conversely, a worker is a member of the ruled (servile or servant) class not, again, because of his intentions or desires but simply because his function in the economy is to serve. Once again, therefore, Burnham arrives at a social interpretation in which the human factor is eliminated or largely ignored. He assumes, in accordance with his pervasive mechanistic doctrine, a concept of class and of class power that rests on the laws which are held to govern an organization's existence. He argues not merely that the function of a class automatically determines its position in the pyramid of power, but that the function a man performs automatically determines his position in the stratification of classes.

Now this, as our previous discussion of Burnham's historical automatism implies, is a proposition that cannot be conceded. Men do not simply fall into a logically prescribed homogeneous class according to some particular deterministic scheme. Class is not simply a logical delineator of type, a categorization of men based on the exclusion of differences and the inclusion of similarities—all, be it perceived, from the standpoint of the classifier. It is this, to be sure, but it is also more. It involves in addition a socio-psychological feeling of loyalty or allegiance from the standpoint of the one who is classified. These may, or may not, coincide, depending at least in part on the particular standard employed.

If, for example, we use economic income as our mark of delineation, we get one set of classes. If we use economic function, we get another. And if we employ economic status or attitude, we get still others. If we turn, on the other hand, to such a factor as political propensity, we obtain yet another set of classes. And a radically different classification would emerge were we to employ as our basic criteria such considerations as religious belief or affiliation, national background or cultural interest, or even so elusive a factor as racial "type." Delineations such as these, moreover, state rather than resolve the problem; for men who belong to one class by virtue of one criterion, say economic income, may belong to another through racial or religious membership. Thus a Negro lawyer who pleads the cause of a juvenile delinquent can hardly be said by virtue of his function as a lawyer to be in the same social class as the white attorney who derives a high income from his services to a large corporation. And thus men engaged in different occupations within a single factory unite on a picket line only to divide again for social or religious or other reasons.[61]

In a memorable chapter in his *Engineers and the Price System*, Veblen bemoaned the failure of the engineers to form a class. Only this, he argued, was needed for them to assume control of the industrial system. But what he—and later Burnham—failed to perceive, was that class does not rest on function alone. There is no objective community of interest among managers or engineers so great as to surmount their many differences and antagonisms. Historically viewed, moreover, the managerial function is not a new function; it was performed by special groups in all societies, yet that performance did not serve to unite them into a single homogeneous class. And it does not serve to unite them today.[62] The divisions of opinion on the Taft-Hartley law, on the retention of price and rent controls, on federal aid to education, on the necessity for legislation prohibiting racial or ethnic discrimination in employment, on these and other important issues in recent years, adequately serve to illustrate this point. These same divisions expose, in addition, the invalidity of Burnham's more general argument that industrial managers, labor leaders, and government administrators, are all members of the "managerial class."

This last point requires a word in comment. If Burnham is right that function is the sole or crucial determinant of class, then to the degree that labor leaders penetrate managerial functions they are members of the managerial class. But as managers their loyalty is to a different "class"—the union members whom they represent— than the owners to whom the managers of industry owe allegiance. Thus we are faced at the outset with *two* managerial classes, not one. Add to this the managers of government, whose primary allegiance is neither to the labor unions nor to the owners of the corporation but to the general public or consumer, and we have *three* managerial classes, distinguished from each other not by function but by attitude or allegiance. The anomalous question then presents itself: How can *three* classes with *three* different allegiances be *a* social and ruling class? Clearly, Burnham's seemingly plausible generality quickly loses its glitter when confronted by inconvenient but very real facts. Function, whatever else it may do to explain the economic process, cannot by itself adequately explain the nature of economic or social power.

To attempt, therefore, as Burnham does, to equate the managerial function with a schematic class delineation, is grossly to simplify and to mistake the nature of a class. It is to confuse the specific with the general, the attitude a man has as a worker in a particular job with the attitude that man has as a total being. It is to ignore the everexistent gap between the logic of the classifier and the allegiance of the classified. And it is to succumb, once again, to that circularity of reasoning which defines an alleged economic oligarchy not in terms of class but in terms of function, and then calls those who perform that function a class, but fails to follow the logical and correct alternative of first defining the class and then demonstrating that those who perform the managerial function belong there.[63] For these and other reasons, Burnham's thesis of the managers as a socially integrated class is patently vulnerable.

Economic power as control of political power. The theory of the ruling class as an economic class rests on the further assumption that those who manage (or control) the instruments of production in a given society possess as a necessary consequence the final say as to what may or may not be done in that society; they determine, that is, the ends to which that society is directed. It is not to be denied that those who control the instruments of production have a voice in that final say; the question is, do they have a controlling or determinative voice? Does economic power—and here again enters Burnham's assumption that control of the instruments of production is alone sufficient to ensure control of economic power—control political and other forms of power? Marx and his followers as well as many of his dissenters have affirmed a positive reply to this query, and in pursuing their insistence Burnham moves on heavily documented ground.[64] But is that documentation conclusive?

Take, for instance, the evidence of the totalitarian experience which Burnham offers in proof of the dominance of managerial control. That the industrial managers of the Soviet Union are influential in the state and formally supreme within the confines of their plants is beyond question; but that they are subservient to the political arm of the state as manifested in Stalin and the political bureau of the Communist party, is even more definitely attested.[65] That the German capitalists and managers played a striking and important role in the formation of the Nazi state is undeniable; but that they too were dominated by Hitler and the leaders of the National Socialist party is equally conclusive.[66] Indeed, it would appear from the experience of these states that those who control political power are enabled thereby to control economic power, that politics dominates economics even more than the reverse.[67] As Hilferding, in a striking departure from his earlier convictions, observed:

"The economy, and with it the exponents of economic activity, are more or less subjected to the state, becoming its subordinates. The economy loses the primacy which it held under bourgeois society. This does not mean, however, that economic circles do not have great influence on the ruling power in Germany as well as in Russia. But their influence is conditioned, has limits and is not decisive in relation to the essence of policy. Policy is actually determined by a small circle of those who are in power. It is their interests, their ideas as to what is required to maintain, exploit, and strengthen their own power that determines the policy which they impose as law upon the subordinated economy." [68]

These considerations underscore the importance of a factor that has been largely minimized by the exponents of economic determinism, namely, the factor of law. One need not resort to the extreme position of a Rudolf Stammler that law is the precondition of economic relationships,[69] to perceive the invalidity of the Marxist contrary extreme, as argued by Achille Loria, for example, that law, fundamentally, is determined by economic relationships alone.[70] To hold that law is merely the mechanical expression of political power, which in turn is the reflection of economic power, is to ignore the very profound sense in which property and government mutually sustain each other. Indeed, from one point of view, it can well be argued that property is, after all, little more than a right, a legal right to exclude others from the use or benefits of that which one may possess, and as a legal right it is necessarily dependent on government; it exists only because government suffers it to exist, because government recognizes and protects it. In consequence, as MacIver notes, while "a particular government may do little more than uphold an already established system of rights . . . in the longer perspective *it is government that creates property*. Property is not wealth or possessions, but the right to control, to exploit, to use, or to enjoy wealth or possessions." [71] And through law this right can be restricted no less than it can be maintained or enlarged.

We can see this truth in the profound impact of the Napoleonic code, for example, on the economic system of France. We can see it in the vast economic reconstruction of England now being effected —through law—by the Labour Government of that country. We can see it, in lesser form, in the state regulation of cartels in Germany in 1923 and 1930, and, more strikingly, in the pronounced shift in the ideological basis of the Soviet state, where law has ceased to be what Marxist theory had long proclaimed it to be and has become —as indeed it always was—an essential method of economic prescription and control.[72] As the statute books of every state amply testify, it is law that effects economic changes no less than it is economic considerations that compel a readjustment in the law.

In fact, the law itself, by granting a privilege to one group and imposing a discrimination on another, frequently creates groups with distinct economic interests that then seek a readjustment in those economic interests through a readjustment in the law.[73] The exclusion of aliens or women or specified religious groups from a particular profession, as in Germany under the National Socialist regime, for example, is a sufficient case in point. Without law economic institutions could not survive; for in a very real sense it is the law and not the economic institution which is reinforced by the military power of the state.

The validity of this view is supported by the fact that even in non-totalitarian states such as England, France, and the United States, those who are the most rigid expounders of the theory of economic determinism—the Communist parties in those states, for instance—endeavor through political (legal) action to effectuate economic change. But if economics controls politics and thereby law, why attempt to influence government rather than, or even in addition to, industry? Why seek control of the state? The inescapable answer is that it is done because control of political power carries with it the means to control economic power. Loria perceived but sought to explain away the significance of this truth; Engels and Lenin, however, both understood and affirmed it. "The Proletariat," wrote Engels, "seizes state power, *and then* transforms the means of production into state property." [74]

Even if we approach this problem from the historical vantage-points Burnham cites, we note that power in its many forms has been derived not only from economic but also from political and military and even religious considerations. Thus in feudal society it was not, as Burnham would have us believe, economic power which gave social power but the conjunction of economic with political power that produced that result.[75] Similarly, the bishops of the medieval church were able to secure both economic and political power by virtue of their spiritual attributes and cultural domination; they did not hold religious power solely or dominantly because of their economic possessions.[76] And the instances in which military conquest brought economic power as a consequence are so numerous that mere mention of Alexander, Caesar, Napoleon, and Hitler should suffice.[77] The difficulty, indeed, of maintaining an exclusively economic interpretation of power in the face of in-numerable historical exceptions is so great that Burnham himself, in a later work, conceded the *partial* impact of the economic phase. "The economic field, after all," he declared, "is only one among many phases of social life. It may be disputed just how decisively this economic phase affects the others." [78]

To insist, then, that economic power is inevitably the dominant form of social power, that economic power always and everywhere controls political power, is to fall into the error of exclusiveness by omitting or minimizing other related factors in the causal process. Where other factors—such as personality, tradition, military and political power, religious influence, and the like—are admitted as necessary, the proposition that the economic is the primary or dominant or basic factor is difficult to sustain. For where a situation is defined by a variety of aspects, where two or more factors are both necessary in the causal nexus, no one aspect or factor is sufficient, no one is always primary, no one is more fundamental, no one "controls." Economic phenomena influence political events, but political phenomena influence the course of economic history.[79] Indeed, the historical fact that modern democracies no less than other forms of state have used political power drastically to limit or to channel the economic power of propertied groups at once serves to negate the contention that economic power is necessarily superior to any other form of social power.[80]

Burnham himself would appear to be somewhat aware of the pro-found significance of the political factor, for in his discussion he attempts to do two things: (*a*) assert that the final power of the managers will come only through their control of the state; and (*b*) argue that there is no real distinction to be drawn between the political and the economic managers, for in the managerial economy the two will be fused.[81] Now the first, it is to be observed, is political and not merely economic power; and the second is, apart from its dubious validity, an equation of the economic and political factors rather than a supremacy of the one over the other. Thus Burnham is in effect admitting the very thing he denies: that control of economic power, while necessary, is not sufficient; political power too must be had if one is to rule. But there is, on the evidences of history—indeed, on the evidence of the totalitarian experience alone—, no less reason to believe that control of the political factor will give control of the economic factor, than there is to believe that control of the economic factor will automatically bring with it control of the political factor. In certain situations, the economic may precede the political; in other cases, the order of priority may be reversed; and in still other circumstances, both may be compelled to surrender to a temporarily greater force, whether it be the legions of Caesar or the magic of ancient Egypt's priests.

C. RULE BY ORGANIZATIONAL NECESSITY

Burnham's concept of the ruling class as economic class results, in essence, from his analysis of the way in which a ruling class comes to power. In this he turns away from the Machiavellian concern for the art or techniques of securing and maintaining power to the Marxian principle that the ruling class comes to power through the organizational imperatives of the social structure. These organizational imperatives are held to stem, on the one hand, from the economic relationships into which men are compelled to enter irrespective of their will; and on the other hand are said to determine, from the very nature of those relationships, who are to rule and who are to be ruled. In Burnham's terms:

"Modern society has been organized through a certain set of major economic, social, and political institutions which we call capitalist, and has exhibited certain major social beliefs or ideologies. Within this social structure we find that a particular group or class of persons—the capitalists or *bourgeoisie*—is the dominant or ruling class in the sense which has been defined [i.e., control of access to the instruments of production and preferential treatment in the distribution of the products of those instruments]. At the present time these institutions and beliefs are undergoing a process of rapid transformation. The conclusion of this period of transformation . . . will find society organized through a quite different set of major economic, social, and political institutions and exhibiting quite different major social beliefs or ideologies. Within the new social structure a different social group or class—the managers—will be the dominant or ruling class." [82]

This, it is plain, is the doctrine of economic determinism, resting not, as with Veblen, simply on the techniques of production and the discipline of habituation ensuing therefrom, but with Marx on the economic relationships resulting from those techniques of production, relationships which are held to be the crucial determinants of the social structure.[83] As Burnham says, it is not the desires of men, not the power of cliques, not even the wisdom of elites, that are the determinative forces of social change; it is the structural factor alone that decides.[84]

What is the validity of this argument? Is it true that human choice can have meaning only in so far as it conforms to the realities of the social structure? And does the social structure give power only to those who control the instruments of economic production?

In giving an affirmative reply to these questions, Burnham asserts a view that has much to commend it. If man is to survive, he must sustain himself; and the process of sustenance is in large measure an economic process. That economic process, moreover, furnishes the means or equipment (at least in part) to whatever goal we seek to attain. These are obvious truths, and we can accept them without cavil. We can agree, even more,

"that our dependence on the economic means determines largely our attitude to the whole social order which yields them to us in scantier or more abundant measure. We can agree that the conservatism or radicalism thus bred is apt to extend to the cultural realm, particularly to the 'stabilizing' cultural factors such as religion. We can agree that the mode in which the economic means are acquired influences the nature of the satisfactions we seek through them, that, for example, the competitive spirit engendered in the economic struggle affects our manner of living, our recreations, our philosophies, our ideals. We can agree that the struggle for the means of living, engrossing and perpetual as it is for the vast majority, must color, according to its character, the whole outlook of men." [85]

We can grant all these things and insist, beyond them, that apart from the economic structure history has no meaning. But, it is important at the same time to add, "in so agreeing we are simply admitting that the economic element is one highly important factor in the whole nexus of interactive influences which determine social phenomena." [86] There is still the central problem as to just what part that economic element plays in the total picture, whether it is the sole element or the dominant element, or whether it is but one of several major considerations that vary in significance according to the particular circumstances of the given situation.

Viewed from this standpoint, the exclusive or dominant role assigned by Burnham to the economic factor is clearly difficult to sustain. It is not easy, for example, to relate the nature or varieties of religion solely or primarily to economic forces. Christianity arose in the Roman Empire and has survived many economic changes. Judaism, perduring many centuries and many lands of persecution, is beholden to no one mode of economic production. The division of Protestantism into numerous sects has in no sense followed alterations in the social structure alone. Indeed, as Max Weber and Tawney have shown, the influence of Protestantism on capitalism is sufficient demonstration of the truth that cultural institutions may shape or influence economic institutions, just as economic institutions may shape or influence cultural institutions. Here, as everywhere, the relation is not simply unilateral.

That social institutions and social change cannot be attributed solely to the forms or relationships of economic production is evidenced too by an examination of primitive societies. The power of a tribal chief, for instance, cannot be explained simply in economic terms, any more than one can adequately interpret the matriarchical system in those terms. The diversity of thought-forms (*mores*) in primitive societies of the same economic levels is as striking a fact as the persistence of thought-forms throughout the ages, despite changes in the economic system or social structure. Even the differences in the status of men and women, Boas notes, are not primarily economic. They are rather the result of a chain of circumstances emerging from differences in the physiological life of man and woman.[87]

Economic systems, in short, are submerged in the social relations of man. They are part of the cultural life but they are not the whole or even, necessarily, the dominant part of it. Under certain circumstances, as under a free-market economy, the economic may indeed be the most valid interpretation; but under other circumstances, as under a controlled economy, it is not. To apply the principle of economic determinism to all human societies, in consequence, is to ignore the complexities of history for a false simplicity.[88] This truth Burnham himself perceived and accepted in a later work, where he bluntly observed:

"Theories of 'economic materialism' or 'economic determinism' . . . are unable to meet the test of the facts. Social and political events of the very greatest scope and order . . . have occurred without any important correlated change in the mode of economic production; consequently the mode of production cannot be the sole cause of social change." [89]

There is a further and no less significant aspect to this problem of organizational necessity that should not go unnoticed here. When we have once recognized the dependence of society upon certain structural or organizational relationships, have we thereby determined which organizational relationships are to prevail? The same social structure, it is evident, produces not only managers but independent trade unions as well, and in addition to these the element of government. If the nature of the organization is to determine, what exactly does it determine? We have already seen the lack of any conclusive demonstration that it is the managers who are destined for social rule; but if it is not the managers, who then are to control? [90]

In the answer to this question we find the crucial weakness of the deterministic theory, for only the human factor can resolve an organizational stalemate. Granted the imperatives of social organization, granted even the anti-democratic tendencies inherent in our present industrial structure,[91] there is yet a wide field in which man himself can move—to select from among several alternatives that which he deems most useful or valuable to himself.[92] Man is not merely the servant, he is also the master of organizational imperatives. He does not merely serve its functional operations; he channels those operations toward goals and purposes he—and not the abstract imperatives—has set. Nor is it any the less untrue to hold that man is bound by a particular mode of production, for where, if not from man, arise the forces that change the mode of production? Does the machine produce changes from within itself? Do techniques of production emerge from one another as by some magical order? And if it is not in the machine or in the techniques of production that we find the source of technological or economic change, but in the economic relationships predicated on those techniques, what are those relationships if not the relationships of men? That man is delimited in the scope of his power and conditioned in the manner of its exercise, is not to be denied; but it is not only the economic, it is also the political and, more broadly, the social organization of a society which effect that delimitation.[93] It is, even more, the habits and patterns of human thought, indeed the civilization itself, which so delimit and condition. Always, however, man, and the ideas that are in man, contribute too to the formation of power.

These considerations help us again to understand why no monistic and mechanical theory of causation can serve as an adequate explanation of social phenomena. There is no gainsaying the profound importance of the economic structure and of the organizational patterns concomitant with that structure. Nor do we serve any useful purpose by ignoring the accouterments of power that attach to those who control, by virtue of their economic positions, segments of that economic structure. But there is at the same time no way thus far known to man to escape the simple truth that these elements alone form but part of a total situation. Those who manage the instruments of production exercise important controls, but so too do those who share in the direction of labor and government; and which of these shall at any one time prevail—which shall exercise final power over the social structure—is in no sense a mechanical determination. So fatalistic a view not only denies the vitality of human choice, constrained though this may oftentimes be; it is in direct conflict with the vast experience of mankind. Similarly, just as economic life does not constitute the whole of social life, so economic power does not constitute the whole of social power. And just as those who control an aspect of economic power do not control the whole of economic power, so those who control the whole of the economic organization do not necessarily control the whole of social organization.[94]

In absolute terms, therefore, the theory that social rule emerges simply and necessarily as a consequence of organizational imperatives is false: it simplifies the total situation by ignoring or minimizing structural factors other than the economic alone; it fails to explain the multiplicity of diverse "superstructures"—as in the realm of religion—that everywhere accompany a similar economic base; and it does not provide for the psychological factor of man himself. As a partial explanation of social power it is, of course, valuable; but as a partial theory it loses both its vitality and its key significance, and fails to sustain the thesis of rule through organizational necessity.

D. THE IMPOSSIBILITY OF DEMOCRACY

The invalidity of Burnham's several assumptions—first, that the ruling class is a principle of historical law; second, that the ruling class is always an economic class, made up only of those men who control access to the instruments of economic production; and third, that this ruling class comes to power simply (and indeed solely) by virtue of organizational imperatives—alone renders invalid his concluding inference, that democracy is therefore impossible. But Burnham, in addition to these considerations, adduces two further structural arguments, which, he holds, conclusively demonstrate democracy's inability to survive. These are (1) the shift in sovereignty from parliaments to administrative bureaus, and (2) the managerial removal of the institutional bases for democracy.

There is involved in this construction, however, a seeming acceptance of the doctrine that democracy does contemporaneously exist and has previously existed, but is only now and in the immediate future destined to disappear. Such a conception argues not the permanent but only the temporary impossibility of democracy, a view for which credence is offered in the following statements from the *Managerial Revolution:* [95]

"There have been many kinds and degrees of democracy. Democracy such as England and France and the United States have recently known is only one kind among many others. . . . The democracy of Athenian slave society is not the same in general social character as the democracy of capitalist England."

and

"The democracy of capitalist society is on the way out, is, in fact, just about gone, and will not come back. The democracy of managerial society will be some while being born; and its birth pangs will include drastic convulsions."

This seeming incompatibility with the absolutist position that all societies are ruled by a ruling class requires a word in clarification before we can proceed to an analysis of the specific structural factors that today operate, according to Burnham, to destroy democracy.

The central question, it is plain, is: What is democracy? To this Burnham replies (and with much validity): "Democracy is a political system where policy is decided, directly or indirectly, by a majority, *and* where minorities, differing in their opinion from the majority, have the right of political expression and the opportunity, thereby, of becoming a majority." [96] But for Burnham the emphasis throughout is not on the factor of majority rule but on that of minority rights. In fact, his employment of this latter factor is so exclusive as effectively to eliminate the majority principle itself.

Now the right of minority opposition is indubitably essential, but it can never be more than the negative aspect of a twofold condition, the positive side of which is the right of the majority to have its way, to effectuate through law its opinions and beliefs. And this Burnham categorically and absolutely denies: in all societies, he insists, not the majority but the minority determines public policy.[97] He restricts this crucial right of minority opposition, moreover, to a minority of the elite, to a section of the ruling class itself. As he went on to state in one of his later works: "It is true that the opposition is only a section of the elite as a whole. It is also true that when the opposition takes governing power that is only a change of rulers." [98] This right of minority opposition, then, a right which Burnham insists is essential for democracy, is no more than the right of a *particular* minority, a minority *within* the elite or ruling class; and this, of course, whatever other relevance it may have, is clearly not the minority opposition democracy requires.

In these terms, however, Burnham's further statement that democ-

racy "is in no way incompatible with class rule in society" [99] begins
to take on meaning, though not thereby validity. Narrowly conceived, the Athenian slavocracy was indeed a democracy. But from
a broader standpoint, based on the inclusion of women and slaves,
for example, the minority who made up the citizenry was a political
oligarchy. The distinction, to be sure, is one of degree, but differences
of degree, when crucial, tend to become differences of kind. And
it is crucial to democracy that no one class or caste should permanently possess political control. It is not class rule but the absence
of class rule that distinguishes democracy from all other forms of
state, that is one of the essential hallmarks of democracy. In democracy we have the one "specific form of government in which political
life cannot be identified with a politically privileged class; a democracy has no political class." [100] If the majority is compelled to move
within the contours of policy set for it by a ruling class, the majority
cannot be said to rule; and democracy, at the same time that it
insists on minority opposition, insists also on majority rule. And if
both the majority and the minority are, as in Burnham's construction, part of the ruling class, then the terms patently cease to have
the meanings democracy ordinarily ascribes to them.

This digression into the meaning of democracy, as the term is employed by Burnham, has been made necessary in order to avert a
possible confusion as to just what is involved in the organizational
theory of the ruling class. It is not merely a denial of democracy
now; it is, even more, an insistence that democracy can never be.

We can now turn our attention to the specific structural factors
which, in conjunction with the previous considerations, are held by
Burnham to ensure the supplanting of democracy by managerial
society.

The shift in sovereignty. According to Burnham, sovereignty in
the modern state has left the area of parliament for that of the
administrative bureau. In this phenomenon, he argues, there is revealed the decisive refutation of the democratic theory and the final
demonstration of managerial dominance. What is the validity of his
claim?

That the rise of the administrative bureau has carried with it a
vast concentration of power is scarcely to be denied. Here, as elsewhere, Burnham has seized upon a truth crucial to any interpreta-

tion of modern society. But that this concentration of power in administrative bodies constitutes a shift in sovereignty is an extension of that truth into a false hypothesis.

It is to be remarked, at the outset, that the problem of sovereignty is not alone a question of locus, of localization, but also of meaning —not merely *where* sovereignty is but *what* sovereignty is. And in assuming that sovereignty is simply the fact of power, Burnham has failed to note a distinction fundamental to politics—the distinction between final and incidental decision, between supreme and derivative power.[101] Sovereignty is not the mere fact of power, not the mere making of administrative decisions. Where a judge in the exercise of his power resolves a dispute, in which the ruling can be appealed to a higher source of power, he is not sovereign; yet he has made a decision. Where an administrator determines to pursue a particular course of action and his decision is subject to review and veto, that decision is not a sovereign one. Where any decision by a leader or group to pursue a certain policy can be reversed by a superior leader or group, the decision in the first instance, in yielding to that in the second instance, cannot be said to be sovereign. And where an official possessing delegated powers makes decisions in accordance with policy previously determined by his superior, his decisions are not sovereign. It is not the act of decision, not the fact of power, but the act of final decision, the fact of supreme or ultimate power, that points the direction of sovereignty.

This consideration helps us to see the inherent defect in Burnham's localization of sovereignty. He assumes that such localization is in the parliaments of democracy; he does not stop to inquire into the source of parliamentary power. Here is a crucial weakness of his argument: the failure to perceive that democracy *as a principle* is not dependent on the particular institutions which seek to actualize it, that democracy *as a principle* is compatible not alone with parliamentary but with legislative-administrative forms as well. The problem for democracy is not that of institutional localization, not whether this or that body or agency should exercise this or that particular power. The problem for democracy is that of *responsibility:* to ensure that the institutional forms respond to the public opinion which sustains them.[102] A shift in power is not necessarily a problem in sovereignty; it may be merely a problem in technique, in method.

To argue, therefore, that "sovereignty cannot be delegated," [103] and that the delegation of power is in consequence the abdication of sovereignty, is to confuse, in the first instance, control of major direction with the control of detail, and to mistake, in the second place, the specific or limited fact of power with the larger or more general fact of sovereignty. It is, even more, to fail to perceive that the essence of democracy is not the institutional patterns through which it is realized but the principle of responsibility, the determination of public policy through the free play of conflicting opinions.

The structural bases of democracy. The inability of democracy to survive, Burnham further holds, lies in the removal by the managers of the institutional bases that make democracy possible.

"There is no democracy without opposition groups. Opposition groups cannot, however, depend for their existence merely on the good will of those who are in power. They must have some sort of independent institutional base in society. . . . In decentralized economies, oppositions are able to base themselves on some section of the economy, since no one and no group controls the economy as a whole. Oppositions can be based on one large branch of the economy as against others, on agriculture as against industry, on heavy industry as against light industry, on labor as against capital. But the centralization of the economy under the managerial structure would seem to remove these possibilities. All major parts of the economy will be planned and controlled by the simple integrated set of institutions which will be the managerial state." [104]

There is involved in this argument two sets of factors: the one, a description of that which is; the other, a description of what must be. To the extent that it anticipates the future, it reverts once again to that mechanistic determinism which admits no deviation from the inexorable march of material (i.e., economic) forces. It proclaims anew a fixed destination and a fixed passage. It paints with bold strokes the history of an era that is yet to be, casting into the dim recesses of insignificance man's intelligence and his aptitudes. Such a doctrine is alien to all but the dogmatic fatalist. It is not a doctrine that can, today, be refuted, for it deals with a future the details of which are still largely inaccessible. Nor is it a doctrine immediately proved or disproved by the pattern of unfolding events. Although the failure of predicted events to materialize does help to defeat the hypothesis, the realization of predicted events may turn on factors foreign to those on which the predictions were based. To affirm that the managers *will* come to power, and that they will do so *only* in a totalitarian structure, is at best an effort in clairvoyance that can only await the considered judgment of historical time. To the extent that Burnham asserts this view, he assumes the guise of a prophet. On the record, his garb is no less tattered than that of other repudiated pretenders to the throne.[105]

To the extent, however, that Burnham argues the necessity of structural decentralization for democracy, he affirms a profound and indispensable truth. Democracy can, indeed, survive only if there is a separation between the state and the community, between the various institutions and bases that make opposition groups possible. And as our earlier analysis showed, there is this necessary separation in the modern American state. Not only management but also labor and government play powerful and significant roles; not only these but agricultural and ecclesiastical elements, and independent owners of small business enterprises. So long as these several forces continue to exist, in greater or lesser degree and strength, and to operate through the media of free political parties and organized pressure, democracy reaffirms one of the conditions of its life as well as a mark of its achievement.[106]

IV

Conclusions on Democracy and the Organizational Theory

The democratic no less than other forms of state is a function of the social order. Without social order, and the organization attendant upon such order, there can be and is no government. Without government, and the organization attendant upon such government, there can be and is no social order. The two are interdependent: where there is one, there is the other. And both imply the fact of organization.

There is, accordingly, a great element of truth in Burnham's argument that we must turn to the organizational factor if we are to understand the workings and indeed the very existence of a particular form of state. But there is, too, an equal if not greater element of error—an error emerging from Burnham's insistence that the organizational factor is not merely to be included but is to be made the sole or dominant factor in the explanation of political power. In such an extension the partial truth becomes a total falsehood. This may clearly be seen if we pause briefly to recapitulate our conclusions on the three arguments that together constitute the foundations of Burnham's larger theory.

Thus there is incontestably a large core of validity in Burnham's construction of the ruling class as historical law; many states in many ages stand in visible or historic support of this thesis. But whatever the relevance and applicability of the ruling class principle to past facts, that applicability can in no sense be interpreted as extending, merely by virtue of its past existence, into the future. So mechanistic a doctrine fails completely to understand the complexity of human motivations and the power of human choice. It neglects the element of contingency in history. It oversimplifies the specific problems of power so as to mold them into a schematic generalization that accords with the similarities but underestimates the differences between societies. It ignores the profound truth uttered by an older and more intellectually mature Michels, that "epochs of history do not lend themselves to photographic reproduction." [107] And it does all this on the fatalistic and indeed fantastic presupposition that the processes of an artificial structure will necessarily operate to enslave men who have already in some measure effected their escape from enslavement. What has been, it is all too clear, need not forever be. If a particular class has ruled before, that alone is no inexorable demonstration that it will continue to rule. Just as Darwin and Lyell wrote the immutable out of nature, so the variability in man and society discredits the idea of a perpetual oligarchy.

Similar considerations point to the invalidity of Burnham's concept of the ruling class simply or solely as an economic class. It is the strength of Burnham's argument that he recognizes the profound significance of the economic element in social organization;

but it is his crucial weakness that he fails both to perceive that the economic is one among several factors and to restrict his valid perception to a portion rather than the totality of power. The economic element is not the only one because labor and government no less than management are vital factors in the composition of economic power. And the economic element is not the total (or even in all cases the dominant) element because military, priestly, and political power have all in the course of history come variously to rule. Economic power is always prominent, indeed essential, power, but it may be secured through other than economic means alone; and it may, above all, as the record of democracy attests, be controlled not only oligarchically by a class but also democratically by the people. Here is a central issue for democracy: not whether economic power shall control political power or political power control economic power, but whether the people, through democratic processes, shall control both.

These reflections expose the weakness in Burnham's further contention that power emanates from organizational imperatives alone. The organizational factor is indeed a paramount one: a change in the economic structure, for example, is accompanied by a change in the thoughts and behavior of men.[108] But this is not to conclude that the organizational factor is thereby the sole or decisive factor. In the first place, the structural factor is itself a complex that must first be resolved. Mosca and Kent reduced it to political organization, Marx and Burnham to economic organization, and these in no sense exhaust the multifarious power elements that pervade every society. In the second place, even the economic structure is a complex of elements—of management, of government, of labor, of agriculture, and so forth—a complex which experience amply suggests is not resolved merely by the operation of mechanical processes. In the third place, if the economic structure is the basic determinant, how is one to explain or reconcile the fact that, as Corey reminds us, "any particular economic organization of society is capable of many superstructural variations"?[109] This consideration alone conclusively establishes the interplay of factors other than those of economic imperatives. And then, finally, the general objection must be entered that any deterministic theory, economic or otherwise, fails to the extent that it does not adequately take into account the psychological variabilities in man. It has been well said:

"Man is a critic as well as a creature of circumstance. . . . We cannot conclude that, because the painter is absolutely dependent on his paintbox, the nature of its contents explains the picture. No more can we conclude that the struggle of the artist to earn his living explains it." [110]

For these several reasons Burnham's doctrine of the impossibility of democracy cannot be held to have been sustained. The complexities of social existence—what Morris Cohen has called the multidimensionality of history—are much too great and numerous to be reduced to any monistic formula, as the more cautious interpretations of even Pareto and Mosca at times perceived. And if we are to understand the social process it will be only through the correlation of the various elements that play significant roles within it, not through a determined insistence on absolute and exclusive theories. The organizational factor is always a necessary but never a sufficient explanation of the social process; and that it precludes democracy has yet to be established.

3

The Ruling Class as Conspiracy of Power

In the seventh book of the *Republic* Plato magnificently portrays the dichotomy between form and substance, between things as men conceive them to be and things as they actually are. Shadows, he perceived, render realities obscure, and men, governed by the illusions to which alone they are exposed, are unable to pierce the veil that cloaks the actuality beneath it. Indeed, because men perceive only the illusions permitted them they regard the illusions as true and press the inquiry no further. In this way the apparent assumes the qualities of the real, and the real itself is apprehended only by the unusual few capable of freeing themselves from the general misconceptions of mankind.

What Plato advanced as a theory of knowledge, some men have advanced as a theory of power. In all societies, they say, not the many but the few prevail. This they hold to be the fundamental political reality; all else is façade. Under the form of oligarchy, they argue, form and substance coincide: the few who are the actual rulers of the state stand forth too as the titular rulers of the state. But in democracy, according to this interpretation, and *only* in democracy, form and substance are no longer one. The many who appear as the rulers are in fact only puppets; the real rulers are unseen and, to the public, unknown. But always they are there, and always they are the few.

Where, for the theorists of the organizational school, the few are those who come to power through the imperatives of the social structure—through their command, say, of the instruments of economic production—those few are, in the power or force interpretation of the state, men who are driven by the will to power, by the greed, the lust, the impulse to dominate and to govern the affairs of other men. They are those who have not only the urge to power but the ability to acquire and effectively to utilize the weapons of power. And the weapons of power are ultimately, in this view, but two— force and deceit.

To talk of the state, therefore, as a problem in active consent, or to look upon democracy as a form of political organization in which the masses of mankind determine, through the free expression of conflicting opinions, the broad ends to which public policy shall be directed, is to return, in this interpretation, to the images in Plato's cave. It is to mistake the form for the substance, the illusion of democracy for the reality of oligarchy. No matter what the ideological representation, no matter what the forms and the procedures, always, these critics of democracy maintain, the core of political organization is rule by the few; always the actual residence or depository of power is in the hands of a dominant oligarchy; always democracy is unreal.

I

THE POWER FACTOR IN OLIGARCHICAL THOUGHT

One of the earliest and most suggestive expressions of this doctrine is to be found in the several *Dialogues* of Plato, not merely in Thrasymachus' famous proclamation that "justice is nothing else than the interest of the stronger," [1] but even more in the dogmatic assurance with which Callicles affirms that rule belongs to the strong, that the strong man with "a nature capable of acquiring an empire or a tyranny or sovereignty" should give full vent to this nature and not admit "custom and reason and the opinion of other men to be lords over him."

"I plainly assert [said Callicles], that he who would truly live ought to allow his desires to wax to the uttermost, and not to chastise them; but when they have grown to their greatest he should have courage and intelligence to minister to them and to satisfy all his longings. And this I affirm to be natural justice and nobility. . . . Nature herself intimates that it is just for the better to have more than the worse, the more powerful than the weaker; and in many ways she shows . . . that justice consists in the superior ruling over and having more than the inferior." [2]

And when Socrates puts the question: "Are the superior and better and stronger the same or different?"; he receives from Callicles the reply: "I say unequivocally that they are the same." [3]

Whether or not these doctrines are characteristic of the Greek Sophists is unimportant for our purposes here.[4] What is important is that they were seriously advanced and tenaciously held, not simply by those to whom Plato attributed them but by a variety of thinkers ever since. Thus we find Machiavelli in the eighteenth chapter of *The Prince* urging his ruler to pursue the ways of the lion and the fox, for the force of beasts, war, he said, "is the sole art that belongs to him who rules." [5] And thus we find Hobbes, formulator of the great Leviathan, stating as "a generall inclination of all mankind, a perpetuall and restlesse desire of Power after power, that ceaseth only in Death." [6] Some, like the sociologists Ludwig Gumplowicz [7] and Franz Oppenheimer,[8] followed Marx in identifying this power factor with a particular class and in regarding the origin as well as the existence of government to be essentially a matter of conquest and domination. Others, like Nietzsche [9] and Spengler,[10] similarly conceived power to be the basis of the state and obedience a matter of compulsion, but held this concentration of power to lie not so much in the hands of a class as in the possession of individuals or cliques impregnated with the will to power and having or acquiring the means to effectuate that will. The doctrine was rationalized into still other forms by nationalist writers such as Treitschke, who regarded the state not merely as personality, not merely as will— indeed, "the most emphatic will that can be imagined"—but also and above all as power, "Power which makes it will to prevail," [11] and by Hegelian writers such as Bosanquet, for whom "the State . . . is necessarily force." [12] But for the restatement of the theory in all its crude and "realistic" essence, we must go to such modern expounders as Pareto and the spokesmen for Italian fascism.

In Pareto's view all governments rest on force and consent. The latter, however, he holds to be secondary, for not only can it be manufactured by cunning and deceit (Machiavelli's foxes), more important it can be governed or suppressed by force. Those who command the instruments of force, he argues, require only leaders adept at chicanery to triumph, "and history shows that such leadership is usually supplied by dissatisfied" leaders from those skilled in the art of guile. It is meaningless "to ask whether or not force ought to be used in a society, whether the use of force is or is not beneficial." The truth is that force is always used, both "by those who wish to preserve certain uniformities and by those who wish to overstep them." And in both cases that force is employed by a minority, by a few (the elite) who dominate rather than respond to the desires of the many. Government, argues Pareto, may claim to be founded on reason, but in fact it rests on force. And government, whatever the form it may assume, is always in substance oligarchic. The sovereign, the parliament, may occupy the stage; but behind the scenes is the everpresent governing class. Especially, says Pareto, is this marked in democracy.

"King Demos, good soul, thinks he is following his own devices. In reality he is following the lead of his rulers. . . . In the fact, whether universal suffrage prevails or not, it is always an oligarchy that governs, finding ways to give to the 'will of the people' that expression which the few desire. . . . [Universal suffrage, indeed,] is no more exactly definable, no less shrouded in mystery, no less beyond the pale of reality, than the hosts of other divinities." [13]

In this Paretian analysis Mussolini discovered what he held to be the true explanation of the nature of democracy. Democracy, he declared, is a form of government that gives the people the illusion rather than the reality of sovereignty. "The real effective sovereignty lies in the hands of other concealed and irresponsible forces." Democracy, nominally without a king, is in fact "ruled by many kings—more absolute, tyrannical, and ruinous than one sole king, even though a tyrant." For a true understanding of political society, therefore, we must look not to the form but to the substance of government. And this, in his view, is always oligarchical rule. [14]

These concepts of the unreality of democracy, of man's lust for power, of force (and its corollary, deceit) as the basis of the state, and of the localization of the control of force in an oligarchy able and anxious to use it, have been given frequent restatement by American critics of democracy. With the resignation of one who yields unwillingly to the inevitable, Max Nomad declared:

"There are only two principles governing all politics. First—to get power by all means, even the vilest; and, second, to keep that power by all means, even the vilest." [15]

Without such resignation but with an equal sense of the inevitable, L. J. Henderson embraced Pareto's interpretations as "a work of genius" and, pointing to the similarity between Pareto and Machiavelli, went on to defend the validity of this Machiavellian position.[16] In a drastic departure from his managerial hypothesis, James Burnham seized upon the power theory of the state as the true and conclusive explanation of political affairs and attempted to expand the doctrine into a science of politics.[17] And in a slender but provocative volume, W. B. Munro presented the argument that the people cannot be effective agencies in government, that oligarchy and not democracy perpetually obtains.[18]

Political life, Munro declared, is governed not by the people or by the opinions of the people but by the operation of certain deterministic historical laws. These laws do more than simply exert pressure; they actually control government. And of all these laws, Munro asserted, none is more important than the domination of the many by the few, the inevitable inclination of all governments to autocracy.

"Every government, whatsoever its form and howsoever guarded, tends to become a government by minority. The attempt has often been made to fasten political power in the hands of the whole people, but it never stays there. It gravitates into the possession of a class— a ruling class. . . . Nothing, indeed, is more impressive in all human history than the relative ease with which, under any and every form of government, the classes have managed to strip from the masses the substance of power while leaving them the outward forms of it. . . . It must inevitably turn out that way. . . . It is the essence of all government that the Few shall lead and the Many follow." [19]

It is inevitable, Munro argued, because men lust for power and organize not merely to arrogate but to enlarge that power. Those who hope for democracy, therefore, are "foreordained" to disappointment, for democracy is no more than "a form of government that goes through the gestures of obeisance to popular sovereignty." [20] Behind the pretensions of democracy, insisted Munro, lie always the invisible forces that actually and eternally rule.

This, then, is the indictment of democracy: that it may be the form but it is never the substance of government; that always the actuality of rule, of governance, is in the hands of a few irresponsible to the many; and that this ruling oligarchy both arrives at and maintains power through the employment of force and deceit, that the state, in the last analysis, is a function of power and not of consent. The elaboration of this argument has thus far been sketched in general and somewhat varied terms; for its full and forceful presentation by an effective American spokesman, let us turn to the numerous writings of Lawrence Dennis.[21]

II

Lawrence Dennis: The Elite As Power

There is one difficulty in dealing with Dennis (and other writers of this as well as other schools) that should be made plain at the outset. This is his frequent practice of confusing that which he thinks is with that which he thinks ought to be. This confusion arises in part from his attempt simultaneously to do three things: first, state the necessity, indeed the inevitability, of irresponsible elite rule; second, prescribe certain values or purposes which he thinks a good elite should endeavor to secure; and third, persuade his readers that they should both welcome and support such an elite. His books, that is to say, are an argument for fascism; consequently he speaks in part of what people should do. On the other hand, he seeks to rationalize or justify this choice of action by arguing that some such choice must be made, that the situation not only is as he depicts it but that it also and always must be, and that in acting according to his precepts we are merely taking cognizance of the reality. In this respect his books also constitute a deterministic argument against democracy. Sometimes it is difficult to tell which facet of the political problem he is presenting—the reality or the desirability. More often, indeed, the sprawling nature of his argument makes it difficult to know just what his central objection to democracy is. For our purpose in this section, however, we shall consider only the negative and deterministic portion of his argument, only, that is, his indictment of the democratic principle as a vain and impossible dream. And we shall seek, in these terms, to ascertain the specific grounds on which he rests his charge.

Unlike those anti-democratic theorists who profess a personal predilection for democracy but argue that detached and scientific observation compels a recognition of its impossibility or undesirability, Dennis, in strict compliance with his avowed policy of "realism, logical consistency, and emotional sincerity," admits categorically his disbelief in democracy. He is, he tells us, "an apologist for the authoritarian [totalitarian] state and a critic of liberal democracy." [22] This acknowledgment of preference, however, should not be taken to imply a prejudiced or preferential interpretation of political phenomena, for, Dennis insists, whatever else his books may do, they approach the subject with the careful scrutiny of the objective analyst. As he puts it:

"The first point to make clear about this analysis and view is that the bases are facts and logical deductions from such facts rather than ethics or preferences. . . . Its method aims to be scientific and logical, not ethical. . . . My preferences are brought in only incidentally to the development of the . . . main theses which are largely interpretative of actual trends and probable events." [23]

As we study the facts, Dennis observes, we note at once a phenomenon of primary importance: this is the division of society into rulers and ruled, elite and mass. The former are the few who actually and "always determine what the masses get." The latter are the many, those who, under all systems, are always excluded from power. Men may battle as to which set of the elite shall rule; they may even join issue as to which system will make that rule effective. But, Dennis insists, "there is no choice as to whether or not some group of the elite shall rule. . . . There must always be a ruling or managing class." [24]

This ruling or dominant class is, according to Dennis, made up of two elements: those of the elite who are in power and those of the elite who are out of power but seek it. The determination of who shall be "in" and who shall be "out," while of interest, is of no real significance to the average man; he "goes on doing as he is told." But to the different sections of the elite that determination is crucial. Both are greedy for power. Both are willing and strong enough to fight for it. And both do. Who the dominant elite shall be, in consequence, "can never be permanently determined by law," by reason, by abstract principles, or theories of justice; these, Dennis insists, can never be the determinants of social order. What is decisive is power, the force factors that emerge as the expression of the conflict of peoples, of group pressures, of human appetites. And the ultimate play of these force factors, "as in war, takes place outside the bounds of law." [25]

This, Dennis holds, is not only as it should, but as it must, be. "Politics is always essentially a conspiracy of power," and law is essentially the means whereby "contests of sheer force or might" are staged. "It specifically makes possible and easy ways in which the strong can use force to crush and oppress the weak." [26] The failure of liberals and conservatives both, Dennis argues, is that they

"still think of politics as a game. *They have not awakened to the fact that it is now a war.* In war, as all military manuals teach in chapter one, the purpose is to destroy the enemy." [27]

Those who, therefore, still think in terms of right rather than in terms of might are oblivious to the naked reality of social order. It is not right that makes might; on the contrary, Dennis affirms, it is always and only might that makes right. This is true under the totalitarian régimes; it is equally true under the liberal régimes.[28]

Consider, for a moment, the nature of a social order. Is it the expression of the will of the people or is it not rather "the expression of the composite will of a dominant class?" Clearly, says Dennis, it is the latter. Is this dominant class in control by virtue of its principles or wealth or property or is it not rather in control through its command of "the instruments of power . . . guns and propaganda?" Again, says Dennis, it is clearly the latter. And is not the operating plan "always an expression of the might of the people"; does it not derive its rightness, "its moral validity and its practicability from the might which makes it effective"; and does it not prevent "contrary might from making it ineffective?" All this, says Dennis, is clear beyond dispute. Plainly, then, rule is power, and power is force, and force is might, and a social order is rightfully the embodiment as it is the reflection of the will of the strong; for, Dennis concludes, "only might can make right right or effective." [29] Thus Dennis, in the manner of the Greek Sophist Thrasymachus, returns to the affirmation that justice is the right of the stronger. "The motivating force," he declares, "is the will to power"; the actualizing force is the expression of power. Always it is power, for in the last analysis "force has always ruled the world." [30]

It is true, Dennis admits, that certain forms of state, such as democracy, do not appear to rest on force, and indeed in America the clique in power does not openly do so. Unlike a totalitarian system such as the Soviet Union, Dennis observes, where the dominant elite can openly and honestly accomplish its purposes through the use of force, the elite in this country must, if it is to maintain the form of democracy, proceed "with guile and duplicity." [31] But it is important, he adds, not to let this curtain of deception obscure the reality of the power which sustains it. At bottom, Dennis insists, the form of democracy becomes the substance of oligarchy. In his words:

"The elite do rule, as liberal theory does not recognize; . . . they, and not the majority of the people, make most of the important choices; . . . their acts are not subject to popular control by the ballot or the enforcement of the Constitution in the way liberal theory supposes possible. . . . The elite are the leaders, the directives lie with them. Directions of social trends are determined by them." [32]

This is not to say, however, that in the form of the democratic state the people are utterly helpless, that the elite are subject to no control by the people, that the elite rule in a wholly capricious and irresponsible way. This, says Dennis, is belied by the obvious fact that when a majority, "as so seldom happens," is agreed on the necessity for a change and is both "capably inspired and led by the out-elite," they do exercise an effective voice in the determination of which elite shall be in power. "In this way," Dennis holds, "the majority can be said to determine a change in rule." But this change in rule, he continues, means no more than the replacement by one elite of another elite; it is in no sense the assumption of power by the people. The majority decision, moreover, is itself, "in the largest number of cases, nothing more or less than the product of a minority interest managing things and wielding power." [33]

And when we regard carefully not the form but the reality of the democratic state, we find, according to Dennis, that it is not opinion but force which fundamentally prevails. The duties and obligations of the individual are determined not by the free play of opinion, not by popular directive or popular consent, but by the forceful power of the ruling class. In Dennis' phrase: "It may be said that the social situation rests on consent only if it is assumed that those who are powerless against the coercion applied consent to what they do not like but cannot alter." [34]

This, Dennis affirms, is the true description of political organization. And never more so than now. For democracy, even as mere form, is "an order doomed by the irresistible trend of prevailing social forces." In its place we shall have fascism, "the inevitable alternative." It is useless to attempt to repair or preserve the old system; we are faced now with "a trend we are clearly powerless to arrest." Do what we will, "present trends must put the state sooner or later in the complete control of some combination of power groups with a will to use the state in the pursuit of ends not embraced within the liberal ideologies." [35]

III

ANALYSIS AND CRITICISM OF THE POWER THEORY

It will be seen that this argument is, in many ways, analogous to the Burnham thesis. Both approach the problems of men in a spirit of alleged objectivity; both profess a method divorced from values and revolving only about facts. Both derive from the application of this "scientific" method a conviction that oligarchy is a universal feature of political society. Both insist that this oligarchy not only has been and is, but that it must either forever or in the foreseeable future continue to be. Both hold that the desires and intentions of ordinary men are irrelevant or unimportant to the determination of public policy and the selection of ruling personnel. Both conclude, in consequence, that democracy as men ordinarily conceive it to be is impossible.

They differ, however, in two significant respects. Where Burnham regards his oligarchy as a closely integrated ruling class resting on a community of economic function, Dennis speaks not so much of a ruling class as he does of an elite, and not so much of an elite (in the general sense of leaders) as of a clique of strong and ruthless men bound together by a common lust or greed for power. And where Burnham conceives his ruling class attaining power as the automatic consequence of economic imperatives, of social organization, Dennis argues that the rule of the elite is the consequence not of its economic position but of its strength, of its superior capacity and willingness to use force and deceit. Both affirm a deterministic doctrine: but in the one case it is a theory of structural (in particular, economic) determinism, in the other a concept of psychological determinism.

This is not, it is important to add, to argue that Dennis is unaware of the impact and importance of economic factors. On the contrary, he builds much of his argument on the premise that democracy is doomed because of its economic inability to survive. Indeed, in several remarkably similar passages he anticipates both the thesis and many of the supporting arguments developed by Burnham in *The Managerial Revolution*.[36] But the stress, for Dennis, as for Pareto, is always on what men think and do, what they believe and how they act. It is never the mechanics of a structure or organization that is, in Dennis' view, the determinative force.

The crucial points of distinction between the two theories are, then, the composition of the oligarchy and the manner in which this oligarchy comes to power and maintains it. And if the validity of Dennis' conceptions of these factors be granted, his conclusion that democracy is impossible—that it may exist in form but never in substance—inescapably follows. Let us, therefore, examine his arguments in some detail.

A. THE PROBLEM OF ELITE

It is unnecessary to consider here the simple historical theory that oligarchy, because it has forever been, must continue forever to be, and this despite Dennis' proclamation that

"Every culture has to be run by an elite. The more complex and the more revolutionary, the more essential the function of the directing elite. This is more or less Michels' 'iron law of oligarchy.' " [37]

It is unnecessary for two reasons: first, the discussion in the previous chapter (sec. III, A) of this aspect of perpetual minority rule applies, broadly, to the contention here; second, and no less important, Dennis himself attaches far less significance to this phase of the deterministic argument than does Burnham. Indeed, in one place Dennis, speaking of the assumption that we are governed by eternal and inexorable laws, specifically declares:

"The assumption is obviously false both as to history and human psychology. Life is not a game to be played under immutable rules. It is, among other things, a grand free-for-all fight over what the rules shall be." [38]

What is significant, in Dennis' construction, is (1) the nature of the elite and (2) the relevance of the elite for democracy.

The nature of the elite. If it is democracy that is illusion and oligarchy that is real, the first necessity in political analysis would appear to be the identification of those who, in the oligarchy, command the instruments of state power. These, Dennis tells us, are the elite. But when we press for a more precise delineation of the elite, for a more specific enumeration of those criteria that will enable us objectively to distinguish elite from mass, we obtain from Dennis not one but a variety of definitions. In some places he speaks of "an aristocracy of management," in others of "the frustrated elite of the lower middle classes," in still others of those having an income (in 1936) of three thousand dollars or more; then again, he speaks of the influential and the powerful, not only of those who are "actually influential and powerful" but also of those who are "potentially influential and powerful," or of the "elite of exceptional natural endowment," or of the greedy as contrasted with the needy. And in one passage he summarily declares:

"The elite may be considered to mean that one-fourth to one-third of the population which, for whatever reasons, is actually or potentially more powerful and influential than the balance of the population. This would include all the professional classes, all businessmen, all farmers, all persons having incomes well above the average, and all who by reason of personal qualities or advantages of any sort have considerably more to say about the running of things than the average man." [39]

The numerous contradictions in this series of definitions are too apparent to require more than passing comment here. Those who comprise the *aristocracy* of management cannot at the same time be those who are both frustrated and of the *lower* middle classes. Those who possess a superior natural endowment—provided we can agree on what is superior and natural and endowed—do not necessarily receive a superior income, nor do those who receive a superior income necessarily possess an exceptional natural endowment. Those who are needy may also be greedy—for power, for riches, or for whatever rewards a society may offer. How, moreover, do we identify those who are "potentially" more influential and powerful before they have "actually" demonstrated that quality? Dennis gives us no specifications, and if we turn to the fact of demonstration for proof of the potentiality, we obviously fall prey to the logical fallacy of arguing in reverse, of falsely assuming that the affirmation of the consequent establishes the existence of the antecedent. Considerations such as these, when conjoined with the statistical ambiguity of such phrases as "*well above* the average" and "personal qualities or advantages *of any sort*" that enable the possessor to have "*considerably more to say* about the running of things than the average man," serve to indicate that Dennis' figure, "one-fourth to one-third of the population," is not so much a carefully calculated estimate based on objectively determined data, as it is an arbitrary delineation designed to encompass the maximum that may yet perhaps remain a minority. Moreover, to say that one-fourth to one-third of the population has considerably more of a voice or influence in the running of things than the average man is to say little indeed. If the statement is to have any relevance to Dennis' thesis at all, it must be shown that this one-fourth to one-third has its say in a very particular way, that it speaks as a ruling class or elite. And this evidence Dennis nowhere puts forth.

To these reflections on the composition of the elite, we may add yet another observation. In close imitation of Pareto, Dennis advances a twofold division within society: one, a division between elite and mass; the other, a division of the elite into "ins" and "outs," or, as Pareto would say, into governing and non-governing elites. These, Dennis insists, are the only significant class cleavages.[40] But as we have already seen, no serious and objective criteria are adduced to enable us to distinguish the elite from the mass, and indeed it is difficult to see how this can be done. Both Dennis and Pareto appear to have ignored the elementary fact that among the "mass" most men are in some respect elite, most men are in some one thing superior to other men; and this being so it is impossible to speak of an abstract superiority as the sufficient criterion of an oligarchical elite.[41] And if it is only the elite of strength with which we are to be concerned, where is the evidence to indicate that those who are strong possess the "class consciousness, pride, and solidarity" that Dennis attributes to them? [42]

Take, as simple illustration, Dennis' inclusion of *all* businessmen in the elite, the strong element in society. We need not dwell on his castigation elsewhere of these same businessmen as "the least intelligent and creative members of our ruling classes," nor on his insistence that "they are less articulate than the average taxi driver or longshoreman, and they make much less sense." [43] We should, however, pause to observe that by this broad inclusion the small retailer and the neighborhood iceman are thrust into the same ruling class as the great industrialist, while the average wage earner whose income may yet be greater than that of the iceman or the grocer or the haberdasher is of the mass. When Dennis goes on to add to this impossible alignment the insistence that the elite (iceman, grocer, haberdasher, great industrialist) are united by consciousness of class, by pride and solidarity, the imagination of the reader may well feel unduly taxed. Similarly, if the strong are, in Lasswell's phrase, those who get the most of what there is to get, we are confronted with the fact that different people not only get different things, and in different quantities, but that those who get more of one may get less of another. Thus we have not one but a plurality of elites, some of whom may overlap as well as conflict with the others.

The failure clearly to delineate elite from mass renders doubly difficult the attempt to distinguish ruling and non-ruling groups within the elite, for how do we determine who are the "ins" and who are the "outs" when we do not even know the supposedly elite group of which they are each a part? By what characteristics are we to recognize the dominant rulers of oligarchy? It cannot be argued that the dominant elite are those who govern (i.e., play a role in the government, real or apparent), for apart from the circularity of such reasoning there is no conclusive evidence that those who govern always constitute a cohesive and coherent group. Nor is there any real indication that it is strength rather than some other quality which sets off the "governing elite" from the "non-governing elite"; for if there is no accurate separation of the various elites, there can be no attribution of specific characteristics to those elites. Yet if any one thing must be shown, it is that the elite is a class, a group of men united by a strong sense of class consciousness and class ambition; for without this sense of solidarity it is impossible —in Dennis' own terms—for the elite to come to power *as a class*. And clearly such a consciousness of class cannot be ascribed to a body which has not been, and perhaps cannot be, defined.

We are, in a word, back to definitions; and the definitions advanced by Dennis—as well as by other theorists of this school [44]— are as contradictory as they are vague. And in politics no less than in logic, confusion is still no guide to understanding.

The relevance of the elite. Let us, however, grant in all its generality and abstractness the reality and the existence of a ruling elite. Let us say, with Dennis, that in all societies there are a few superior to, and more influential than, the many, and that the distinguishing characteristic of these few (the elite) is their superior or greater strength. What, the important question becomes, is the relevance of this admission for democracy? According to Dennis, the mere fact that there is an elite is sufficient to deny the possibility of democracy; for the elite and not the people, he insists, actually rule. But is there a necessary incompatibility between the elite principle and the theory of democracy?

The answer, on reflection, is patently in the negative, for leadership is as necessary in democracy as it is in any other form of state, and this leadership must be that of a minority. Only a minority can at any one time conduct the manifold affairs of state and manage the actual machinery of government; only a minority can effectively resolve the innumerable specific issues that constantly confront governments with a demand for immediate decision. There is leadership everywhere—in clubs, in churches, in armies, in industries, indeed in all aspects of social life as well as in all levels of government—and leadership implies a division between the few who make up the vanguard and the many who make up its train. In this respect democracy equally with other forms of state accepts as basic the fact of elite. Indeed, from this point of view, democratic government may be regarded as an institutional device for securing proper and adequate leadership. It is not, in consequence, the fact of leadership, the mere existence of elite, that is the crucial distinction between democracy and oligarchy. The central point at issue is the fact of responsibility: whether the leadership derives its power from the freely given assent of the people and whether the policies pursued by the leadership conform to the changing tides of public opinion. These, the components of political responsibility, and not the mere fact of minority leadership, are the essential criteria of forms of government.[45]

Those who, therefore, as Dennis and Pareto, look to the existence of elite as the sufficient denial of democracy, build unrealistically on the very simple consideration that the elite—broadly regarded as leadership by the "superior" few—exist in all states. They fail to apprehend the rudimentary truth that it is not the fact of elite as against non-elite that is the demarcation of governments, but the kind of elite that may in any one society happen to prevail— whether it is a democratic leadership or an authoritarian leadership.

B. THE DOMINATION OF POWER

It is the essence of Dennis' argument, however, that the elite is always an irresponsible elite and therefore never a democratic elite. What we regard as democratic leadership, he holds, is in reality but the external obeisance that disguises the true avoidance of popular rule. The elite, he insists, is not the agent of authority but the authority itself. And it is an irresponsible (oligarchical) authority because it is made up of those men whose ruthless will to power carries them into the seats of government and who, once there, deny through the imposition of force the full degree of freedom and political opposition that democracy requires. In this construction there is advanced a twofold doctrine—one, a theory of psychological determinism, the other, a power or force interpretation of the state—the conjunction of which is held to explain both the manner in which the elite comes to power and how that elite rule is maintained. What is the validity of this view?

That this twofold doctrine does account for much of what has happened in history is immediately apparent. The machinations of Dionysius the elder and Agothocles in ancient Syracuse give striking support to Grote's observation that "the machinery of fraud whereby the people were to be cheated into a temporary submission, as a prelude to the machinery of force whereby such submission was to be perpetuated against their consent—was the stock in trade of Grecian usurpers." [46] And we have but to recall the unsavory history of Cesare Borgia and his father Pope Alexander VI in Renaissance Italy, or the political adventurism of Cromwell, Napoleon, Mussolini, and Hitler in modern Europe, or the tyranny and deception of local Caesars who still flourish in American communities, or the strategy of wars and the chicanery that accompanies them in the guise of diplomacy, to note the evidence that argues powerfully in support of the guns and guile theory of the state.

But to recognize the validity of such an interpretation in numerous historical instances is not in itself to argue that the interpretation is therefore sufficient. In the first place, it may be irrelevant to other situations, historical or contemporary. And in the second place, it may be not the full but the partial explanation even in some of those situations where it does apply. To sustain the contention that it is *always* the true explanation, that political power is always and everywhere essentially a matter of force and deceit, it is necessary to go considerably beyond the mere recital of historical events. It is necessary to show that the explanation applies as a matter of logical or inherent inexorability, and that it is the fundamental or dominant if not the exclusive interpretation. Let us consider in these terms Dennis' central concepts.

The will to power. To the extent that Dennis lays stress on the will to power doctrine as a necessary factor in the interpretation of political rule, there is clearly no ground for objection. The few revelations by anthropologists that primitive communities exist in which the power motive is absent or minimized,[47] while of interest to an understanding of the development of that power impulse, do not remove the obvious fact that in the world's great civilizations the drive for dominance has been everywhere present. Whether we conceive of that drive as an instinct inherent in the organic structure of man,[48] or as a childhood reaction to frustration,[49] or as a socially developed means to the attainment of particular ends, there is sufficient agreement among the several psychological schools that it is a drive of major and dependable significance.[50]

This was perceived even by such expounders of the organizational doctrine as Mosca and Michels, both of whom employed it as a necessary adjunct to their primary doctrine, without however attempting to rest it on psychological grounds more specific than the greed for power on the part of the leaders and the apathy of the masses. It was an insight vigorously emphasized by Sorel, as when he discoursed of the voraciousness of political appetites.[51] And for Machiavelli and Pareto, of course, it was the core of all political analysis. When Dennis argues, therefore, that the clue to the understanding of political power is in the will to dominate, he rests his case on a necessary foundation.

What is peculiar to Dennis and other anti-democratic theorists of this school, however, is that they do not stop here. They recognize that the mere existence of the power impulse in man in no way dictates the inevitability of oligarchy, for democracy can, through the imposition of restraints, readily reconcile individuals or groups having a flair for dominance with its special forms of government. What Dennis claims, over and beyond this, is the residence, the localization, of that will in a particular group (the elite) only. According to him, the inert masses, lacking both the capacity and the urge to rule, are never the leaders but always those willing to be led. The elite group, on the other hand, possessing both the capacity and the will to rule, is able—by virtue of such possession— to impose itself on the masses. What we have, in consequence, is a broad and simple alignment of dominant versus recessive groups, a situation in which those who have the will to power dominate those who do not have the will to power.

So sweeping a generalization, however, is as vulnerable as it is immediately suspect. To divide mankind into two categories, elite and mass, is one thing; to assert that the division corresponds with the possession or non-possession of a particular psychological trait is quite another. And when we find in all of Dennis' writings no evidence calculated to sustain the latter proposition, nothing beyond the mere statement that it is so, we have adequate cause to question its validity. The real vulnerability of the argument, however, appears in connection with the simple fact or challenge of democracy itself. If democracy exists at all, it does so only on the basis of a resistance psychology, on a refusal by the masses to permit the unrestrained exercise of political power by men not answerable to the people. But this resistance could not be manifested unless the masses too, no less than the elite, possessed the will to power. And if the masses, equally with the elite, have the will or impulse to power, we arrive at a constant psychological factor which cannot possibly explain the variations in political rule. The very fact or being of democracy, therefore, is the conclusive negation of Dennis' sweeping doctrine.

If it be argued in reply that this objection overlooks the central point at issue in that it assumes the existence of the non-existential (democracy)—that it takes for granted the reality of democracy and then argues from the assumption that democracy exists back to the psychological grounds on which that assumption can be maintained—the obvious rejoinder is to point to the admitted necessity for democratic pretensions. If the masses are apathetic and lack the will to power, why are force and deceit necessary to this oligarchical theory of the state? Surely force need not be exercised against a people incapable of revolt; and just as plainly deceit need not be employed against a people whose opinions, even if different from those the rulers desire them to hold, could not result in a thrust to power. The sheer necessity of maintaining the "façade" of democracy is sufficient proof that the will to power is not restricted to the members of the elite alone. And when we conjoin with this the very real rise of the democratic movement, particularly since the great French Revolution of the eighteenth century, we note beyond peradventure the inability of Dennis' broad generalization to stand.

This point may perhaps more readily be seen if we approach the problem from a slightly different view, if we consider, for example, some of the many-faceted relationships in which power has its being. For our purposes, three such relationships are crucial: (*a*) the relation of the leader to his followers (the problem within an elite); (*b*) the relation of the leader and his group to other leaders and their groups (the problem among or between elites); and (*c*) the relation of the leaders and their elite groups to the people (the problem of elite to non-elite).

(*a*) In a complex world no one person can alone possess the manifold resources and instruments of power. In consequence, the drive for political supremacy necessarily becomes a collective enterprise. To this degree political domination becomes at once a social as much as it does an individual function, for "only that individual can exercise domination who has the ability to integrate the interests of powerful factions or special interest groups of which the domain is composed." [52] This involves at the very least the creation of a balance-of-power situation with the masterful individual at the top. But the masterful individual is not at the top simply because he has a will to power. If he has a will to power, so have those who associate themselves with him; and in the sharing of a mutual endeavor it is rare or unknown that conditions fail to be exacted. The masterful individual attains ascendancy because of his ability to compromise the differences among his followers, which means that the allegiance he secures is predicated on his promise or ability to satisfy their demands. This goes beyond the mere conjunction of the will to lead, on the one side, and the will to follow, on the other. It is the resultant of a process of barter, under which circumstance the will to power even of the most domineering of men is necessarily curtailed, delimited, or in some way modified and channeled by wills outside of himself. The leader or dominator, then, no matter how great the degree of his power, is never an absolute monarch. Always he is part of a collective movement and always he is in some measure controlled no less than he is sustained by those whose support he seemingly has. "The leader," in Max Lerner's phrase, "not only rides the movement but is ridden by it." [53]

(*b*) What is true of the leader in relation to his own group is equally true of the leader and his group (as one part of the elite) vis-à-vis other leaders and their groups (other parts of the elite). Unless there is a merger or unification of many diversified interests in a greater and more cohesive class interest, the "elite" will contain groups in conflict as well as in agreement with each other. And Dennis, as we have seen, has in no sense demonstrated the class cohesiveness of the elite. Indeed, his inability even to delineate with any degree of accuracy the nature of the elite underscores the fact that if there is such a thing as the elite it is not one but many elites, and if there are many elites there are many currents of opposition. From such a situation, it is plain, no one will to power can emerge untrammeled; the pressure and pull of multitudinous wills means the curbing of any one. Especially is this true where a particular will emerges into temporary ascendancy so that all other wills concentrate their energies upon it for purposes of concession or control.

(*c*) Most important of all, however, is the relation we have already noted as central: that of the elite to the people. It is simple enough to say, as Dennis and the fascists do, that it is the duties rather than the rights of the masses with which the rulers of the state (the elite) are concerned. But this is to overlook the obvious fact that the masses frequently do not share such ideas on the subject. A people so permeated with fear as actually to believe that Attila the Hun might be what he styled himself to be—"the scourge of God"—are hardly the same as those who swept the lilies of France into the streets of Paris. A people prepared for an authoritarian *Führer* by the mystical doctrines of a Hegel, a Spengler, and a Houston Stewart Chamberlain, are not the same as those who ridicule and cast aside a Huey Long, a Fritz Kuhn, a Charles E. Coughlin. If Nietzsche is right when he says that the will to power is the very essence of existence, he must also be right when he says

that the will to power is in the weak no less than the strong; for
existence is common to all men, not only to supermen. Thus his
proclamation, "Wherever I found a living thing, there found I a will
to power, and even in the will of the servant, found I *the will to be
Master*," is an admission that the masses too will drive for power.
As Melekian observes:

"In strict logic, the refutation of Nietzschean individualism is furnished by its very assumptions. If the strong few have a desire for
power, so have the weak majority. What should prevent them from
making a collective resistance, nay, even a collective attack on the
dangerous assailers, and aim at their subjection or even their
annihilation? If the will to power is their very nature, how can they
deny it for the sake of the few? Would this not be the denial of
nature itself?" [54]

The will-to-power theory, in brief, is a double-edged weapon that
can just as readily be applied to one half of the elite-mass dichotomy
as it can to the other. And because the masses also, in the logic of
this doctrine, lust for power, the successful leader or section of the
elite is not he who defies or ignores the support of the people, but
he who seeks and employs it. And if he is to get that support he
must, as Dennis and Pareto argue, either win or compel it. If he is
to win it, he will patently do so only if he succeeds both in satisfying
their demands and in guarding their conventions, in which circumstance his is a will subject to popular control. The increasing
measure of that control, as indicated in part by the degree of his
responsiveness and the number and quality of his concessions, is
the measure of the democracy that thereby prevails. And in this
respect the will-to-power theory in no way contravenes the democratic principle. If, on the other hand, he seeks to compel it, he is
faced with the logical alternative, as Hobbes said, of a war of all
against all. For in these terms there is always a conflict of wills:
always those who wield power are confronted with the opposition of
those over whom that power is wielded. "Just as there is a continuous desire for power, so also there is a continuous desire to make
that power the servant of the bulk of the individuals it affects." [55]
Aristotle warned the monarch of this danger in urging him to keep

his ear to the ground and to satisfy his subjects lest they rebel; for absolute coercion, he well perceived, is a practical impossibility.[56] The will to power can never live unrestrained.

These several considerations serve to indicate the inadequacy of the will-to-power theory as a general and conclusive explanation of the inevitability of oligarchy. The road between will and power is as arduous as it is long; and in the attempt to conjoin the two many deep-seated currents have to be met and explained away. The nature of these currents and the problems involved in their resolution are issues that would take us too far afield to permit examination here.[57] Enough has been said, however, to make plain this one truth: that the will to power moves always in an ethos governed by many wills, and is, in consequence, inescapably subject to social (as it is amenable to democratic) controls.[58] Those who, therefore, as Dennis and Pareto, postulate a simple one-way relationship of imposition and acceptance, admit marriage to a psychology of power itself almost completely divorced from the realities of human behavior.

The state as power. The governing elite, Dennis further argues, attains and solidifies its power not merely through the supremacy of its will but through the employment of two central weapons: force and deceit. Indeed, Dennis insists, if we are to understand the true nature of the state, we will do so only through a correct appreciation of the dominance of force; for not only are right and wrong matters of might, the fundamental social conflicts themselves, he holds, are essentially those of naked power. Government, in a word, is always the rule of the strong, and force, always triumphant, is the basis of the state as it is the sovereign of the world.[59]

We need not delay unduly over the fraud factor in this construction, for this, while necessary—as Machiavelli and Pareto insisted—is clearly subservient to the element of force itself. Where discussion is free, deceit is doubly vulnerable: it is combatted by other deceits and it is exposed by truth. To ensure the victory of a particular deceit, in consequence, it is necessary to prevent freedom of discussion, and this means the application of force. As Mussolini bluntly expressed it:

"My desire is to govern if possible with the consent of the majority; but, in order to obtain, to foster and to strengthen that consent, I will use all the force at my disposal. . . . For it may happen that force may bring about consent, and, if that fails, there is always force." [60]

The crucial and ultimate factor, then, is the force factor, and that this is one of the cardinal features of social existence is attested full well by its widespread, indeed almost universal, use in history. It was not for lack of substance that philosophers like Thrasymachus and Thomas Hobbes, political engineers like Machiavelli, and mystical theorists like Fichte, Nietzsche, and others who flourished in modern Germany, were able to build a doctrine dedicated to the justification of the strong. Nor was it for lack of familiarity or of reason that early eighteenth century poets such as John Gay could put into the mouths of protesting highwaymen words such as these:

"Why are the Laws levell'd at us? are we more dishonest than the rest of Mankind? What we win, Gentlemen, is our own by the Law of Arms, and the Right of Conquest." [61]

Indeed, so pervasive and paramount a factor is the element of force that when a recent anti-democratic writer, Wyndham Lewis, advanced the proposition that the ruler himself—ostensibly for the sake of the ruled—should be "forced to rule by force," [62] his argument found ready support in the obvious examples of contemporary and near-contemporary totalitarian states.

To deny the strength and the vitality of the force factor is, in point of fact, not only historically but logically impossible. As T. H. Green observed, force is the outward visible sign of every state; it is the very mark of the supreme or independent coercive power that is lodged in political government. [63] Without force, no government can perdure; with force, government stands buttressed by an essential attribute of state. But to admit the reality of force as a characteristic of the state is no sufficient warrant for the conclusion that force is thereby the essence of the state. There is still the ineluctable fact that force is but a part—not even, necessarily, the dominant part—and not the whole of power. There is still the crucial consideration that, for the state, as for man, force is essentially an instrument, not end but means. And as an instrument it can be used equally to destroy or to sustain a state, equally to divide or to unite a people. These are truths both powerful and profound; they can no more rightly be excluded from valid theories of the state than can the force factor itself.

Consider, for example, the element of force in relation to power. According to Dennis, these are equivalent and interchangeable terms: those who hold force—and in his conception force is a matter of guns, sheer might—also hold power. But how then are we to explain the successful stand of the Roman Catholic Church against the onslaughts of Mussolini, he who had both the guns and the declared will to employ them? How are we to account for the power of money, of property, or for the power that accrues to men as the result of organization? If intelligence is of no avail, why do men resort to strategy rather than surrender to a numerically greater or stronger group? Whence came the power, the moral force, of Gandhi? Whence came the spiritual influence of rabbis, ministers, and priests, the veneration accorded men of learning in China? These, and questions like these, but begin to suggest the many difficulties inherent in so narrow a view of power as that which equates it with might alone. And if we consider for a moment simply the role of opinion, we note the thorough-going inadequacy of this interpretation.

When a man with a gun demands your money, it is not the mere presence of the gun but your belief that he will use it that compels your obedience. When a band of armed men responds to a leader, or a platoon of soldiers to an officer, it is not the force of the single gun that secures their acquiescence; on the contrary, if the many so willed, they could turn their own guns in overwhelming might against the inconsequential physical force embodied in the one. What determines the behavior of the ruled is opinion, belief, not force. Even where that opinion is rooted in fear, even in fear of force, still it is opinion and not brute force that most commonly decides. Bodies may cringe, but generally in anticipation; fists may clench, but they remain, as Michels said, in the pockets. Force as direct, brute, physical strength is but one of the instruments of coercion. Opinion too is a force, according to Mill "one of the greatest active social forces." [64] In this respect Sorel was far wiser than Dennis and Pareto, for he recognized that ideologies which move men are far more important as historical forces than the actual might which is employed to sustain or eliminate those ideologies. Caesar may destroy Christ, but not the idea that Christ taught. Gentile may destroy Jew, but not the faith which governs him. White may put down Black, but the drive for justice is not thereby wiped away. And guns may hold down men, but only while men sleep.

Might is but one of the several forms or kinds of power; it is not the whole of power, nor is it even the whole of force. Yet there are those, for example Marx and Oppenheimer, who would prove that the state is peculiarly force by pointing to the origin of the state in force. This, however, is an explanation no more accurate today than it was in the time of Aristotle. That unique mind suggested then that the true emergence of the state is a function of the family, and the evidence of anthropologists and sociologists in the two millennia since he wrote has amply borne out the validity of his insight. Equally untrue is the argument that the state is force because it has developed in force. As Rivers and Thomas have shown, government in primitive tribes can in no sense be equated with force alone.[65] And as the transformations of governments in history indicate, change comes not merely through revolutions of violence or the domination of an imposed will. Opinion, education, technology —these too leave their impress on governments and forms of state.[66]

These reflections enable to us perceive the second and no less crucial weakness in Dennis' conception of force as the basis of the state, namely, the simple fact that power and force are not solely ends but also means, that the state cannot rest solely on force because force is itself frequently the manifestation of something outside itself. Dennis would appear to recognize this when he says, typically: "The chief objective of this conspiracy [government as monopoly of force] is everywhere today, and usually has been in times past, the realization of a given scheme of social values which were both rationalized and cherished by those in power." [67] But elsewhere he repeatedly insists that the issue is solely that of naked power, of guns versus guns, of might to rule the world. The state, he maintains, is essentially the monopoly and the exercise of power.

Now this combination of ideas, as Barker remarked of Treitschke, raises difficulties. "If the fundamental cause of the existence and preservation of the State is culture [or, as Dennis puts it, a given scheme of social values] then the essential attribute of the State is not power but culture; and the State should be defined not as power, but as the organ of culture, which only uses power as a means to culture, and so far as it is such a means." [68] This, however, implies the subordination rather than the exaltation of power. It admits the role of force, but only as servant, not as master. Indeed, this could not be otherwise. "Force is the sword of government, but what nerves the hand that wields the sword is not and cannot in the last analysis be force." [69] The real issue then is the conflict of values, in which force moves as a weapon which may or may not, depending upon the peculiar circumstances of the moment, prove triumphant. To talk of force as the basis of the state is to ignore or to misapprehend the fact that what makes a state is not the mere exercise of supreme coercive power but the exercise of that power in a particular way and for particular ends. When Dean Inge declared, "A man may build himself a throne of bayonets, but he cannot sit on it," [70] he captured, though admittedly in a crude and somewhat overstated epigram, the essence of the true principle that force alone can never accurately depict the nature or substance of the state.

Why, then, proponents of the force theory argue, does the state arrogate to itself the full right to the exercise of force? If the state is not founded on power, on force and violence, why does it insist on the monopolization of the force factor? Is not this sufficient proof that the state rests on force alone? The answer to this question is, in a sense, the decisive refutation of the doctrine of those who advance it. For the state, paradoxically, monopolizes the factor of force in order to prevent and to end the rule of force. Actually, of course, the state never completely monopolizes the element of force: the church, the family, the school, miscellaneous groups of diverse size and aims and composition—all retain and utilize some part of it. But what the state does is to secure as near a monopoly of force as it possibly can. And the state does this primarily, as we have said, to prevent others from using it. If the state failed in this endeavor, if men were free to employ force in the resolution of their affairs, then not peace but war, not reason but strength, would prevail. The state must, in consequence, as a very condition of its existence, legitimately apply its force so as to prevent others from utilizing it, as in the attainment of political rule. Through the denial of force the state maintains the conditions of social order so that law rather than individual might shall determine the conflicts among men.[71]

Nor is this all. The state, through the positive application of its force concentration, is able to neutralize, to cancel, to overcome the force employed by those who would reject the supremacy of law and resort to adjudication by battle. Here, it is true, in this exercise of force against those of its citizens who would rebel or otherwise seek to deny the law, is the strongest evidence to sustain the force or power theory of the state. But one does not, as Dennis would urge of democracy, halt an analysis merely at the surface manifestation of a phenomenon. If the state is to survive at all, it will do so, commonly, only because it has the voluntary support of its people, only because its citizens acquiesce in a community of consent. Men do not customarily obey the law merely because the police stand ready to enforce it; they obey because they conceive it proper to obey, because they *will* to do so.[72] Where that will is lacking, the force of the state is rarely able to secure compliance, as the turbulent histories of American prohibition and of the Irish under English rule amply demonstrate.

It is true, of course, that even a loyal citizen occasionally ventures to evade and even to oppose the law, for example, in such matters as tax and traffic regulations. But such instances are as minor as they are unusual, and they scarcely constitute what we mean when we speak of the defiance of the state's authority. The fact that the state may resort to force in denying citizens their attempt to evade the law is merely the proper discharge of the business of government. It no more makes the state "force" than appeal by a citizen to the law to compel the fulfillment of an obligation previously undertaken by another citizen, makes the citizen "force." The state no less than the community itself cannot function if men are free to disobey whatever laws they personally dislike. This is not to argue, in the manner of Hegel, that men are therefore obliged to obey every law, irrespective of its content or the circumstances that brought it forth, that men must always render absolute and undivided allegiance to the state. It is simply to recognize that the state must, for the fulfillment of its purposes, require and obtain universal compliance. To this end compulsion is necessarily applied. But the use of compulsion remains always secondary: it is incidental to the laws previously and commonly assented to and it is employed only in a marginal sense. As Lindsay observed:

"Government and the organized force of government in the support of law are *possible* because most people give government their loyal and unforced support and because *most* people *mostly* wish to obey the law. But the acts of government and laws have to apply to everybody all the time. Most people usually wish to obey the law. Everybody has to obey it always. . . . It is necessary to fill up the margin between most people and everybody, between usually and always." [73]

And the employment of force in this marginal context is, obviously, hardly the same as the employment of force as the normal operating routine of government.

What we are arguing, in effect, is that, in T. H. Green's famous dictum, "Will, not force, is the basis of the state." Authority does not, as Woodrow Wilson once thought, rest on force; [74] rather does force rest on authority. And authority is always a function of active consent, of voluntary will.[75] It is not force that, in a democracy, secures minority acquiescence to majority rule; it is not, as Walter Lippmann and Treitschke and others declared it to be, a matter of counting heads rather than of breaking them.[76] It is not this because force is not, in the first place, simply a matter of numbers alone, and second, and more important, because the acquiescence of minorities derives from the greater and more pervasive factor of generalized consent, from social attitudes deep-set in the very natures of the people, from the habits and customs of the community.[77]

There is, indeed, a kernel of validity in the doctrine of the state as force, but only to the extent that force is exposed as the distinctive characteristic of the state, only to the extent that force is made the necessary attribute of the state. To go beyond this, to make the corollary the substance is to gloss over the elements of consent, fear, habit, utility, and the like, in order to make central an isolated and instrumental factor which is in a very real sense not the strongest but the weakest of the enduring bases of the state.[78] No one need deny the vast significance that force has had in history to realize that that significance has accrued to it only as the concomitant of other factors—the purpose, the will, the intelligence of peoples—never as the manifestation of sheer force itself.

"Sheer force has constructed nothing, certainly not the building of great states and empires. It is no accident that the great empires of the ancient world, Egypt, Athens, Rome, were those of the people who in their own times contributed most to the products of the mind. The states that have reached and maintained greatness have applied force to assert advantages that were prior to their force, advantages without which their force would have been as vain and short-lived as the shadows of the passing clouds. On the one hand were their economic opportunities and resources; on the other their enterprises, their character, their mental energy, their skill, their initiative, their adventurous intelligence. When these advantages failed, their force failed also." [79]

This was what Socrates had in mind when he denied Thrasymachus' claim that justice is the right of the stronger. This was behind Rousseau's consummate argument that strength alone, even that of the strongest, "is never strong enough to be always the master." [80] Strength as the adjunct of right, yes; but strength as substitute for right, never. For it is not, nor can it ever be, true that might makes right. "Might is an instrument alone, neutral in itself." Joined to a true cause, might reinforces right; joined to an untrue cause, might reinforces wrong. The opposition is never between might and right; it lies always "between right and wrong only, between might and weakness only." [81] Force can never, by the very logic of its being, create right; it can but serve or abuse it.

To argue, therefore, as Dennis does, that the state is force, which alone enables the state justly to prevail, is to advance a postulate that cannot be sustained either in logic or in history: not in history, for democracy, unlike dictatorship, is rooted in the freely rendered consent that is authority; not in logic, for might is an instrument that bears no necessary relationship to right.

IV

CONCLUSIONS ON DEMOCRACY AND THE POWER THEORY

According to Dennis and other theorists of his school, democracy is impossible because it is unreal, and it is unreal because political power always lodges in the hands of a few (the elite), never in the hands of the many. This elite, he tells us, is a clique of strong and ruthless men who are driven insatiably by the psychological will to power and who employ in this drive the crucial and indeed irresistible weapons of force and deceit. The conjunction of these several factors, he holds, operating as they do on the ignorance and apathy of the masses, renders oligarchy perpetually secure.

That this analysis supplies a necessary ingredient or aspect to a valid understanding of the political process cannot be gainsaid. Men are driven by a will to power. Force and deceit are employed both as a means to the attainment of power and as a means to the maintenance of that power once it is secured. Numerous illustrations have been assembled in the course of this chapter to attest to this element of validity, and if further evidences were required they could amply be drawn from the totalitarian or Latin American dictatorships of our own day.

But to note the relevance and importance of this aspect is one thing. To make it the totality is quite another and altogether different thing. For in this latter construction the ingredient that makes oligarchy possible becomes the totality that makes oligarchy inevitable; the elements that emphasize certain of the difficulties attached to democracy now assume a preponderance that renders democracy incapable of realization. Here we no longer have a partial and allegedly possible interpretation of the state. Instead we are confronted with a complete and deterministic doctrine that allows neither for chance, choice, nor democracy. It is not the particular circumstances of the moment, it is not a particular state at a particular time, that this theory attempts to explain. On the contrary, the theory is put forward as an explanation for all states and for all time. And it is in this latter and broader sense, in this absolute and deterministic construction, that the theory cannot be sustained.

It fails, in the first place, because it neither defines its ruling class, the elite, with any sufficient degree of adequacy nor establishes the solidarity, the class consciousness, of that elite. By the very standards and delineations of those who insist on elite supremacy, indeed, the elite is not merely ill-defined, it is divided. And it is not only divided but, as the history of the democratic state has established, it can be rendered responsible. To say, therefore, that the few always rule is in itself but to recognize a physical necessity of government. So long as the few who rule do so with the consent of a freely formed majority, one of the fundamental conditions of democracy is actually met, not denied.

In the second place, it is by no means clear that the lust for power resides only in members of the elite. Not only is there no psychological or historical proof that this is so, the very fact or rise of democracy is sufficient to disprove the doctrine. Were it not, indeed, for the reality of that will to power in the many as well as in the few, the few would have no need to resort to the stratagems of fraud and the violence of force. That they must employ such methods of control to survive is ample indication not only that the masses too have the surge to power, but that it is the oligarchical rather than the democratic state which dissembles, which is forced, despite its pretension to rule by law, to rule by force. It is compelled to do so by the twofold fact that it denies its subjects the right to challenge its domination through the legal processes of an opposition party or to resort to challenge by force. Democracy's government, on the other hand, though it rules by law, is itself ruled by law; hence its policy is a function of the free opinion maintained under that law, and not a function of force.[82]

These reflections make plain a third failure of Dennis' argument, namely, the lack of any serious substance in his claim that only force and deceit are the bases of the state. It is true that as a temporary measure one or both may prevail, but in the long run it is not force but belief that sustains a state. Force can never triumph over dissension; in the very moment of its victory it breeds further dissension. Force alone is the most precarious of political foundations; left to itself, it will be destroyed by another force, a truth that Hitler and Mussolini learned only when it was too late. It is authority alone, an authority resting on consent, on will, that can bind the entities that together make a state. And where there is authority, force stands revealed as the tool, not the basis, of the state. So also for the principle of deceit. Only where conflicting opinions are suppressed can deceit perpetually obtain. Given even a modicum of the unrestrained organization and expression of human thought, the propagation of deceit is exposed to the searching glare of criticism. Under such conditions there can never be assurance that a particular deceit will prevail. Many men and many groups have conspired to gain power, and in the pursuit of their conspiratorial goal both force and deceit have been generously employed. Of these conspirators a few have succeeded, but many more have gone down to catastrophic failure. The pages of history as well as the emergence of democracy bespeak the truth that those who lust for power do not always obtain it.

A seeming objection may be entered at this point. Granted the invalidity of the power theory alone as a conclusive demonstration of democracy's impossibility, it may yet be affirmed that the conjunction of this theory with that of the organizational doctrine would so operate as to preclude the realization of the democratic principle. Where those who conspire to seize the power of the state, that is to say, are also those who control the instruments of economic production, democracy, it is held, is unlikely to survive.[83] Such an argument, however, is a specious one, having at most a limited applicability. Those who have controlled the means of production have always been among those who have sought political control, yet they have not inexorably won. The legions of Caesar have conspired too, and their endeavors have not seldom been fruitful. Moreover, those who advance this joined theory fail to note the incongruous fact that to fuse the two doctrines is not to affirm but to deny them. It is to negate the theory of economic determinism—that political power always, in Harrington's phrase, follows economic power—in that it admits into play other and non-economic factors. And it is to disavow the equally absolute and exclusive theory of power as conspiracy of will in that it recognizes the significance of the social mechanism.

There is no evasion of this one great truth. The element of validity that is generally contained in even the most rigid of deterministic views is distorted, by the very fact of its absolutism and inevitability, into an untruth. There are always complications that no man can foresee, always variables that no man can control. He who would construct today an order fixed and inevitable, a system of principles that *must*, by the sheer necessity of their being, determine in an inescapable way the resolution of human affairs, finds himself deluged tomorrow with a host of unaccountables that renders his order no longer fixed and no longer inevitable. It was this understanding that Macaulay brought to the doctrines of Machiavelli when he said: "Every man who has seen the world knows that nothing is so useless as a general maxim." [84] And it was with no less insight that Guicciardini, Machiavelli's great antagonist, wisely declared:

"Bear in mind what I said before about these maxims, how they are not always to be put into practice without discrimination; in some special cases they are not serviceable. And what these cases are is a matter that cannot be comprehended by any rule, neither is there any book which can teach them; but this is a thing which must be learned first from nature and then from experience." [85]

Democracy may, indeed, fall beneath the challenge of the oligarchs. But if it does, it will be only because men have failed adequately to implement their faith; because men have failed so to organize themselves and the structure of their society that no man or group of men can capture easily all the instruments and forms of social power; because men have yielded in their intelligence and their alertness to false and greedy leaders. These things may truly come to be, as they all too long have been; but they are not inevitable. The answer is still in the sagacity and the character of the people.

Part Three

THE UNDESIRABILITY OF DEMOCRACY

4

The Incompetence of Democracy and of The Average Man

Those who dissent from the democratic principle do not rest their case on deterministic arguments alone. Indeed, the bulk of the critics of democracy accept the premise that democracy is possible but argue instead that it is an undesirable system of government. Various reasons have been advanced to support or to justify this charge and various aristocratic and authoritarian alternatives have been proffered. Underlying all these analyses, however, is the common acceptance of a basic indictment of democracy. This is the alleged incompetence of democracy and of the average man.

I

THE THEORY OF POLITICAL INCOMPETENCE

Government, according to this view, must be rational and in the hands of competent men if it is to succeed. The average or common man, however, it is held, is neither rational nor competent. "Stirred to fury and swayed by passion," [1] he abjures reason and follows blindly the dictates of his licentious nature, of what, even under the most favorable of circumstances, can only be described as his mediocrity. It is not, in this construction, simply the fact that the average man is uninformed. He lacks, even more, the capacity to accumulate the necessary knowledge on which to base an intelligent opinion. By definition not a superior man, he is said to be essentially an imperfect, even inferior man. A government that rests on the presumed competence of this inferior, average man, in consequence, is of necessity an irrational and incompetent government. And this, the theorists of this school insist, is the essence of democracy.[2]

This indictment of democracy is not, of course, new. It is a theme as common to the writings of the ancient Greeks as it is to the pronouncements of modern anti-democratic theorists. Aristophanes, for example, in a memorable passage from *The Frogs*, has his Chorus denounce democracy's assumed reliance on average men in these words:

"I have often noticed that there are good and honest citizens in Athens, who are as gold is to new money. The ancient coins are excellent in point of standard; they are assuredly the best of all moneys; they alone are well struck and give a pure ring; everywhere they obtain currency, both in Greece and in strange lands; yet we make no use of them and prefer those bad copper pieces quite recently issued and so wretchedly struck. Exactly in the same way do we deal with our citizens. If we know them to be well-born, sober, brave, honest, adepts in the exercises of the gymnasium and in the liberal arts, they are the butts of our contumely, and we have only a use for the petty rubbish, consisting of strangers, slaves and low-born folk not worth a whit more."

And the thought thus expressed has received frequent restatement ever since.

It is found, to take a random yet not unrepresentative sampling, in Hegel's declaration that "if 'people' means a particular section of the citizens, then it means precisely that section which does *not* know what it wills."[3] It is found, again, in Spengler's oft-quoted adage that "the mass is the end, the radical nullity."[4] Calvin embodied it in his doctrine of the irrationality and depravity of man,[5] and Burke made it the foundation of his attack on the French Revolution.[6] In Spain it was given extended exposition in the writings of Ortega y Gasset,[7] while in France a friendly critic like Le Bon[8] found himself allied with hostile critics like Faguet[9] and Sorel [10] in this general condemnation of democracy. Victorian writers like Carlyle [11] and Maine [12] lent their voices to the swelling chorus of discontent, as in America, Hamilton,[13] John Adams,[14] Fisher Ames,[15] and others had done before them. Indeed, in the virulent language of Fisher Ames, as in his polemic *The Dangers of American Liberty*, we find a high point of this fulmination against democracy conceived as the rule of incompetent, average men.

"The most ferocious [said Ames] of all animals, when his passions are roused to fury and are uncontrolled, is man; and of all governments, the worst is that which never fails to excite, but was never found to restrain those passions, that is, democracy. It is an illuminated hell, that in the midst of remorse, horror, and torture, rings with festivity; for experience shows, that one joy remains to this most malignant description of the damned, the power to make others wretched." [16]

There is, in fact, no period in the history of political thought when there have not been those who have protested against democracy on this ground. And in the period with which we are primarily concerned, that of contemporary American thought, such protestations have been unusually prolific.

Thus so anti-democratic and cynical a critic as Mencken, in speaking of what he called the common man's "congenital incapacity for the elemental duties of citizens in a civilized state," declared:

"The vast majority of men . . . cannot take in new ideas, and they cannot get rid of old fears. They lack the logical sense; they are unable to reason from a set of facts before them, free from emotional distraction. But they also lack something even more fundamental: they are incompetent to take in the bald facts themselves." [17]

This attitude was shared by W. K. Wallace, who looked upon democracy as a leveling doctrine, one which led to the deadening monotony of uniformity,[18] and by Atwood, for whom democracy— defined as "too much participation by the people"—resulted in mobocracy, in "demagogism, license, impulse, agitation, discontent, anarchy and chaos." [19] It was enunciated by Everett Dean Martin in several volumes, the common theme of which was the identification of democracy with the crowd-mind, the undifferentiated mass.[20] It was given a more specific psychological setting by Harry Elmer Barnes, who contended that "differential psychology has proved the intellectual inferiority of the masses," and concluded therefrom that "the average citizen is not only deficient in cerebral power but [is] also the victim of his emotions in public affairs and political 'deliberations.'"[21] Alleyne Ireland reaffirmed the doctrine when he argued that the common man is "absolutely incompetent" either to form an opinion or to select someone competent to form one.[22] And it was set forth in biting fashion by Albert Jay Nock who inveighed against "the current sublimated drivel about the preciousness of 'democracy'" and expounded the "idea of invincible ignorance" in these terms:

"We do not behave like human beings because the great majority of us, the masses of mankind, are not human beings. . . . They are merely the sub-human raw material out of which the occasional human being is produced. . . . 'Mere reason and good sense,' said Lord Chesterfield, 'is never to be talked to a mob. Their passions, their sentiments, their senses and their seeming interests are alone to be applied to. Understanding, they have collectively none.' . . . This observation of Lord Chesterfield constitutes one of the most serious arguments against representative government. In my opinion it is by far the most serious argument; indeed, I believe a century of experience has shown that it is the only argument needed. One may confidently rest one's case on it."[23]

Even some of those generally friendly to the principle of democracy have accepted the validity of this alleged incompetence of the average man and have pointed to what they consider to be certain of its unsatisfactory consequences. Thus we find Willoughby, for example, concluding that "democracy leads to mediocrity of statesmanship."[24] In Schumpeter we read that the typical citizen, on entering the political field, descends to a level of mental performance that is infantile. "He becomes a primitive again." In consequence, Schumpeter argues, democracy requires a political aristocracy if it is to succeed.[25] In Kent there is a forceful expression of this doctrine of the unintelligent, incompetent, average man; [26] and in Ascoli we are told that democracy is incompatible with intelligence.[27] But of all the friendly critics of democracy none has so incisively set forth this indictment as has Walter Lippmann.

Proceeding on the assumption that democracy rests on the capacity of the average man to run the specific affairs of government, Lippmann endeavored, in a pair of effectively written volumes, to show that the average man has no such capacity. Public opinion (the expression of this presumed competence), Lippmann argued, is neither public nor opinion, for there is no such thing as "the public." [28] No man, he insisted, can possibly keep up with all the manifold problems of public life and the average man, in particular, doesn't even want to do so. As a result, "he does not know what is happening, why it is happening, what ought to happen." There is and can be no such thing as the omnicompetent, sovereign citizen. That is at most ideal, never reality. The citizen cannot, as a matter of actual fact, govern; he can only assent to those who do govern. What we mean by public opinion, Lippmann declared, is merely "the voice of the interested spectators of action," not the voice of the actors themselves. A democracy that rests on the average man or on the majority of average men, in consequence, is logically confused and unsound; for it is not the average man or the majority that fashions public policy. It is always particular individuals. "I set no great store," Lippmann observed, "on what can be done by public opinion and the action of masses." [29]

In these several restatements of what is probably the oldest of the criticisms of democracy, we find the curious anomaly that some of the friends no less than the enemies of democracy have yielded assent to the indictment. Both have, in effect, seemingly begun by taking the general position that there is a lack of efficiency and competence in the normal workings of a democracy as compared with the rule of a strong man or an elite, assuming—and this is, of course, a large assumption—that the strong man or the elite is intelligent. For some, as for Nock and Mencken, this consideration has become the main count in their evaluation of democracy; it has reduced their estimate of democracy to the point where they reject the principle as undesirable. For others, as for Lippmann, it has become a qualification, an incidental or secondary defect that weakens but does not compel a repudiation of the democratic principle; it permits a general acceptance of democracy together with an acceptance of some of the criticism. Both views rest on a common foundation: that democracy is rule by the average man or by the majority of average men, and that the average man is incompetent either to rule or to select a government competent to rule.

For a full statement of this criticism, we will do well to turn to the work of Ralph Adams Cram, a professional architect whose prolific political tracts have reproduced in forceful terms the several arguments leveled against democracy on this ground.[30]

II

RALPH A. CRAM: THE NEMESIS OF MEDIOCRITY

It is, in Cram's view, the business of the architect, more than any other practitioner of the arts, to apprehend and interpret the society in which he dwells; for if man is to build for society he must first understand it. And as architecture is more than the mere making of designs or the addition of stone to stone, so society, political society, is more than the mere making of laws or the construction of administrative machines. These are important, to be sure, but only as the products or the manifestations of the essential core of reality; they are never the core itself. That core, says Cram, is always man. As it is man who makes a cathedral, so it is man who makes a society. And as it is not the quantity of men that determines the beauty and well-being of a cathedral, so it is not the quantity of men that determines the goodness and health of a society. For both it is the *quality* rather than the quantity of men that is vital. Here, Cram asserts, is the first principle of architecture, here is the central truth of politics: the realization that the determining factor in government, as in life, is the human factor, and that the significant element within the human factor is quality.[31] For society, it is plain, is essentially a cathedral of man.

Considered in these terms, the history of man is, according to Cram, "the history of an eternal conflict between the quantitative and the qualitative standards."[32] This dichotomy is not an abstraction existing only in the insights of the philosophers. On the contrary, says Cram, it is a real condition, a fact of human existence, localized within the minds and the natures of men. There are some, for example, who embody the qualitative standards. These, Cram observes, are the men of character and intelligence, the men best able to fashion the best laws and to organize the best society. They are the men "who by nature or divine direction can speak and act with and by authority." They are the men "competent to see clearly, capable of thinking constructively, and with the will to lead capably." They are the natural aristocracy central to "any social fabric that has reached a moderately high state of integration." [33] They are the "bright figures of men and women" who have behaved "like our ideal of the human being. . . . They are not what man *is*, they are, perhaps, what he might be." [34] These, Cram insists, are the men pre-eminently fit to rule.

There is, on the other hand, a quite different category of men. These are the vast majority of mankind, the men who lack quality but embody by their sheer numbers the fact of quantity. These, Cram tells us, are "of the mass," and "the great mass of men is and always has been of the Neolithic type." [35] They are those who possess "the limited, superstitious, second-rate proletarian mind." [36] Lacking both capacity and comprehension, when asked to judge of measures or of men they "do not know what they want." This is because they are unable to comprehend either "the merits or demerits of most of the political measures put before them, or the character and capacity of the many candidates." It is true, Cram remarks, that they "undoubtedly wish the State well, but so vast, complex and highly specialized have become the interests and functions of the nation, they simply cannot understand them, nor do they very much want to do so." They are, in a word, those men who "do not measure up to standard." They are capable "neither of organizing a sane, just and workable society, nor of self-government through a parliamentary system based on universal suffrage." [37] They are, Cram concludes, the men pre-eminently *unfit* to rule.

If we are to have a constructive government, a good society, then, it is to the qualitative rather than to the quantitative element that we must turn; for in the former we find not simply the fact of leadership but the quality of leadership, not merely the expression of opinion but the quality of an informed opinion. These, Cram insists, are the essentials of a sound political order.

But when we so regard democracy we find, according to Cram, that neither of these essentials exists. In democracy, "the art of leadership, and the fact of leadership, have been lost." [38] In democracy, leaders "of an intellectual or moral capacity above that of the general mass of voters" are neither created nor desired. In democracy, all mankind has been reduced "to a dead level of incapacity . . . while society itself is unable, of its own power as a whole, to lift itself from the nadir of its own uniformity." In democracy, not leadership but universal mediocrity prevails.[39]

What democracy has done, Cram says, has been to institutionalize the domination of quantitative standards by transferring political power from the superior few to the inferior many, from "the classes" to "the masses." [40] It has entrusted political power to those unfit to exercise it, and the consequence has been the election of mediocre rulers to office. As "that very wise Frenchman," Faguet, observed, the people are incompetent yet want to govern. Through democracy they have satisfied that desire, but only at a very great price; for the mediocrity of the rulers conjoined with the mediocrity of the people have destroyed leadership and established "the reign of mediocrity." The final result, Cram forebodingly states, can only be oblivion, death.[41]

Democracy, then, is "not a blessing but a menace." It "has achieved its perfect work" of level uniformity. It "has crashed, and bids fair, unless something is done about it, to drag culture and civilization with it." [42] What can be done?

At the outset, Cram says, we must recognize that "the first law in the Book of Man is inequality" and, in accordance with this primary law, establish a political order "of status and of diversified function, under an hierarchical, not an egalitarian system of organization. . . . It will be conditioned not by the quantitative but by the qualitative standard." [43] Second and no less important, we must abandon the concepts of universal suffrage and majority rule. These, Cram argues, have worked badly and are wholly matters of expediency. "The question of abstract justice and the rights of man does not enter into the consideration." [44] Only by doing these two things, Cram believes, can we hope to establish true democracy, the "High Democracy" of the Middle Ages. "For its fulfillment . . . and its regeneration, the real democracy demands and must achieve the creation and co-operation of a real aristocracy." [45]

In fine, it is quality and not quantity that should prevail. It is competence and not incompetence that should rule. As Cram in one place concludes:

"By rights, and for our own best interests, power and direction and leadership should rest with those who have risen above their Neolithic environment, and conversely, there is no greater mistake that can be made and no greater disservice rendered to themselves, than to place in the hands of the incompetent, powers and privileges they cannot adequately administer. . . . The whole question is, which moiety is in control, which establishes the standards, makes the laws, directs the outer lives of mankind as a whole? If it is the minority then culture develops and society continues; if it is the majority, civilization may progress for a time, but culture declines and in the end there is the *débâcle* that presages a fallow period and then the arduous building up of a new era on the wide ruin the old has wrought." [46]

For this above all is true: "Democracy is possible only when there is a king on his throne." [47]

III

COMMENTARY ON THE THEORY OF POLITICAL INCOMPETENCE

We do not require the elaborate and painstaking investigations of the social psychologists to tell us that man is an irrational animal. He has given conclusive evidence of this in his behavior at political no less than at non-political conventions, in his worship of false idols, in his susceptibility to fraud and deceit, in his pious justifications of the poverty and ill-being of his fellow-men, in his racial and religious prejudices and acts of discrimination, in his all-too-ready evocation and at times even glorification of war. It is unnecessary further to document this obvious as well as profound truth; such instances can be multiplied by innumerable examples from the experience of every man.

But all of this is merely partial explanation; it is to touch, but not to exhaust, the aspects of man. Man is not only irrational, he is also a rational man. He has learned how to harness the elements to his social convenience, how to educate and care for himself and his children, how to join with his fellows in co-operative enterprises that redound to the benefit of all, how to write great books and create noble music, how to simplify through specialization the complexities of modern life, how to settle through the arts of peace problems once soluble only through recourse to war, how to limit and control not only the ambitions of despots and kings but the power and government of man over man. These are attainments of the greatest moment; they are a monument to the glory and ingenuity of man.

Man is thus both a rational and an irrational animal.

The critics of democracy hold, however, that it is the peculiar essence of the democratic state to deny power to the rational, the educated, and intelligent man, and to give power to the irrational, the average, incompetent man. In this conception a dichotomy is drawn between rather than within men, a dichotomy which permits the critics of democracy—friendly and hostile alike—to portray a world in which there are two distinct camps: one, the camp of superior, rational men; the other, the camp of inferior, irrational men. On the basis of this division, they then advance their several arguments against the democratic principle on either or both of two levels: (*a*) that the average man is incompetent to conduct the affairs of state; and (*b*) that a government chosen by democracy is incompetent as compared with a government not chosen by democracy. In the first of these constructions there is the further twofold thesis that democracy is rule by the average man and that the average man is incompetent either to rule or to select a government competent to rule. In the second hypothesis there is the contention that democratic government is as a matter of record less competent, less rational, and therefore less desirable than other forms of government. Let us consider these several doctrines.

A. THE INCOMPETENCE OF THE AVERAGE MAN

Democracy as rule by the average man. It is Lippmann rather than the anti-democrat Cram who most effectively sets forth this phase of the criticism, though Cram no less than other expounders of the theory gives it full support. The people cannot, says Lippmann, themselves "create, administer, and actually perform the act they have in mind." They can only "say yes or no to something which has been done, yes or no to a proposal." Consider the bewilderment of the man who must render a decision one day on subways in Brooklyn and another day on railways in Manchuria, one day on rural credits in Montana and another day on the rights of Britain in the Sudan. "He cannot know all about everything all the time, and while he is watching one thing a thousand others undergo great changes." [48] If he does not know all, how can he govern? The answer, according to Lippmann, is that he cannot. Especially is this true

"when the public runs into millions and the issues are hopelessly entangled with each other. It is idle under such circumstances to talk about democracy, or about the refinement of public opinion. With such monstrous complications the public can do little more than at intervals to align itself heavily for or against the régime in power. . . . By their occasional mobilizations as a majority, people support or oppose the individuals who actually govern. We must say that the popular will does not direct continuously but that it intervenes occasionally. . . . We must abandon the notion that democratic government can be the direct expression of the will of the people. We must abandon the notion that the people govern." [49]

The difficulty with this line of reasoning is that it both assumes and tries to prove too much. In the first place it equates the principle of democracy with the rule or government of the many or of the people as a whole. But in a democracy neither the people nor the many ever actually govern in the sense that they decide the innumerable specific issues of policy that constantly arise. A democracy no less than other forms of state is a government by leaders, and it is the leaders who resolve the immediate, day-to-day problems of government. But where oligarchy renders those leaders unaccountable to the many or to the people as a whole, in democracy they are both elected by (or appointed by those elected by) and answerable to that "many." What the many or the people can further do, moreover, is to decide in broad terms the general direction in which governmental policy is to move. In this respect they do more than merely occasionally intervene; through their determination of the contours of policy they continuously direct. Beyond these two functions the public, in the normal pattern of events, is not likely to go. To indict democracy, therefore, as Lippmann does, on the ground that the public governs, but is incapable of governing, the myriad of political details, is completely to misapprehend the nature of the democratic principle. Such criticism is irrelevant criticism, for it builds not on reality but illusion.[50]

A second difficulty with this type of argument is that it tends to confuse democracy with majority or mass or mob rule. Thus Cram, for whom Ortega y Gasset is "the great prophet of the coming age, as he is the truest exponent of the character and content of . . . the democratic era," [51] followed Ortega in his denunciation of democracy as rule by the mass, the average man multiplied and made mediocre. And so Lippmann, with Cram and other spokesmen of this school, protested against majority rule, "the fundamental principle" of democracy.[52]

But in a democracy none of these concepts strictly applies. The people are a mass only in the sense that they are numerically many; they are not thereby necessarily a mob or an irresponsible and inchoate multitude. Consider, for example, the words of Herodotus:

"A mob is altogether devoid of knowledge. . . . It rushes wildly into state affairs with all the fury of a stream swollen in the winter, and confuses everything." [53]

And compare with this the activities of a group of scientists attempting to resolve a problem in physics, or a group of politicians debating a controversial issue in the houses of Parliament, or again a group or multitude of people gathered about a street-corner lecturer in Hyde Park or Union Square. These are not, as anyone who has stood among them can well attest, merely by act of congregation a mass or a mob. They do not submerge their individuality in the near-hysterical emotionalism of Ortega's mass mind. They listen, they speak, they frequently weigh with telling effect the contrasting sides. In exceptional circumstances, to be sure, when multitudes fall under the temporary sway of a leader or demagogue, men may, as in periods of crisis such as revolution, abandon the practices of reason and resort to the ungoverned behavior of the "mass" or "mob." In these circumstances, indeed, men may exhibit such suicidal tendencies as will, when craftily played upon by the demagogue, lead them to vote democracy out of existence. But these are the unique rather than the customary patterns of human behavior. They emerge, generally, from newly established, highly imperfect, and extremely unstable experiments operating under the handicap of a long anti-democratic tradition, as in Germany under the Weimar Republic, for example. They are, moreover, the movements that deny rather than express democracy. And when we add to these several considerations the crucial fact that it is not mass rule that is the distinguishing feature of democracy but control by the mass—and here again it must be emphasized that it is mass only in the strict numerical sense—of those who do rule, of those who immediately determine state policy, then it is plain that both the concept and the indictment advanced by these critics of democracy are false and irrelevant to the issue at hand. The mass no more than the many does not itself rule; it sees only that rule is rendered responsible.[54]

The equation of democracy with majority rule is a more delicate and understandable affair, for whatever else democracy may involve it does require that the ultimate choice, the final act of decision, be that of the majority. There are, however, certain considerations which must be attached to this recognition. It is apparent, from what has gone before, that the majority cannot, *as a majority*, rule; it is but the medium through which the people determine who are to rule and to what general ends.[55] Secondly, it is not always easy to determine precisely what is meant by a majority, and then consistently and practically to apply the determination. Do we mean, for example, a majority of the whole people or only a majority of those who vote? Are those who vote only to be the adult males or are we to include women; and if we extend the suffrage only to adults at what age shall we debar the young? If we agree that the mentally defective and the insane are unfit to exercise the suffrage, what shall we say of the criminal, and of the various kinds and degrees of criminality? And when we have resolved all these troublesome problems, what shall we then decide of the applicability of that majority process? Is it to be invoked every year, or every few years; and if a longer rather than a shorter period, how are we to know whether the government in power is after a particular decision or series of decisions still supported by a majority? These are but a few of the technical difficulties involved in the strict majority process, difficulties which, while by no means insurmountable, suggest a less rather than a more extreme insistence on the absolute workings of the majority principle.

A third and perhaps more crucial consideration is the fact that majority rule is compatible with democracy only when it is a shifting rather than a fixed and permanent majority. A dictatorship may and, if we are to accept the results of its plebiscites, frequently does have the support of a majority. Does it thereby become a democracy? A government democratically elected may through regular electoral processes exclude from citizenship the minority which opposed it. Does it thereby remain a democracy? In both instances the answer is plainly negative, yet in both the majority may be said to rule. Clearly, then, simple and absolute majority rule is not the hallmark of democracy. It is essential, yes; but it is only one of the essentials, not the sole and complete condition of democracy. With majority rule must go minority rights, most of all the right of minorities freely to organize and to express themselves so that they in turn may become a majority.[56]

These misconceptions of what democracy is remove much of the ground from under the criticism leveled against it. If democracy is not the rule of the many, then it is beside the point to argue that the many are incompetent to rule. If democracy is not mass rule, it is irrelevant to hold that the mass "is and always has been of the Neolithic type." If democracy is not simply the rule of the majority, then it is meaningless to point to democracy as "the tyranny of majority rule." And so it is with the concept of democracy as rule by the average man.

In a democracy it is not the average man who rules. Foregoing for a moment the precise delineation of "average man," even accepting for a moment the broad description of the vast majority of the electorate as average men, it is still plain that it is not the average man *as average man* who sits in positions of leadership. The average man may and does have a voice, even in these terms a majority and therefore controlling voice, in the determination of who shall rule, but he himself does not rule. He selects from among the various candidates put forth by the political party system those particular few who shall rule. Indeed, in this very fact of limitation, in this restriction of his choice to those few who become candidates, we perceive the first clue to the invalidity of the charge that the average man is alone responsible for the mediocrity of his leadership. Where the selection of candidates is in large part the result of manipulation and intrigue by interested pressure groups and political bosses, it is profoundly unrealistic to ascribe responsibility for those selections to the average man. His is a choice that enters primarily after the alternatives are set. Within those alternatives, however, he is free to move. He may select wise rulers or unwise rulers, men of limited mental capacity or men of great intellectual stature, poor men or rich men, men of business or men of labor, men who walk in the path of a particular deity or men who recognize no force or power outside themselves, liberal men or conservative men, selfish men or men devoted to the common weal. These are not average, common, general men; they are particular and in some one respect at least uncommon men. They differ somehow one from the other; they are never in all things uniformly alike. Thus the average man in exercising the suffrage does not himself as average man assume the reins of government; he merely decides who among the limited number of candidates shall be given those reins.

As it is with the selection of men, so it is with the determination of policy. It is not the average man who decides all issues of state; it is the leaders who so decide. And this is as it should be.

"It is no part of any reasonable theory of democracy that the people should decide the endless specific issues that confront governments. Many of these the people cannot under any circumstances decide; others they should not decide because this mode of operation is too slow or too cumbrous or because the public lacks the expertness necessary for an intelligent decision. But the function the public really fulfills is precisely one that Mr. Lippmann denies it. It is the broad determination of policy." [57]

What the average man can and in a democracy does do is to judge of the alternative programs or "platforms" presented for his choice which are right or just or preferable and which are wrong or unjust or undesirable. His judgment may in any one instance be erroneous but it is not thereby totally incompetent, for competence is never the same as infallibility. All that is expected and desired in the democratic state is that the common man express in broad terms his preferences or dislikes. This expression—through organized political parties and pressure groups, through elections, through the various media of communication, and the like—determines the contours of public policy. And it is this determination that is the unique contribution of the democratic principle to the political organization of man.

Thus we see that Lippmann, despite the unquestioned validity in his insistence that many of the problems of government are beyond the purview of the common man, fails to sustain his indictment of democracy, and for two central reasons. One is that democratic government, contrary to his assumption, does not require the average man to resolve all the miscellaneous and specialized problems of state. The other is that democratic government does not require the average man to rule. To talk of democracy as rule by the average man, therefore, is to talk in a completely unrealistic and irrelevant vein. It is to beg the whole question of what democracy is, has been, or can be. Democracy is not rule by the average man. It is, in essence, control by all men of political power exercised by a few.

The average man as determiner of public policy and personnel. The fact that democracy is not rule by the average man is conclusive refutation of the irrelevant and unrealistic doctrine that democracy is undesirable because the average man is incompetent to rule. The indictment of democracy does not, however, pause here. If it is not the average man who rules, it is, in Cram's view, the average man who determines who is to rule and to what ends. This, according to Cram, is in fact the method of democracy, a method at once "corrupt, incompetent and ridiculous," of "sublime incapacity." [58] And since it is an incompetent method, resting on a basis of incompetent men, it can, Cram argues, but produce incompetent results.

In these terms, it would appear, the case against democracy as rule by the average, incompetent man remains undestroyed. It is still the people who in a democracy have the final say as to what may or may not be done, and the people are, for Cram, always the inferior many, never the superior few. The people as a whole, he says, typify, indeed embody, the fact of the average man. And what is the average man if not an incompetent man? "No democracy," wrote Mosca's editor, "would endure if it followed the 'will' of the ignorant peace-loving masses instead of the aggressive leadership of the enlightened few." [59] The masses lack the intelligence and the understanding to perceive either the proper ends of government or the means to the attainment of those ends. Left to themselves they determine bad policy and select mediocre leaders. To rest control of the state in the hands of the people, therefore, is, Cram insists, to deny the rule of "character, intelligence and capacity" and to ensure the domination of "the dead level of the average." [60]

That the people determine through the free expression of competing ideas the broad patterns of policy and the composition of central personnel is undeniably the very heart of the democratic principle. But that "the people" are, as Cram contends, "average men," is a proposition subject to serious disputation. In the first place, just who or what is this "average man"? Is he alike or uniform in all things to all men or is he simply representative of most men in one or more particular ways? Is he a carefully calculated median or mean or even rough average of the body of mankind, or is he an ambiguous delineation designed to blur rather than to illuminate the different natures or categories of men? A moment's reflection will serve to reveal the deceptive character of the phrase. There is nowhere a man or a group of men to whom we can point and unqualifiedly say: There is average man. On the contrary, what we find is that men are alike in some things and unlike in others; no man is alike to another man in all respects.

Take, for example, the factor of competence or rationality. Do we find these qualities present in some men and absent in others as a matter of general possession, or do we not rather find—barring the extreme forms of imbecility—that men are competent or rational in some things but not in others? Consider the Southern citizen who discusses with every trace of reason the methods of judicial appointment yet who, when the issue of miscegenation is thrust into the fore, loses that reason in a wave of emotionalism. Consider, again, the neighborhood cobbler, familiar after many years of intimate contact with the several local politicians and competent to judge who among them is likely to defraud and who to benefit the people of the community; then note his inability to offer, say, a reasoned judgment on Mussolini's adventure in Ethiopia because of certain emotional attachments he may have to the people and rulers of Italy. Or regard the cloistered scholar, not quite so cloistered and so immune to the swirling currents of political activity as his forebears of legendary note, yet still—despite his expertness in an esoteric field—in some ways incapable of comprehending the degradations to which men are still prone to subject other men. A man competent to judge music may be incompetent to evaluate the merits and demerits of a tax proposal. A man capable in business may evince little understanding of the problems of juvenile delinquency. A local labor union official may know nothing of monopolies and cartels. In all walks of life and in all categories of men, there are those who expatiate with knowledge and understanding on subjects clear and familiar to them. Yet it is a matter of common observation that these same men become the most irrational and emotional of disputants in matters of which they know little yet feel deeply.

The conclusion is inescapable; most men are competent in some particular thing, at least in those things that are within the purview of their experience; most men are rational in some particular respect, at least in those matters that command their understanding and do not disturb their prejudices. Yet none is omnicompetent and none—not even the most learned and wisest of men—is all-wise. These are attributes given to all men in varying measure or degree. As Dodge and Kahn point out:

"The chances of an individual's being superior in all human traits are infinitesimal, and the same holds true of his being inferior. The general population is made up of people who are statistically superior in some traits and inferior in others. Since no two personalities are identical the combination of the many traits characterizing a human personality, and the various degrees of superiority and inferiority of those traits show great diversity. The number of variations is equal to the number of individuals." [61]

Even in a prison or an army, where men are dressed and housed and otherwise so largely treated alike, or in the extreme forms of totalitarian dictatorship, where large bodies of men are forced into the same molds, we do not find uniform or average man. Each has and maintains his own individuality; each is in some particular way or thing an uncommon man.[62] And nowhere is this more true than of men in a democracy, where human diversities are given free play in a realm of cultural freedom that permits the development of man in a myriad of specialized ways. The concept of the average man is not merely an abstraction; it is, as an accurate measure of the diversities among men, a treacherous and unwieldy abstraction. Dean Inge put this eminently well, albeit in a somewhat different context, when he said:

"In judging of a man's character, it is not fair to sum him up as a gambler, or a miser, or a wine-bibber. He may be what we call him; but he is many other things besides; the label is not descriptive of the man, but only of one corner of him." [63]

Unquestionably there are men who share in common a certain habit or trait or attitude, but these same men differ from each other in other habits, traits, attitudes, and the like. Identities in this respect are always particular, never general; and politics, if it is to respond to realities, cannot ignore inconvenient particulars for less exacting but more accommodating generalities. Democracy knows no common or average man. Democracy knows only man. In this light the argument against the competence of the average man is an argument against the competence of man; and from government by man there is no escape.

There is a second consideration that militates against Cram's hypothesis on this point. This is the fact that in democracy it is not so much man as it is opinion that determines the direction of public policy and the composition of key personnel. This is not, of course, to deny that opinion emanates from man; such a contention would be as meaningless as it would be absurd. It is rather to shift the emphasis from the factor of individualized man to that of general opinion. And in the formulation of general opinion it is not man as an individualized creature any more than it is average man who alone decides. All men—whether they be superior, inferior, or "average" men—contribute to that formulation.

This is, indeed, an unavoidable process. Since opinion is the expression of interests and values, and since these are related to social organizations, it follows that the group opinion which emerges is in no sense the opinion of one average man writ large. It is, instead, the result of prolonged discussion, in which alternative possibilities are set forth and examined, in which interests are measured and diverse opinions are weighed, and in which the final consensus is a group-, not an individual-product. Hence the idea that men vote as a heap of disjointed individuals or, in the opposite construction, as a mass, is totally misleading.

Let us probe a little further into the process. To argue that public opinion is average opinion—the opinion of an average man multiplied—is to presuppose not only the existence of such an average man but his mental independence of other men and groups as well. But this is clearly a fantastic presupposition. In the real world each man has the benefit through discussion of the wisdom, knowledge, and relevant experience of other men. To the resolution of a particular problem are brought the opinions of men who differ not merely in intellectual capacity but in occupation, education, interest, activity, and so forth. The ideas of the mechanic are subjected to the scrutiny and criticism of the small businessman, and both to the peculiar experience and training of the lawyer. The academic viewpoint of the scholar is challenged by the realistic necessities of the politician. And each gleans information and enlightenment not merely from the arguments of the other but from disputations among themselves. Lawyers no less than scholars disagree, and mechanics no less than businessmen have varied responses to common problems. From public discussions in lecture halls and private conversations across the dinner table, from incidental talk in the barber shop and passing comment in the street car, from the multitudinous organs of propaganda—from the press and the radio and the pulpit and the harangues of the street-corner orator—men derive new and sometimes challenging ideas. The expert too contributes his specialized knowledge to the flow of ideas in the endeavor to influence his fellow-men, thereby enabling the uninformed citizen soon to acquire that which he does not already know. When we add to these influences the pressures of organized groups and of political parties, of men in all walks of life and degrees of intelligence, each anxious to press his particular claim, then it becomes plain that the resultant opinion—what we call "public opinion"—is never adequately defined merely as the sum of the detached opinions of the individual or "average" man. Public opinion is not average opinion but opinion, opinion made up of the thoughts of all manner of men. It is not a series of opinions added together; it is a synthesis, a merger, a blend, a new unity composed of the inseparable currents of thought that constantly pervade men's minds.

It is sometimes urged, however, that the opinion of the expert (the man who knows) is superior to the opinion of the common man (the man who doesn't know), and that we should therefore rest the power of final decision in the expert alone. But this is hardly a tenable argument. It mistakes, indeed, the very nature of the expert's knowledge. The expert knows *how* to do something, not *what* is to be done. This latter is the effective range of every man. Consider, for example, the simple problem involved in the purchase of a house or of an automobile. To do either effectively it is not necessary for the ordinary man to become an architect or a bricklayer or a machinist or a mechanic. On matters of technical competence he relies instead on the expert, who advises, performs, and when necessary repairs the house or the automobile. But the ordinary man himself makes the decision, both as to whether he should have the house or the automobile and which house or automobile it shall be, and who shall build or supply the house or automobile. This is the age-old and still central distinction between ends and means, values and techniques, policy and administration. The ordinary man decides what is to be done and who shall do it; the expert determines how it is to be done. In what has by now become an almost classic phrase, "the expert should be always on tap but never on top." [64]

That the subordination of the expert is a necessary and proper course for the democratic state to pursue, becomes even more apparent when we bear in mind several additional considerations. First, the expert is subordinated in the determination of public policy not to some "average man" but to public opinion, in the formation of which the expert himself plays no insignificant part. Second, the more a man becomes an expert in a given field, the more narrow and specialized his knowledge or expertness generally becomes. In the popular expression, he knows more and more about less and less, and is, in consequence, hardly qualified to render a definitive judgment on affairs outside his specialty. Third, experts no less than allegedly incompetent men differ among themselves. What, for example, is the expert opinion on the control of the business cycle? How would the experts abolish unemployment and do away with war? What institutional mechanism will enable us permanently to reconcile individual freedom and political order? Bring any group of experts together on these problems and in all probability one will be given as many expert opinions as there are experts. Fourth, experts act not merely on the basis of abstract knowledge but also on interest. And since questions of public policy are not neutral but highly charged questions, it cannot be expected —nor indeed has history disclosed—that experts will decide these questions in some purely objective way. They too are swayed by passion and governed by ideals.[65] Fifth, the peculiar possession of the expert is knowledge, but knowledge is not necessarily wisdom. As one writer observed: "A head for facts is often half a head when it comes to judging, ruling, handling men." [66]

Policy, in a word, is the domain of interest and value, not of technique. This last—and this last alone—is the province of the expert. No more striking illustration of this vital yet frequently ignored truth need be adduced than the problem presented by the atomic bomb in our own day. Would an oligarchy of atomic physicists, for example, necessarily make a wiser decision regarding the control and uses of atomic energy and the atomic bomb than a group of democratically chosen representatives? What would happen if this same oligarchy decided it was possible to supplant all power installations by atomic power plants overnight, while a board of expert economists agreed that the labor so displaced would require twenty years to re-absorb? Obviously the ultimate decision would have to be made in terms of values and interests, and if this government by experts made such a decision it would be acting as a government of politicians, not experts.

Once again, therefore, we are compelled to return to the force of opinion—not the opinion of a specialized few but the opinion of all. And since it is the opinion of all, the question of the competence or incompetence of the average man is plainly irrelevant to the principle of democracy. It is neither average man nor average opinion that is, in the democratic state, the crucial determinant of public policy and major personnel. Indeed, even to speak of the average man is to mistake and grossly to simplify the nature of human reality, for a man is at most average in a particular trait, never in the totality of his personality. And whatever the limitations inherent in the restricted knowledge and experience of the "average" individual, it is in no sense a proper description of democracy to say that that "average" man and his limitations are the molders of state policy. It is all men, common and uncommon, who contribute to the fashioning of that policy.

Nor is it less untrue to argue that if it is not the average man alone it is the average man multiplied. Cumulative opinion is not a mere exercise in arithmetic. Democracy does not simply build a cathedral out of stones which represent, each in individual form, the detached opinions of particular men. The give-and-take of conflicting ideas, the varying contributions of men who differ profoundly one from the other in some particular or group of particulars, the shifting currents of knowledge and belief under the impact of new illuminations—these are not a matter of pluses and minuses. So to construe the formation of public opinion is unduly to artificialize the social process. Public opinion is at the very least a synthesis, and in this synthesis groups and the leadership within those groups, man and all the varieties that are in man, thought and all the nuances and instruments of its conveyance, play a vital and it may be indefinable role. In this way the limitations of any one man are transcended in effective degree. In this way leadership and the free passage of competing opinions have their full day in court. In this way democracy lives.

B. THE INCOMPETENCE OF DEMOCRATIC GOVERNMENT

The indictment of democracy rests on yet another facet of the theory of political incompetence. Here the argument is directed not so much to the incompetence of the average man as it is to the incompetence of democratic government. Thus Cram, surveying the course of democracy in the last century, declares:

"It is useless to deny that government, in the character of its personnel, the quality of its output, the standard of its service and the degree of its beneficence has been steadily deteriorating during the last century and has now reached, in nearly every civilized country, a deplorably low level. Popular representatives are less and less men of character and ability; legislation is absurd in quantity, short-sighted, frivolous, inquisitorial, and in a large measure prompted by selfish interests; administration is reckless, wasteful and inefficient, while it is overloaded in numbers, without any particular aptitude on the part of its members. . . . The whole system is in bad odour for it is shot through and through with the greed for money and influence, while the cynicism of the professional politician and the low average of character, intelligence and manners of the strata of society that increasingly are usurping all power, work towards producing that general contempt and aversion that have become so evident of late and that are a menace to society no less than that of the decaying institution itself." [67]

This is as serious an indictment as it is detailed, a charge which, if sustained, would go far toward weakening the case for democracy. But by itself it is inconclusive. By itself it tells us nothing of the relative competence of non-democratic governments. To say that government chosen by democracy is incompetent is to deal with but a phase of the problem, to gaze, as it were, upon a single face of a two-sided shield. It is still necessary to consider the other phase, to examine the alleged competence of oligarchical governments, and to relate the forms to each other in the light of these findings.

In the restricted realm of politics no less than in the broader realm of communal life, few things are either all of one or all of the other, few all good or all bad. If we prefer democracy to dictatorship or to hereditary monarchy or to rule by clergy or to other forms of oligarchy, we do so not because the system of our preference is superior in each and all of the thousand and more facets of its operation but because we conceive the system as a whole to be more desirable—in terms of the particular values we hold dear—than any other system. Thus, to defend democracy against the charge that it is as a matter of historic fact an incompetent form of state, it is not necessary to set up absolute and idealistic standards and then attempt to establish in these terms the competence of democratic governments. It is enough to show that those who argue the incompetence of democracy have failed to establish the superior competence of oligarchy, that they have ignored, in the vehemence of their attack, not only the positive achievements of democratic governments but, more important, the grounds on which the presumed competence of oligarchical governments can be maintained. Here is the crucial field of disputation, here is the conclusive test.

But when we move into this field we find it relatively unexplored. Not by the historians, to be sure, who have recorded in voluminous detail the facts relating to the competence of oligarchical governments, but almost completely by the critics of democracy. And when we survey the record it is not difficult to understand why.

Consider the alternatives to democracy. If government is not democratically chosen it may, in the first place, be self-perpetuating, as is the case with hereditary monarchy. Now this form has, granted certain questionable assumptions as to the necessity or desirability of oligarchy, several significant virtues, not least among them the stabilization of rule essential to the very existence of the oligarchical state. But unless we are prepared to argue that kings and the descendants of kings are always competent men, it is difficult to see how these several attributes are in any way related to the factor of competence. Stabilization merely preserves what is, but as Philip VI of Valois abundantly showed, what is, need not be competent government. And we cannot argue successfully the inexorable competence of kings in the face of such monarchs as George III, who presided with all his colossal blunders at the abdication of the greatest of all colonies, and Louis XVI, who succeeded in losing not only his kingdom but also his head.

That these are not isolated and unusual instances of incompetent monarchical rule is evidenced by the history of kings in every country and in every age. Take, for example, Leopold II, king of Belgium and sovereign of the Congo Free State.

"During a quarter of a century, he did not build in his African possessions as much as one school; there was a cruel scarcity of hospitals and doctors; he took no care for a proper use of the land, for the encouragement of sound business enterprise, for the education and uplifting of the negroes. . . . Such was the man who had made himself owner of twenty million blacks. When he died, there were only ten millions of them left." [68]

Or take the governments of monarchical Spain. "Afflicted with a series of kings, whose increasing incapacity culminated in the imbecility of Charles II," this country set up a colonial empire in South America that represented the very quintessence of venality and incompetence.[69] Or take, again, China under the later Manchus, or France before the revolution, or Russia under the Czars—the critics of democracy can find little here to sustain the wisdom and competence of non-democratic governments. The record of monarchy, indeed, is conclusive evidence that the self-perpetuation of rule enjoys no necessary relation to the factor of political competence.[70]

A non-democratically chosen government may, on the other hand, be that of a clique based on a particular class. This was the case, say, with the theocracy of ancient Egypt or the consuls of pre-imperial Rome or the factions that plagued medieval Florence. But in all these cases the selection of government was made not in terms of competence but in the light of considerations largely irrelevant to that factor. A competent man who was not of the Egyptian priesthood was excluded from political rule, for it was not competence but membership in the priestly class that was the basis of selection. A competent man who was also a slave or not of the citizen class of republican Rome was permitted no share in the government, for it was not competence but birth and wealth that gave primary access to political rule. A competent Florentine who was not of the Guelphs or the Ghibellines, or who was a member of one when the other was in power, encountered almost insurmountable difficulty in attaining to political rule, for again it was not competence that was the fundamental selective factor. Class rule of whatever form rests on the exclusion from political power of all not in the particular class; that men of competence may thereby be excluded is irrelevant to the principle. And as the record of oligarchical cliques throughout history—the gerontocracy of Sparta, the Medici of Italy, the military cliques of modern Latin America, and the like—amply attests, no clique looks to the factor of competence as a test of its capacity or right to rule. Instead the resort to conspiracy and the employment of force are the central determinants.

Dictatorship is yet another form of non-democratically chosen government, though it is a form very close indeed to that of a clique based on a particular class. As Hitler and Mussolini and Stalin incisively show, no matter how absolute and extensive the power of the dictator may appear, his power is always rooted in the clique which not merely sustains, but dominates together with, him. Hitler without a Goering and a Goebbels and the rest of the Nazi inner circle is unthinkable. Equally so is rule by Stalin without a Zhdanov, a Kaganovich, and the remainder of the executive committee of the Communist *Politbureau*. Yet the intense glorification of the Leader, the mystical aura with which he is carefully surrounded, mark this as a distinct type. It is a type, however, that does not select its government on the basis of competence alone. In Nazi Germany one may have had to be competent but one had also not to be a Jew, and then beyond this to be an avowed member of the National Socialist party. In Italy one had to be a Fascist, and in the Soviet Union a Communist. In all totalitarian dictatorships it is not competence but acceptance of the faith that is the basic prerequisite for a share in political government. Indeed, he who is competent but not of the faith is not merely denied a place in the government; he is occasionally, despite his competence, denied even the right to live.

These considerations underscore a feature common to all forms of oligarchy. Whatever their separate and occasionally several merits, whatever their promises and their deeds, this one thing is clear: those who rule do not come to power simply by virtue of a selection made in terms of competence. And if oligarchical governments are not chosen in terms of political competence, plainly it is irrelevant if not meaningless to charge democracy with a failure to select its governments on that basis. All that such a charge—even if we were to grant its truth—would establish is that no governments are selected on the basis of competence. And in these terms the indictment, by the very fact of its universality, loses both its force and its applicability.

The competence that does not attend the selection may, however, manifest itself in the results. If, that is to say, the critics of democracy could show, by historical induction, that the rulers of non-democratically chosen governments have been or are better or more competent than the rulers of governments chosen by democracy, then their indictment would rest in some degree on valid ground. But it is a striking fact that they do not show this. Nor, indeed, can they on the basis of history or contemporary experience do so.

It is true, of course, that they are able to point, on the one hand, to kings and dictators such as Alexander, Caesar, and Napoleon, and on the other hand to undistinguished leaders of democracy such as Harding, McKinley, and Coolidge. But it is not less important to record, together with this, that if there has been a Caesar there has also been a Nero, and if an Alexander also the Seleucids of Asia and the Ptolemies of Egypt. Conversely, democracy can point with no mean pride to a Wilson and a Franklin Roosevelt, to a Holmes and a Cardozo, to a Robert La Follette and a George Norris. Neither form can lay exclusive claim to competence or to greatness of leadership; but by the same token neither form is the sole possessor of mediocrity and ineptitude.

The burden of proof is here on the critic of democracy. By his indictment of democracy as incompetent he implies, and in Cram's argument explicitly states, that non-democratic governments are competent, at least more competent than democratic governments. But incompetence and corruption are features characteristic of all forms of government known to history, and a feature common to all cannot logically be employed against one alone. Especially is this true when we bear in mind the further fact that democracy precisely because it is democracy is more prone than oligarchy to reveal its aspects of incompetence. Non-democratic governments can, by virtue of their control over the organs of publicity, succeed for long periods of time in concealing their inefficiency and corruption, and thus give credence to a belief in their competence. But democratic governments, because they contain the necessary corrective mechanism of public criticism, because they constantly turn the searchlight on public practices, expose their errors of commission and omission, reveal the malpractices of their officials, indeed make such revelations the very business of the public and particularly of the opposition. It is therefore never enough merely to show that democratic governments are in some ways incompetent. It is necessary to show, beyond this, that oligarchical governments are more competent than democratic governments, that democratic leaders are less capable than oligarchical leaders. And this the critics of democracy have failed to do. They have failed not because they have not tried but because the evidence is overwhelmingly against them.[71] Indeed, the very existence of democracy is in a profound sense the institutionalization of man's protest against the proved incompetence of dictators and kings.

It is sometimes urged, however, that there is one realm where the rulers of democratic government are demonstrably less competent and less efficient than those who come to power through non-democratic means. This is the realm of business. And in these terms certain of the critics, in echo of Spencer, advance their indictment of democracy.

Thus we read, in a special edition of Spencer's *Man versus the State*, a series of denunciations by various American commentators of the incompetence of democracy as compared with business.[72] Thus we find, in a more recent work that rails against "a totally incompetent Congress, chosen and guided by a nation of economic illiterates," a demand for business domination in the person of another Hamilton.[73] Thus we are assured, in a massive two-volume report by the Economic Principles Commission of the National Association of Manufacturers that government enterprise is generally less efficient than the enterprise of individuals and groups.[74] And thus we learn, from Munro, from Nock, and from a variety of business leaders, that democracy does not and indeed cannot conduce to efficiency.[75]

Despite its many supporters, however, this is at best a specious argument, and for two conclusive reasons. In the first place, the comparison is not fairly stated. Business is a highly specialized field of endeavor, the realm of the expert familiar with a very limited aspect of communal life. No matter how great the scope of its activity, so long as it remains a business it remains always an economic and therefore a restricted institution. Government, on the other hand, is a broad and highly diversified activity, of which business is only a part. It is the realm of the economic but even more of the non-economic life of man. It is not business but government that concerns itself with the total well-being of its people, that provides sanitation facilities, that establishes educational and health services, that enters into the innumerable aspects of man's existence, seeking throughout to contribute to his welfare and to ensure the opportunities for his further development.[76] Business is to government as the finger is to the hand; they are in no sense comparable institutions.

The comparison is unfairly stated, again, because the standards of evaluation are different. The primary function of business is the pursuit of private gain. The primary function of government— apart from the maintenance of public order—is the satisfaction of the needs of the community. No single standard of competence or efficiency can apply to institutions devoted to unlike ends, for the means employed to the attainment of one are not seldom eschewed by the other. Consider, for example, the problem of human costs versus production costs. For a long time industry concerned itself almost exclusively with the latter, regarding as irrelevant the human costs of labor—the fatigue of excessive work, the monotony ensuing from an absence of novelty, the denial of self-expression, the employment in unhealthy surroundings of children, of women, of the aged, and so forth.[77] These considerations, however, government cannot and has not ignored. Consider, again, that many of the functions of government are in no sense directly related to profits, for example, agricultural research, soil conservation, flood control, education, public works of various kinds, the informational or promotional function of governmental agencies such as the Women's Bureau or the Bureau of Labor Standards in the United States Department of Labor, and the like. "In general," a noted economist declared, "economics must be on its guard against applying to one type of efficiency the conceptions that belong to another." [78] And particularly is this true of such diverse institutions as government and business.

The argument is specious, in the second place, because it is by no means established that business is as a matter of historic fact superior in competence or efficiency to democratic government. Regarded solely in profit-and-loss terms, the argument is of course not an implausible one. The sacrifice of human and even of social resources may be held to be irrelevant to the efficient utilization of those resources for profits, just as the catastrophic failures of businesses in a capitalist depression may be regarded as a supremely efficient purgative which cleanses the system periodically of the various maladjustments that accumulate over a period of expansion. But from the standpoint of the community, such a basis of calculation cannot long be tolerated. Here the standard of evaluation must emerge from some conception of the social welfare, in which the elements of time and cost, for example, may be of secondary importance.[79] In these terms, the cycles of depression, which plunge millions of people into unemployment and misery as well as force the closing of factories in devastating numbers, are in no sense calculated to sustain the competence of businessmen to run the economy. The constant and rarely unsuccessful drive of business for governmental aid in one form or another—tariffs, patents, waterways, use of the military to protect profits and investments abroad, subsidies direct and indirect, and the like—suggests that business without government is inadequate to conduct even what it considers to be its own affairs. Indeed, it is precisely because business operators have proved incompetent and inefficient that public ownership has in many spheres been made necessary. It is by no means insignificant that in Britain (as in other European countries), long before the advent of the Labour party to power, all three major parties contributed to the development of government proprietary corporations; all were led by "the logic of circumstances . . . to the same solution, at times even against declared principles." [80] And in this country there is emerging an increasing body of evidence to indicate that business—both internally, in relation to costs and profits, and externally, in relation to government—is as a matter of operating routine far less competent and efficient than it has been popularly conceived to be.[81]

The argument against the competence of democracy is thus again seen to be an argument without foundation. Neither in relation to the governments of oligarchic states nor to the "governments" of business are the governments chosen by democracy demonstrably less competent or less efficient. And if they are not demonstrably less competent it is irrelevant to offer as indictment against them merely the fact that they are incompetent. This is as one-sided as it is inadequate a criticism.

IV

DEMOCRACY AND THE AVERAGE MAN

It is the contention of the critics of this school that democracy is an undesirable form of government because it is an incompetent form of government, and that it is an incompetent form of government because it places the affairs of state in the hands of the average man who is an incompetent and irrational man.

No defense of democracy can, it is plain, ignore this central consideration; no philosophy of political liberty can or should evade the direct impact of its charge. To attempt, however, to list and assay the numerous and detailed counts in the indictment would be as futile as it is unnecessary. Let us grant, for the sake of the argument, the major points in the charge. Let us admit, for the moment, that the average man is an incompetent man and that the governments chosen by democracy have been and are incompetent governments. Of what consequence is this for democracy? Is it a conclusive condemnation of the principle?

The answer, as Mill perceived, is plainly in the negative. In the first place, democracy neither implies nor rests upon the competence of the masses, the many, the average man. Democracy does not presuppose that the man in the street any more than the "average" representative has the capacity to judge and to administer effectively all the miscellaneous and specific issues with which governments are faced. All that democracy requires is that those empowered with the resolution of such issues be rendered responsible to the people, that the public "should pass its decisive verdict on the program and the achievement of its agent, the government entrusted by it with power." [82] And in the making of that verdict it is neither average man nor average opinion that applies. It is all men, it is general opinion, that rules.

The condemnation of democracy is inconclusive, again, because it argues not the inadequacy of the principle but that of the particular institutions or agencies which seek to embody or actualize that principle. Democracy as a principle of government, as the institutionalization of political responsibility, is one thing; democratic governments made up of particular men or institutional forms are quite another. To expose and to attack the inadequacies, the incompetence, the several deficiencies of democratic governments, is at most to argue for a change in, or substitution by other elements for, those men or agencies; it is in no sense an attack upon the principle of democracy itself. This can be destroyed only if it can be shown that governments chosen by democracy are demonstrably, indeed necessarily, less competent than governments chosen by non-democratic forms. But this the critics of democracy cannot do. Whether it be a dictatorship, a clique resting on a class, or a self-perpetuating form such as hereditary monarchy, oligarchy neither makes its selections in terms of competence nor does it by its deeds establish a claim to superior competence. In both respects, therefore, the argument against democracy cannot stand.

These considerations comprise both the necessary and the sufficient rejoinder to the attack on the competence of democracy and of the average man; they serve conclusively to refute the untenable allegations of the critics. There are, however, two or three passing comments which should perhaps still be made against those who indict democracy on this ground.

In reply, for example, to the charge that public opinion is in democracy weak, confused, vacillating, unwise, one need not attempt a blanket denial. There are limitations to democracy and not least of these is the susceptibility of the public to false arguments and demagogic leaders. But when this has been admitted it is necessary still to point out that other forms of state do not escape this difficulty. Instead they frequently, as in dictatorship, aggravate it. All governments, whatever their form, are rooted in the general consent of their people.[83] What democracy does is to take formal cognizance of this fact and seek, through the fullest participation of all, the free exchange of knowledge and ideas, thus paving the way for the greatest enlightenment of the people and consequently for the maximum wisdom in their judgments. What dictatorship does, however, is to deny this enlightenment to its people lest they, in the wisdom of their understanding, do away with the dictatorship. It not only denies freedom and individual development to the many; it not only corrupts the few; it ensures, beyond these, that the errors committed by those vested with irresponsible power shall continue undisturbed. Whatever the weaknesses of democratic opinion, it justifies itself by this one great virtue: that the defects of power are through freedom of discussion exposed and in time repaired.

In reply to the alleged incompetence of the average man it is important to note three things: first, as we have already said, that the charge is irrelevant to democracy since democracy is not rule by the average man; second, that the concept itself is a misleading abstraction—there is no average man as a categorical absolute, there is no rational man in juxtaposition to an irrational man; and third, that even if we accept the idea of the average or common man in broad, non-analytical terms, he is, whatever his degree of incompetence, still competent enough through the instrument of public opinion to do two things: (*a*) determine the general ends to which governmental policy is to be directed, and (*b*) determine who is to compose the government. Through the performance of these two functions the average man makes power responsible, and he does so in his own interests. It is often said by the critics of democracy that what is important is not so much rule *by* the people but rule *for* the people. It is the precise quality of democracy, however, that it not merely permits but ensures that government shall be wielded for the benefit of the whole. None but the average man can enunciate his own desires; none can so well guard his own interests. It is still the greatest of truths that he who wears the shoe is best able to judge of its discomfort.

There is yet a final argument to be made for democracy on this ground. This is the very practical and perhaps crucial consideration that man, whatever his actual abilities and capacities, conceives himself to be competent. To say that the average man is a stupid or incompetent man is one thing; to attempt to impose that judgment by denying him a share in political power is quite another. For men fight for what they want or think they want, and they frequently want what they think they are entitled to have. If, therefore, the "average man" regards himself as politically competent, as he does, he will fight, as he has, to obtain a political voice. To deny him that voice, consequently, is to assure conflict and perhaps revolution.[84]

5

The Concept of the Best: A Preliminary Note on the General Theory of Aristocracy

In the *Iliad* of Homer there is a line that, rudely spoken, captures in brief compass the very essence of the aristocratic theory. It is this: "Good sir, sit still and hearken to the words of others that are thy betters." [1] In the *History* of Herodotus a Persian potentate, addressing a group of fellow conspirators, puts the matter with equal simplicity: "Let *us* choose out from the citizens a certain number of the worthiest, and put the government into their hands." [2] In the *Republic* of Plato there is a somewhat longer but no less incisive statement of the same idea. [3] In these and other writings many of the ancients made clear their dislike for democracy and their preference for the rule of the best, a preference that has been given extended and repeated affirmation by theorists ever since.

That this should be so is not entirely difficult to understand, for in olden days, when education was given only to the few and the majority of the people lived in gross poverty, there were stronger grounds on which to rest a repudiation of democracy. And there is, in addition, as Hobhouse perceived, a rational element in this system that forcefully commends it to the minds of men. [4] What government, after all, can possibly be better than the government of the best? Who can know better than the best what ought to be done? Who can act better than the best to see that it is done? Clearly no one, else he or they would be better than the best and would therefore be themselves the best. The argument is simple, and effective. On reflection, however, certain objections intrude that are not readily stilled. In the first place, who are the best? How are they defined? In the second place, how are the best to be selected, and by whom? What criteria will distinguish them from the non-best? What method will ensure their ascension to political rule? Let us consider these questions in turn.

I

THE DEFINITION OF THE BEST

If the best are to rule, they must first be known. Platitudinous though this comment may seem, it yet marks the central problem of the aristocratic theory; for, it is striking to note, while the theorists of aristocracy have long attempted to resolve this primary question, there is still the greatest of disagreement. They agree as to the need for the best. They agree further that there is a best. But they differ widely and vigorously as to who are included in that best. Take, for example, the classic definition of Fisher Ames: that the best are the wise, the rich, and the good. The crevices in this concept are so patent that it could not, as it did not, withstand the scrutiny of reason. As a modern critic observed: "The wise have rarely been the rich, and . . . the rich have almost never been the good." [5] Take, again, the trinity advanced by Spengler: that the best or good are "the powerful, the rich, the fortunate." [6] Little evidence need be adduced to show the obvious inapplicability of this description: the beheading of Didius Julianus only sixty-six anxious and precarious days after his purchase of the Roman Empire from the Praetorian guards, for example, is a striking illustration of the truth that men can be rich without necessarily being either powerful or fortunate or good; while the characteristic tale of the *condottiere* who, after freeing the Republic of Siena from foreign aggression, was put to death and made a patron saint rather than rewarded while alive with the lordship of the city, shows that power and fortune are not inseparable qualities.

That Spengler himself perceived the invalidity of his conception is indicated by his repeated references elsewhere to blood and race as the central qualities or characteristics of the best.[7] But Mallock, who accepts wealth, is indifferent to race;[8] while Stoddard, who accepts race, finds only a mediocrity of intelligence in the presumed aristocracy of wealth.[9] Ludovici, on the other hand, seeks his aristocracy in those who embody the canon of "taste," in his view the means to a flourishing life; while Babbitt and More, to cite but one further illustration, find cause only to admire certain men of restrictive or puritanical standards.[10] Clearly there is no unity of definition among these several theorists of aristocracy. Nor is there, on examination, such unity or even major agreement on any of the other innumerable qualities men have cited to identify the minority of the best.

Yet there are those who, like Mosca, while they admit the inadequacy of the conception, insist nonetheless on its use in a broad and inclusive sense. What is meant by the best man, Mosca tells us, "is the man who possesses the requisites that make him best fitted to govern his fellow men."[11] But this is plainly no more than an exercise in tautology, for it is precisely these requisites that we seek. And when we read elsewhere in this same writer that this special aptitude or fitness to govern is the peculiar concomitant of "wealth, education, intelligence or guile,"[12] we realize that once again we are but returned to an enumeration of qualities on which total or dominant acquiescence is impossible to secure.

No more convincing evidence of this inability of aristocratic theorists clearly to define the best is required, indeed, than the remarkable passage in which Ortega y Gasset makes his plea for the concentration of power in "superior minorities." He does not explain who these minorities are, for this, he perceives, is a question that may be discussed *ad libitum*. What he urges us to do, however, is to accept their existence and to trust to their rule; for "without them," he says, "whoever they be, humanity would cease to preserve its essentials." But why, the skeptical mind may here inquire, should we accept the existence and the rule of those who cannot be identified? Because, Ortega answers, "we are not dealing with an opinion based on facts more or less frequent and probable, but on a law of social 'physics,' much more immovable than the laws of Newton's physics."[13] Yet the contents of the law remain ambiguous.

Such a claim is indeed a gentle extension of the requirement for precision in affirmation.

It may be objected at this point that the aristocratic theory does not depend for its validity on any absolute standard or unity of definition. That men differ in defining the best, it may be argued, may merely mean that they conceive the best in terms of a particular culture, or according to a particular period or stage of historical development. Thus in a military society, it may be said, soldiers are the best; in a capitalist society capitalists are the best; in a priestly society priests are the best; and so on. But this objection carries with it two major errors. In the first place, it confuses a specific function or aspect of society with the totality of that society. Warfare, for example, is always a phase—even where it is the major phase—never the whole of a culture; and soldiers who are best for fighting are not necessarily best for ruling. In the second place, the argument assumes the very thing to be proved. It is a priestly society because priests rule, but why should priests rule? How do we know they are the best? Where religion flourishes priests are needed and may perhaps be proved the best—*for their function as priests*. But this in no way demonstrates their superior capacity to rule man in the variety of his social relationships. The one is as distinct from the other as the rule of the presumed expert is from the rule of the alleged "average man."

II

The Selection of the Best

If the best cannot be defined there is clearly no way to provide for their selection and elevation to power. One cannot resort, for example, as Plato urged, to an elaborate system of moral and intellectual tests, for what evidence is there that these alone are the qualities that render a man best qualified to rule? Who, moreover, is to devise and apply these tests, and who is to select him who is to do the devising? If it is the people, do we not thereby invoke a kind of suffrage akin to democracy? But if it is not the people, if it is the "best" who elect themselves, how did they become the best in the first place? And for how long do they remain the best? What assurance do we have, further, that those to whom the tests are applied have been afforded an equal opportunity to prepare for them? Where some of the people are rich and some are very poor, where some are given free access to schools and jobs, theatres and clubs, while others are discriminated against because of irrelevant racial or religious differences, where these and other artificial barriers cause some to be privileged and others underprivileged, there is patently no basis for objective measurement. How, again, do we know that such tests accurately measure these or other qualities they are represented to measure? Reflections such as these but begin to suggest the many difficulties inherent in this problem of the selection of the best, yet they serve perhaps to explain why no satisfactory solution has ever been advanced.

Consider the alternative proposed by Madariaga. It is pointless, he says, to concern ourselves with this problem of how to select the best. It is done for us.

"No one appoints, elects, or chooses the aristocrat. He knows himself to be one because he hears himself called to his high and arduous endeavor by an internal voice—his vocation. There is no voice with more commanding power; none which can obtain more punctual and loyal obedience. Chief and soldier within one soul, under one will, within the same executive body, the aristocrat obeys his vocation without any possible excuse or evasion. He is his own slave. . . . He is his own police, judge, and executioner." [14]

Noble though this conception is, it yet raises certain difficulties. Who, for example, is to decide between conflicting claims of competing aristocrats? Who is to distinguish the "legitimate" internal voice of the "true" aristocrat from the "illegitimate" but no less vigorously affirmed internal voice of the "false" aristocrat? What if the aristocrat does wrong—as aristocrats of every complexion known to history have done wrong—but refuses to arrest, imprison, or execute himself? We cannot look to another aristocrat for the remedy, not merely because the other aristocrat may also have done wrong, but because by the logic of this construction only the aristocrat himself can judge himself. Yet reason and the experience of mankind both attest that bondage to oneself, when conjoined with power over others, is no sufficient brake on man's capacity for injustice to other men.

Similar considerations expose the several fallacies in such a view as the Spencerian notion that the best will, by their survival, prove themselves. In the first place, the argument builds on one of the most elementary of all logical errors, that of circular reasoning. It assumes that what is fittest to survive, survives but does not know what is fit to survive until after it has survived; then the argument holds it was fit to survive because it survived.[15] In the second place, it wrongly confuses the tiger ethic, the combat of the jungle, with the nature of man's social relationships. There is struggle or competition, to be sure, but there is also the play of other factors—of sympathy, of co-operation or, as Kropotkin put it, mutual aid. Men do not always use the most vicious means at their command, especially, be it noted, if they are the best men. Intellect and emotion soften the brutality even of the strong.[16] In the third place, fitness and survival are alike general and relative terms. What is fittest depends on the quality measured. The best scholar is not necessarily the best athlete; the best businessman is not necessarily the man best qualified to govern a state. What survives, similarly, is in no sense always the best. The trader who adulterates his goods often succeeds where more reputable traders fail. The soldier who flees the battle may survive while less cowardly or less fortunate soldiers die.[17] In the fourth place, the fact of survival in no way establishes the fact of pre-eminence, and it is this latter that is the decisive element in the theory of aristocracy. To take a far-fetched but not entirely implausible illustration, it has been shown that death-rates for women are generally lower than those for men throughout the whole life span; yet we do not argue that this superiority in longevity thereby entitles women to be the sole rulers of the state. Men of no startling competence frequently find themselves at the top while admittedly better men labor below them. They are there, it is plain, because someone put them there, not because they best deserve to be there.[18] For these and other reasons the theory of the survival of the fittest as a method of selection cannot stand.

These several reflections emphasize again the inability of aristocratic theorists either to define the best or to devise some method that will select the best and assure their elevation to political power. Because of this, aristocracy—the rule of the best—is patently unattainable. Democracy, on the other hand, builds at most on the rule of the second-best. It attempts to keep open—in principle at least—the avenues of opportunity so that those who have special skills or talents may be free to secure their recognition, and it provides, through its system of the free operation of conflicting ideas, means whereby all varieties of the "best" and near-best can exert their influence on the rest of the community.

Some theorists of aristocracy, however, still insist that there is a specific and rational definition and method of selection of the best, and offer alternatively the criteria of race, heredity, and nature. To an examination of these major alternatives, therefore, we now turn.

6

The Concept of Racial Aristocracy

I

RACE AS A PRINCIPLE OF POLITICS

The concept of racial aristocracy asserts, in essence, that some races are superior in intellectual capacity and political genius to other races, and that one race, indeed, is superior to all the rest. All that the right state need do, in consequence, is to grant to this superior race exclusive and permanent political power and to deny to the inferior races any share in the government. In this way, say the theorists of this school, the democratic alternative of rule by average or inferior men will be avoided and the conditions of a progressive civilization will be assured. If, on the other hand, the racially superior are subjected, as in democracy, to the rule of incompetent, average men, then clearly the just state cannot long survive; rather will it hurtle, in the picturesque language of one of the spokesmen, "down the road to destruction." [1]

This concept of race as a principle of politics rests on the conjunction of two central ideas: first, that race is to be identified not merely with certain physical but also with certain psychic (essentially moral and intellectual) characteristics or qualities presumed to be unique and innate attributes of that race; and second, that the welfare of a state, indeed the preservation and advancement of a civilization, depends on the maintenance of the purity of that race which is inherently superior to the other races of mankind. From these premises the racial theory evolves its argument that political power should be restricted to that race most capable of exercising it.

That the argument is an old and pervasive one requires little demonstration: the peoples of the ancient world—Hebrews and Greeks, Romans and Orientals—no less than those of the modern subscribed in some measure to the doctrine of superiority of kind—always, of course, in the sense that each people thought itself superior. And this heritage of the past has been extended into the present in the theories and practices of such regions as the American South, the Union of South Africa, the Belgian Congo, and the Germany of the Third Reich.

Where, however, the theory of racial inequality was nurtured in ancient times by folk or group egoism, in the contemporary age it is also, paradoxically, a function of equalitarianism. On the one hand, the equalitarian creed enables those who can no longer uphold their place as equals on other grounds—the poor whites in the South, for example—to maintain their self-esteem and feeling of equality with respect to those who, like the upper-class whites, would otherwise regard them with disdain. And on the other hand, though equalitarianism would seem to call for the suppression of the dogma of, say, the Negro's racial inferiority, it indirectly makes it possible to employ that same dogma to justify a blatant exception to the equalitarian creed. This is a dubious paradox of modern racialism: that it institutionalizes a doctrine of inequality (as between races) to sustain a doctrine of equality (as within a single race).[2]

The racial theory is found not only in the practices and rationalizations of peoples. It is also given expression in the writings of individual theorists, from Tacitus in ancient Greece to the French count, Joseph Arthur de Gobineau, who presented the first systematic exposition of the modern doctrine. Writing in the middle of the nineteenth century, Gobineau argued that the advance or retrogression of a civilization is fundamentally determined by the factor of race, that the white race is the highest of all races, and that the supreme branch of the white race is the Aryan.[3]

In Europe, this thesis of Aryan supremacy was amplified and extended by Houston Stewart Chamberlain into a peculiarly Teutonic philosophy of history, in the course of which he denied the right of scientific evidence to dispute the facts of intuition [4] and held that

"if . . . the Teutons were not the only peoples who moulded the world's history, they unquestioningly deserve the first place: all those who from the sixth century onwards appear as genuine shapers of the doctrines of mankind, whether as builders of States or as discoverers of new thoughts and of original art, belong to the Teutonic races. . . . Our whole civilisation and culture of to-day is the work of one definite race of men, the Teutonic . . . the work not of philosophers and book-writers and painters, but of the great Teuton Princes, the work of warriors and statesmen. . . . The Teuton is one of the greatest, perhaps the very greatest power in the history of mankind." [5]

Chamberlain's doctrine of Teutonic supremacy was given vigorous affirmation in Germany by a vast array of speculative thinkers, as the utterances of Spengler, Treitschke, Rosenberg, Hitler, and others bear witness.[6] But it had already been anticipated in America, in some measure, in the writings of those who, like Calhoun and George Fitzhugh, sought to justify the Southern system of slavocracy,[7] and in the writings of later spokesmen such as the Reverend Josiah Strong [8] and the political scientist John W. Burgess. Indeed, in Burgess' most ambitious work, *Political Science and Comparative Constitutional Law,* we find developed to the full the consequence of identifying political genius with a particular people or "race." Thus, in a striking and typical passage, he declared:

"My . . . conclusion from the facts . . . is that the Teutonic nations are particularly endowed with the capacity for establishing national states, and are especially called to that work; and, therefore, that they are intrusted, in the general economy of history, with the mission of conducting the political civilization of the modern world. The further conclusions of practical politics from this proposition must be, that in a state whose population is composed of a variety of nationalities the Teutonic element, where dominant, should never surrender the balance of political power . . . to the other elements. Under certain circumstances it should not even

permit participation of the other elements in political power. . . .
The Teutonic nations can never regard the exercise of political
power as a right of man. With them this power must be based upon
capacity to discharge political duty, and they themselves are the
best organs which have as yet appeared to determine when and
where this capacity exists." [9]

The assurance with which Burgess enunciated this doctrine of
racial inequality, a doctrine reaffirmed by philosophers like Santayana [10] and historians like Julian Hawthorne,[11] found renewed
expression in the dogmatic utterance of H. L. Mencken, who in 1910
declared:

"The educated negro of to-day is a failure, not because he meets
insuperable difficulties in life, but because he is a negro. His brain
is not fitted for the higher forms of mental effort; his ideals, no
matter how laboriously he is trained and sheltered, remain those of
the clown. He is, in brief, a low-caste man, to the manner born, and
he will remain inert and inefficient until fifty generations of him
have lived in civilization. And even then, the superior white race
will be fifty generations ahead of him." [12]

This sentiment was echoed profusely in the work of Ralph Adams
Cram [13] and Albert Jay Nock.[14] It was fashioned into a law of
politics by Professor Munro,[15] and set forth by Irving Babbitt and
Lothrop Stoddard as a warning against "the rising tide of color." [16]
The latter's prolific writings, indeed, develop in striking and elaborate form the contemporary theoretical warrant for the continued
application of the Southern doctrine of white supremacy, as well too
as the more specific plea for Nordic supremacy.

"The white race [writes Stoddard] divides into three main sub-
species—the Nordics, the Alpines, and the Mediterraneans. All three
are good stocks, ranking in genetic worth well above the various
colored races. However, there seems to be no question that the
Nordic is far and away the most valuable type; standing, indeed,
at the head of the whole human genus." [17]

In this incisive statement the racial theory is expressed in its modern and almost complete form. It insists, as with Gobineau, that of all races the white is the superior; and it also insists, though now with a slight departure from the French expounder, that of all the white races the Nordic is the highest.

For a full and forceful exposition of this theory in contemporary American thought, let us turn to the volumes of Madison Grant,[18] a corporation lawyer and one-time chairman of the New York Zoological Society.

II

THE RACIAL NORDICISM OF MADISON GRANT

Writing under the auspices of Professor Henry Fairfield Osborn, for whom race is the key to history, and aristocracy the only intelligible means of saving democracy,[19] and building closely on the work of Gobineau and Chamberlain, Grant employed the theory of racial superiority to condemn the principle of universal suffrage and to denounce democracy.

The trouble with democracy, Grant argued, is not alone its failure to preserve purity of stock, but, even more, its "transfer of power from the higher to the lower races, from the intellectual to the plebeian class."

"In the democratic forms of government [Grant declared], the operation of universal suffrage tends toward the selection of the average man for public office rather than the man qualified by birth, education and integrity. . . . From a racial point of view it will inevitably increase the preponderance of the lower types and cause a corresponding loss of efficiency in the community as a whole. . . . [This is so because] the tendency in a democracy is toward a standardization of type and a diminution of the influence of genius. A majority must of necessity be inferior to a picked minority and it always resents specializations in which it cannot share." [20]

Democratic theories of the state, therefore, Grant believed, are unscientific and fatal to progress, for they fail to recognize that heredity and not environment is the controlling factor in human development.

"Races vary intellectually and morally just as they do physically. Moral, intellectual, and spiritual attributes are as persistent as physical characters and are transmitted substantially unchanged from generation to generation." [21]

A society that fails to base its political system on the realities of racial differences, in consequence, is a society foredoomed; for "to admit the unchangeable differentiation of race in its modern scientific meaning is to admit inevitably the existence of superiority in one race and of inferiority in another." And if one race is superior to another, it is clearly the essence of political wisdom to entrust political rule to that superior race. But it is the nature of democracy, Grant observed, to deny this primary principle of political behavior. "Instead of retaining political control and making citizenship an honorable and valued privilege," the American has, through democracy, "intrusted the government of his country and the maintenance of his ideals to races who have never yet succeeded in governing themselves, much less any one else." This, Grant insisted, is the American crime; it can lead only to national suicide.[22]

Consider the races of mankind. Some, according to Grant, are obviously inferior and unsuited to govern. These should be denied all share in political rule. Other races are clearly superior and competent to govern. Of these the best or most superior alone should rule. This, in Grant's view, is the "Nordic aristocracy," that "ruling and restless strain." Of all human races, Grant declared, the superior are the white; and of all the white races the highest is the Nordic. This can be shown, Grant said, not merely by Nordic achievements but by the supremacy of the Nordics as a "race." If we examine cephalic index, for example, which Grant held to be the best method of determining race, then the dolicocephalic or long skull is incontestably the best. And this is the Nordic, made up of the Scandinavian, Teutonic, and Aryan groups. Or take light eye color and blond hair. These, Grant contended, are characteristic of the Nordic and patently demonstrate his superiority, as do also his fair skin and tall stature. Indeed, Grant continued, even the term "Aryan race," while really not of racial but of linguistic significance, is a concept that is rightfully limited only to the Nordics, for they alone are the true descendants of the original Aryans. On all counts, therefore, the Nordic is "the white man par excellence." The Nordics are above all "a race . . . of rulers, organizers and aristocrats, . . . characterized by a greater stability and steadiness." [23]

In these terms, Grant declared, it cannot be argued that amalgamation of the races will elevate the inferior. On the contrary, history amply proves that "the result of the mixture of two races, in the long run, gives us a race reverting to the more ancient, generalized and lower type." The product of a racial mixture is one who inherits an unstable brain from the lower race plus flashes of brilliance from the upper race. There results, in consequence, "a total lack of continuity of purpose, an intermittent intellect goaded by its spasmodic outbursts of energy." To prevent this lack of harmony, Grant argued, "races must be kept apart by artificial devices," such as sterilization and segregation; for "democracy is fatal to progress when two races of unequal value live side by side." [24]

As Grant wrote in summary form,

"The backbone of western civilization is racially Nordic. . . . If this great race, with its capacity for leadership and fighting, should ultimately pass, with it would pass that which we call civilization. It would be succeeded by an unstable and bastardized population, where worth and merit would have no inherent right to leadership and among which a new and darker age would blot out our racial inheritance. Such a catastrophe cannot threaten if the Nordic race will gather itself together in time . . . and reassert the pride of race and the right of merit to rule. . . . Democratic ideals among an homogeneous population of Nordic blood, as in England and America, is one thing, but it is quite another for the white man to share his blood with, or intrust his ideals to, brown, yellow, black, or red men. This is suicide pure and simple." [25]

For the preservation of civilization, then, Grant held, it is imperative that we abandon democracy and give political rule to the supreme race, the Nordic.

III

ANALYSIS AND CRITICISM OF THE RACIAL THEORY

If one were to question the validity of the racial theory of politics, he would be met at the outset by the sheer fact of its survival through many centuries of human history. This is, by any standard, an immense achievement, but one that is lessened in significance when we remember that it survived not as a theory relating to the *same* race, but as a theory to justify the acquisition of power by different "races" at different times. It is not, then, simply a single doctrine. The inquirer would be challenged, too, by the long list of writers and statesmen who have lent their support to the doctrine. But here again, the individuals cited have not all subscribed to the *same* doctrine; nor do names, merely by virtue of quantity, establish the truth of the proposition with which they are identified. There is still the problem of demonstrating the validity of the proposition itself. There is also the problem of reconciling the long list of names in opposition.

The racist would confront the questioner, again, with the incontrovertible fact that there are races and that there are race differences. But it is clearly one thing to recognize a delineation of races based on physical criteria; it is altogether another, and very different, thing to associate those physical differences with inherent social or intellectual characteristics. Moreover, difference as a statistical concept implies neither superiority nor inferiority *except by imputation*. And it is with the validity of the imputation that we are here concerned. The racist would cite, again, the undeniable fact of race supremacy, the evident truth that the white race in the American South, for example, is supreme over the Negro. But supremacy is not superiority. It invites justification in the name of superiority, but it does not prove it. By itself supremacy affirms only the fact of domination.

These considerations make it plain that the racial theory of politics, so confidently put forward by Madison Grant and others, requires careful and extended scrutiny. Not rhetoric but the findings of anthropological and psychological research should govern our conclusions; not the speculative thoughts of men trained in literature and the law but the bald data of careful and competent investigators should guide our decisions. In these terms the problem before us might well be met on two broad levels: first, the theory of a hierarchy within the white race, to determine whether or not the evidence establishes the superiority of a "Nordic race"; and second, the theory of a hierarchy among all the races of mankind, to determine the validity of the claim of white superiority.

A. THE CONCEPT OF NORDIC SUPERIORITY

According to Grant, the supreme mark of the "Nordic race" is its political superiority. In proof of this he cites three things: the superiority of Nordic intelligence; the superiority of Nordic achievements; and the distinctiveness of Nordic racial characteristics. These evidences merit exploration.

The superiority of Nordic intelligence. It is significant to note, in reviewing the validity of the Nordic claim to intellectual superiority, that nowhere in Grant is there to be found any sort of comparative statistical survey of Nordic and non-Nordic intelligence. The doctrine of intellectual superiority is affirmed; it is not demonstrated. And the one real attempt made by investigators to prove Nordic superiority in intelligence—that based on intelligence test scores obtained from immigrant groups in the American Army in World War I—has since been thoroughly discredited. What the tests did, it has been shown, was to measure achievement rather than intelligence, and achievement, it is clear, is affected by cultural opportunities and background as well as by native ability. In addition, as one of the interpreters of these tests later admitted, the tests were in no way suited for comparative studies of various racial and national groups.[26]

A more careful attempt to investigate the alleged superiority of Nordic intelligence was made by Klineberg in his study of European "racial" groups. Accepting for purposes of his study the racial standards of the Nordic theorists, and making allowances for the problems involved in constructing a valid test for diverse national groups, Klineberg tested a series of rigidly selected "racial" samples. His findings, in terms of the distribution of "general intelligence" or performance ability, are indicated in the following table.[27]

Group	Average	Median	Range
Paris	219.0	218.9	100–302
Hamburg	216.4	218.3	105–322
Rome	211.8	213.6	109–313
German Nordic	198.2	197.6	69–289
French Mediterranean	197.4	204.4	71–271
German Alpine	193.6	199.0	80–211
Italian Alpine	188.8	186.3	69–306
French Alpine	180.2	185.3	72–296
French Nordic	178.8	183.3	63–314
Italian Mediterranean	173.0	172.7	69–308

Apart from the fact that urban children obtained higher scores than rural children, irrespective of "race," these results indicate that the three "races" are substantially equal in intellect. It is true that if we employ averages, the German Nordics appear the best and the Italian Mediterraneans appear the worst. But this would be a superficial and incorrect reading of the "racial" differences. As Klineberg observes:

"Closer examination shows . . . that the Nordic-Alpine-Mediterranean hierarchy is by no means maintained throughout. The second group, separated by a fraction of a point, is the French Mediterranean . . . group; then come the three Alpine groups; and only then the other Nordic group. Moreover, when *medians* instead of averages are used in the comparisons, the best country group is the French Mediterranean, then comes the German Alpine . . . group, and only then the German Nordics,—all of which indicates, as does also the very small reliability of the differences between these three groups (not more than 75 chances in 100) that the German Nordics, the French Mediterranean, and the German Alpines tested in this study, representing three different 'races' and two nations, should be regarded as equal." [28]

This conclusion is reinforced by the several additional breakdowns Klineberg derives from his data, demonstrating, for example, that the variability within each of the three "races" is so great that by selecting a particular sample the "racial" hierarchy is completely reversed, as in France, where it is the Mediterraneans who are the best and the Nordics who are the worst. Even more significant is the fact that when the three "racial" groups are combined, and both averages and medians taken, the differences are revealed to be practically negligible and the overlapping practically complete.[29]

The validity of Klineberg's test—as indeed of any intelligence test purporting to measure peoples of diverse cultural backgrounds —is, of course, seriously open to question. But if we accept the twofold premise of the racists that there is a "Nordic race," and that intelligence tests applied to diverse national or racial groups will establish the superior intelligence of this "Nordic race," then clearly by the racial theorists' own standards they are convicted of error. When we add to these considerations the care observed by Klineberg to maximize the validity of his tests and procedures, the conclusion seems inescapable that, whatever the intuition of the racists, there is no scientific evidence to substantiate the thesis of Nordic intellectual superiority. There is, on the other hand, in the painstaking survey by Klineberg, reasonable evidence to suggest that the three white "races" are not demonstrably unequal.

The superiority of Nordic achievements. The argument that the "Nordic race" is responsible above all other races for the great advances in civilization, and particularly for political organization, is a statement of alleged fact rather than a philosophy of history. But what do the facts show? If one argues, as Chamberlain does, that unlikeness proves likeness—that Dante, for example, is a Teuton as evidenced by Luther's "powerful head which in every particular is the very opposite of Dante's and by this very fact betrays the intimate relationship" [30]—then all the achievements of men, whether "Nordic" or "non-Nordic," can somehow, no doubt, be ascribed to the members of the "Nordic race." But if one excepts this pathology of thought and remains, for the moment, with the strict racial classification of the Nordic as expounded by Grant, then the question of achievement is not quite so clear. Ample warrant, it would appear, exists for the belief that many of the significant advances in civilization were effected by other than Nordic peoples.

Consider, for example, the contributions of the early Egyptians, or of ancient Palaeolithic man before them. Or take the civilizations of Sumeria, of Babylonia, of Phoenicia, of Chaldea, of the Hebrews, of the Indians, of the Chinese. The contributions of these peoples have been of immeasurable significance, and they are in many cases the contributions of races not even white, let alone Nordic. As Toynbee points out in his *Study of History,* the Nordics have contributed only to four, at most five, of man's twenty-one major civilizations, while the Mediterranean peoples alone, in striking contrast, have contributed to no less than ten.[31] This is surely not evidence to sustain the Nordic claim to superiority in cultural achievement.

If we look, moreover, to political organization itself, there is little or nothing in the history of the Teutonic tribes prior to the comparatively recent advent of the Prussians (whose racial composition is itself one of the most disputed points in anthropology) to compare, say, with the vast governmental achievements of the Persian Empire under Cyrus the Great and Darius, or of Old Babylonia under Hammurabi, or with the development of the territorial state in ancient Egypt. Indeed, the histories of Greece and of Rome, as of the Renaissance many centuries later, suggest that if any branch of the white race has a claim to being the creator of civilization it is not the Nordic but the Mediterranean.[32] Even if we go to the Germans themselves, we find conclusive evidence that the greatest of these include non-Nordics—men like Beethoven and Kant, Schiller and Leibniz and Goethe—all of whom were moderately or extremely round-headed, with cephalic indices ranging from eighty-four to ninety-two.[33]

Not only is the alleged Nordic superiority in state-building unsupported by the evidences of history, it is repudiated by the thoughts of intellectuals in ancient as well as in modern times. Aristotle, for example, was convinced that the Germans were a politically inferior people, and in a striking passage put forward an alternative theory of his own.

"Those who live in cold countries [he said], as the north of Europe, are full of courage, but wanting in understanding and the arts: therefore they are very tenacious of their liberty; but, *not being politicians*, they cannot reduce their neighbours under their power; but the Asiatics, whose understandings are quick, and who are conversant in the arts, are deficient in courage; and therefore are always conquered and the slaves of others; but the Grecians, placed as it were between these two boundaries, so partake of them both as to be at the same time both courageous and sensible; for which reason Greece continues free, and governed in the best manner possible, and capable of commanding the whole world, could they agree upon one system of policy." [34]

This passage from Aristotle underscores by its striking irrelevance to contemporary affairs the necessity of maintaining a historical perspective, of avoiding a limited temporal view in the formulation of a philosophy of human history. Burgess and Chamberlain and Grant, it is clear, see history from the vantage point of the turn of the nineteenth century. But a similar theory advanced in the seventeenth century would cite not the Germans or the Nordics but perhaps the French as the political elect. In A.D. 200 it would in all probability have been the Romans; while in the year 1800 B.C. it might have been the Egyptians. Who will be "fit" to rule in the year 3000?

Not only can we legitimately infer nothing of the superiority of a race by its supremacy at a particular moment; we are equally unjustified in attempting to set forth the hierarchy of races in the future. The Scandinavians of the ninth century were noted for their achievements as the feared, aggressive Vikings of the sea, yet today they are extolled as the non-aggressive exponents of democracy and the middle way. The Japanese were once regarded as a pacific people, yet their record in the past century might well lead men to a contrary description. A great and creative people today may survive tomorrow only in the reflected glory of their ancestors; a poorly regarded or as-yet-unknown people may someday become the bulwark of a noble and flourishing civilization. The factor of race alone cannot explain cultural change. [35]

One last point before we abandon the theory of Nordic superiority in achievement. It is a matter of particular pride with Grant and other expounders of the racial doctrine that the early founders of the American commonwealth were almost completely Nordic. Indeed, Grant claims in one place, "over ninety-eight per cent were Nordic." [36] But as Hrdlička's exhaustive study of the early Americans shows, there is little or no evidence to support this contention; the aggregate comprised various physical types and nationalities, and there is no certainty as to their exact proportion. "Moreover," says Hrdlička, "these groups were not distinct 'races' of man, but mixtures of various older ethnic elements." [37] The fallacy in Grant, it is plain, has been to confuse nationalistic with racial composition, a confusion as common as it is unwarranted.

The distinctiveness of Nordic racial characteristics. It has been seen that the claim of Nordic superiority in intelligence and achievement is in no sense borne out by the facts. The significant question still to be answered is: Is there a Nordic race? How do we recognize it? What are its characteristics?

The positive reply advanced by Grant revolves about three factors: low cephalic index, blondness, and light eye color, with a frequent appeal to tall stature. But even if we exclude from consideration the questionable accuracy of diametric measurements,[38] there is little to show that dolicocephaly is a valid index to Nordicism or to social characteristics. Grant himself recognizes the frequency of a low cephalic index among the Negroes, and Sorokin points out that it is common to the Eskimos, the Hottentots, and the Kaffirs, as well as to many primitive peoples, none of whom are Nordic and none of whom exhibit signs of what the racists would call mental superiority.[39]

Grant insists the Nordic is characterized by blondness of hair, yet he also argues that this category includes all varieties of brown, even up to very dark brown hair. This, of course, is more a definition of convenience than it is one of scientific accuracy; but while it enables the inclusion of great men not otherwise Nordic, it cannot by the same token exclude mediocre and inferior men not otherwise Nordic. Grant fails, moreover, to mention that many who are blond of hair are also round of head, that blondness is not uncommon to mental defectives and criminals, and that no one has yet demonstrated a correlation between color of hair and intelligence.[40] Even if Grant were to argue that blondness and long-headedness applied as *average* rather than as *absolute* considerations, as a *tendency* rather than an *iron law*, he would be on no stronger ground; for as Myrdal points out with reference to the American people, "no anthropometric measurements . . . have ever been undertaken on such a large scale and with such methodological precautions that valid comparisons between one sub-group and the rest of the population are made possible." [41]

Similar considerations operate with respect to eye color and physical stature, which are found in numerous and varying combinations both with color of hair and with long-headedness. Take, for example, Grant's statement that "it may be taken as an absolute certainty that all the original races of man had dark eyes." [42] If this were true, how could we then explain the emergence of blue eyes in the light of the demonstrated hereditary dominance of dark over light eyes? And if dark eyes are dominant, wherein lies the superiority of light eyes? It is interesting, if confusing, to note that Grant goes on to render tribute (but not explanation) to the genius of Alexander, who had mixed eyes, "the left blue and the right very black." [43]

Concerning physical stature, two things may be particularly noted. First, the biological determination of stature is not simply a matter of race; it is also, in part at least, the result of heterogeneity. The fact, for example, that in northern Italy there are tall people with light hair and in southern Italy short people with dark hair is, in Boas' words,

"merely an expression of the heterogeneity of the Italian people. It has nothing to do with a biological relation between stature and hair color. . . . In a homogeneous population tall people are proportionately slimmer than short people. . . . For the population of Italy we find conditions reversed for the reason that the tall North Italians are of broad build, while the short South Italians are of narrower build. For the whole population we find, therefore, that the tall people are broad, the short, slim. Here the biologically determined relation is reversed owing to the heterogeneity of the series." [44]

Secondly, researches by competent investigators have demonstrated no reliable correlations or differences between physical stature and mental traits.[45] Even if, therefore, it could be shown that the Nordics are the giant Vikings that Grant proclaims them to be, it is not thereby established that they possess, *ipso facto*, equally giant minds. And it cannot be shown that the Nordics possess even a unique physical stature; for "every 'race,' even the most homogeneous one we know, consists of individuals differing considerably in bodily form." [46]

It is clear, then, that the Nordic claim to exclusive or distinctive racial characteristics rests on spurious evidence; and this renders untenable indeed the position that there is a "Nordic race." What race implies is, at the very least, a classification based on the hereditary transmission of physical traits; and what we find is, at most, only local types, some of which may approximate the Nordic ideal but all of which are different not merely from each other but, even more, within themselves.[47] The Nordic is not, in strict accuracy, a race but at the very most a type; and physical types are at once unstable, dispersed, and rarely if ever found in pure form.[48] To attempt, therefore, to identify a man as a member of the "Nordic race" because of the language he may speak,[49] or because of the particular nation to which he may belong,[50] or because of his outward physical characteristics,[51] or because he exhibits certain moral and intellectual qualities,[52] is a procedure impossible to sanction in terms of the science of race.

B. THE CONCEPT OF WHITE SUPERIORITY

Though we refuse, on the basis of the evidence, to accept the claim of Nordic superiority with respect to any other branch or type of the white race, we have yet to consider that phase of the racial argument which postulates a hierarchy not within but among the races and which insists that the white race as a whole is superior to the other races of mankind.

Generally speaking, anthropologists have, on this level, admitted the existence of distinct races, the usual divisions being the Negroid, the Mongoloid, and the Caucasian. But to recognize the existence of physical races is not necessarily to identify those physical differences with particular social attributes.[53] Nor is it to establish the superiority or inferiority of one to the other. It is merely to state the fact of physical differences. To equate those physical differences with mental or social differences or to infer therefrom a hierarchy of values, is a procedure that requires documentation and proof on its own grounds.

For Grant, this documentation and proof are to be found in the alleged superiority of white intelligence and in the alleged superiority of white civilization. If one inquires, however, as to the proof of superior white intelligence Grant offers not statistical evidence but affirmation, and the "fact" of superior white culture. But to prove aptitude or intelligence by achievement is to assume the very thing under inquiry, namely, whether the achievement is in reality the result of greater aptitude or whether it can be attributed to other factors. Even more, it is to avoid the question whether demonstrated aptitude is itself not in part the consequence as well as the cause of the supposedly "higher" culture.

It is important to state these considerations at the outset, for it is on the basis of this one central assumption that the racial theory rests. Thus Grant can argue, as he does, that since white culture is highest, white intelligence is highest; and since white intelligence is highest, the white race is physically and mentally highest; any deviation from the white race, therefore, necessarily represents the characteristic feature of a lower race.[54] These three propositions, so advanced in reverse argument, form the core of the racial thesis of white superiority, and, as such, require examination.

The superiority of white culture. In any consideration of cultural achievement it is impossible to ignore the profound contributions of pre-historic peoples—in art, in agriculture, in the invention and manufacture of mechanical tools, in the domestication of animals, in trade—peoples whose civilizations, by their very lack of historic record, cannot possibly be attributed to a particular race. Nor is it possible to exclude from consideration the evidences brought forward only in comparatively recent times by studies of primitive societies, especially of those whose colored peoples have developed cultures both varied and highly complex. Thus, if we inquire into the cultures of the West African Negro, we find, according to Herskovits, that

"they manifest a degree of complexity that on this ground alone places them high in the ranks of the nonliterate, nonmachine societies over the world, and makes them comparable in many respects to Europe of the Middle Ages. Some of the traits of these West African civilizations are: well-organized, intricate economic systems, which in many areas include the use of money to facilitate exchange; political systems which, though founded on the local group, were adequate to administer widespread kingdoms; a complex social organization, regularized through devices such as the sanctions of insurance, police, and other character; involved systems of religious belief and practice, which comprise philosophically conceived world views and sustained cult rituals; and a high development of the arts, whether in folk literature, the graphic and plastic forms, or music and the dance." [55]

Similar results have been yielded by researches into the cultures of other primitive and non-white races, as, for example, those of the Indians of North and South America.[56]

Yet it is Grant's conviction that citizenship should be denied both the Indian and the Negro on the ground that they lack the inherent capacity to effectuate our complex culture.[57]

Now the very indefiniteness of the source of pre-historic cultures and the fact that both the Negro and the Indian have developed highly complex cultures which differ from those of the modern white world primarily with reference to time suggest at the very least the maintenance of an attitude of caution. This suggestion is reinforced by the recognition of the vital distinction between differences of degree and those of kind. Complexity is not merely a matter of more or less; it is also in the nature of the object. If we were to restrict the concept of complexity to the quantitative factor alone, the racist's view might have some merit; for it is undeniable that we have today more in the way of buildings, and especially of larger buildings, more in the way of clothing and money and mechanical tools and devices, more in the way of commercial amusements and the arts, and the like. Still one cannot but wonder if we have at the same time more in the way of human understanding and the capacity to live in peace, more in the way of contemplative thought and the ability wisely to command the mechanical devices we have created. The quantitative factor, moreover, is, as we have noted, essentially a difference in time. The fact that Negro and Indian, and indeed Oriental, civilizations have produced cultures so very much like those of the whites at an earlier stage of evolution argues that the explanation is to be found not in racial capacity but in historical development.[58]

It is not in the quantitative factor, however, that we find the decisive test of a culture; rather is it in the manner in which that culture satisfies the needs of its people and promotes the conditions and the vision of the good life. Here complexity is relative to the special requirements of a people, and these in turn vary from one people to another. As a consequence, the complexity or nature of one culture is at most *different* from the complexity or nature of another culture. Whether or not it is superior or inferior is a value judgment relative to the standards of a particular people. It is difficult, perhaps impossible, to effect the comparison of diverse cultures on the basis of a common standard when those cultures are by their very differences rooted in unlike standards. All we can reasonably do is to record the differences and the similarities; we have no more reason to presuppose the superiority of the white set of variations than the colored races have to affirm the superiority of theirs. What one regards as superior, the other may scorn. It is not, therefore, in any way true that the more complex society is thereby the superior. "Real social superiority," in fact, may even be claimed as an attribute of simpler races or peoples. To go beyond relativism, in this regard, is a denial of wisdom.

To these considerations we should add the recognition that civilization or culture is not the prerogative of a particular people or race, but that all peoples in all ages have contributed in one way or another to the enrichment of human life. This is evidenced by the simple fact that the same cultural traits are dispersed among many races, while within a single race there are to be found many cultural differences. And since culture and race are thus independent of each other, culture cannot be the product of any one race; nor can any one race be the exclusive creator of a particular culture, be it "superior" or "inferior." The claim, therefore, that the culture of the white man is as a matter af racial heredity superior to the culture of the colored man is a proposition unsupported by the evidence of anthropological science and of history.[59]

The superiority of white intelligence. Grant's evidence for the superiority of white intelligence is, as we have noted, the alleged "fact" of superior achievement. This argument is defective not merely because its reasoning is circular but because the "fact" of superior white achievement has not been established. There is, however, a more serious and rational espousal of the theory which, as with McDougall, rests generally on the evidence gathered from intelligence test scores and finds particular proof of white superiority in the lower intelligence test scores of the Negro as compared with the white. Thus Grant could well point to those results in support of his contention that "the immense mass of Negroes [is] intellectually below the standard of the average American." [60]

It must be admitted at the outset that the Negro, today, really is inferior. Not only is he, on the average, poorer in economic standing; not only is he, on the average, more often below standard in health; he is also, on the average, lower than the white man in intelligence performance. This, Myrdal says, is a correct observation, sustained even under scientific study.[61] And just as the white man is generally revealed to surpass the Negro in intelligence performance, so also he is revealed, on the basis of the intelligence tests, to surpass the American Indian.[62] But when all this has been admitted, it will still remain incorrect to deduce therefrom that the inferiority is biological in nature.[63] Not only is such a deduction inadmissible as an obvious *non sequitur*; it ignores several crucial questions that have still to be explored: first, as to whether or not there have been important exceptions to these general findings; second, whether or not there is dependable evidence as to the validity of the tests cited; and finally, whether or not these results are to be interpreted exclusively in terms of hereditary differences or in terms that allow for environmental influences.

First, let us consider the exceptions. Here—if we again proceed for a moment on the racist's assumption that the intelligence tests are valid and therefore an accurate representation of what they purport to measure—the work of Klineberg is highly suggestive. In testing Indian, Negro and white groups, he found that while the white children were superior in speed or time reaction they gave no evidence of superiority—in some cases, indeed, they evidenced inferiority—in accuracy of performance. More than this, he found that the Indian and Negro groups were "at least the equal of the whites in the ability to learn, or to profit by experience." [64] In another study Klineberg considered the argument of the racists that the superiority in intelligence (as revealed by higher test scores) of the northern Negro as compared to the southern Negro was the result of selective migration, and found no evidence whatever to substantiate this view. On the contrary, his investigations revealed

"quite definitely that the superiority of the northern over the southern Negroes, and the tendency of northern Negroes to approximate the scores of the Whites, are due to factors in the environment, and not to selective migration. . . . There is . . . very definite evidence that an improved environment, whether it be the southern city as contrasted with the neighboring rural districts, or the northern city as contrasted with the South as a whole, raises the test scores considerably; this rise in "intelligence" is roughly proportionate to length of residence in the more favorable environment. . . . As the background improves, so do the scores of Negroes approximate more and more closely the standards set by the Whites. The final and crucial comparison could only be made in a society in which the Negro lived on terms of complete equality with the White, and where he suffered not the slightest social, economic, or educational handicap." [65]

There is still another factor that must be considered in any evaluation of the results of intelligence tests. This is the great overlapping that exists among the races. So great is this overlapping, in fact, that statements made about a race will in no way necessarily apply to any particular member of that race. Even if it were agreed that whites are intellectually superior to Negroes, it would not thereby be established that all Negroes are inferior to all whites. Nor could this be established, for on the basis of the intelligence tests accepted by the racial theorists both Negroes and Indians have given evidence of genius and near-genius intellectual capacity. The differences between individuals of the same race are so great that it is impossible to prove a constant racial characteristic in intellect, a consideration whose decisiveness becomes even more strikingly apparent when we bear in mind, with this fact of great individual differences, the additional fact of great differences between family as against racial lines.[66]

These considerations demonstrate that there are serious and important exceptions to the results of the intelligence tests as cited by the theorists of racism. And not only do exceptions logically disprove the rule, they also, in this instance, demonstrate both the invalidity of the tests in fact and the fallacy of interpreting the results of such tests exclusively in racial or hereditary terms.

That the intelligence tests employed in inter-racial measurement are essentially invalid is confirmed by numerous careful and exhaustive analyses. These studies show, for example, that the tests have failed to isolate the environmental or cultural factor and do not, in consequence, tell us what part of the test score is the result of that environmental impact and what part is attributable to hereditary endowment alone.[67] These studies also show that the tests have failed, overwhelmingly, to control such factors as schooling, language and cultural differences, sampling, temperament and speed, differences in social and economic status, motivation and rapport, and the like—factors which, taken together, may very well be uncontrollable when dealing with heterogeneous groups. It is one thing to measure individual differences within a homogeneous group; but it is quite another and far more difficult task to measure differences between such dissimilar entities as races. Psychologists are now, in fact, generally agreed that such testing is unlikely ever to be made perfect, for no common test can accurately measure divergent environmental backgrounds.[68] And that there are vast differences in the environmental backgrounds even of races living in the same general community is no longer, if it ever has been, open to doubt. Myrdal, Gunther, and Fine amply sustain the findings so tellingly put forth in the Reports of the President's Commissions on Civil Rights and on Higher Education.[69]

In the light of these considerations, we are forced to the conclusion that, in an unequal society, intelligence tests unavoidably reflect the unequal and dissimilar environments of the races tested. The results of such tests, in consequence, can hardly be regarded as a decisive indication of racial differences in intelligence.

The problem of racial mixture. Conjoined with the racist's belief that the white race is innately superior both in intelligence and in achievement to the colored races is his insistence that the races must be kept apart and distinct, that the result of the intermingling of blood, "the blackest and most imbecile crime in the human calendar, . . . can only be universal mongrelism and the consequent end of culture and civilization." [70] Subscribing without qualification to this view, Grant went on to assert that "the intelligence and ability of a colored person are in pretty direct proportion to the amount of white blood he has," [71] a position reinforced by the authority of Galton, McDougall, and even Sorokin.[72]

The weight of the authority is indeed impressive; yet the inability of the theorists of racial aristocracy to prove the superiority of white blood either in intelligence or achievement is alone sufficient to defeat the argument. If white blood is not demonstrably superior blood, there can be no legitimate ground for the belief that colored blood, which is *not* inferior blood, will through admixture lower the intelligence or the achievement of white blood. And if we turn to the studies of the anthropologists, we find that this is precisely what the evidence indicates.

The investigations by Herskovits into the problem of racial mixture and intelligence, for example, revealed no evidence of any correlation. He found, indeed, that "the relationship between test scores and physical traits denoting greater or less amounts of Negro blood is so tenuous as to be of no value in drawing conclusions as to the comparative native ability or relative intelligence of the Negro when compared to the White." More than that, he found that the apparent superiority of the lighter-colored or mixed Negro to the darker-skinned Negro was in reality a social rather than an intellectual advantage, a discrimination within the American Negro community that could adequately be explained in terms of their peculiar social and historical development.[73]

Equally conclusive is the study by Klineberg, who discovered "no definite evidence for any inverse relationship between Intelligence . . . and degree of Negro blood." More directly, "there is no evidence for an improvement in score on the performance tests as the proportion of white blood in Negroes or Indians increases." [74] And in the work of Friedrich Hertz we find not only an imposing enumeration of the achievements of men of mixed blood—men such as Pushkin and Dumas—but, even more, a decisive refutation of the legend that racial mixture results in racial disharmony and degeneration.[75]

Approaching the problem from the other side, Ralph Linton points out that "every civilized group of which we have any record has been a hybrid group, a fact which disposes effectually of the theory that hybrid peoples are inferior to pure-bred ones." [76] For if history advances no pure races, how can it be asserted that the lack of racial purity produces degeneracy and decline? And history does not bespeak pure races; all are mixed racial types. "In every single nationality of Europe," states Boas, in a proposition whose truth destroys the pretensions of the "Nordic" theorists as incisively as it does the argument that racial mixture produces racial decline, "the various elements of the continental population are represented." [77]

It would be difficult, indeed, to deny the historic fact of racial mixture in the light of so definitive a finding as the presence of the several hereditary blood types in a single population.[78] And it is this lack of racial purity, now and in the recorded past, which impels Klineberg and others to urge that we abandon completely the concept of pure race, as well as its artificial corollary, pure racial type. There is neither a pure race nor a pure racial type, and there are neither proved advantages nor disadvantages of racial mixture. It is impossible, therefore, to attribute to a non-existent pure race, material qualities of superiority or inferiority. It is logically possible to argue, on the other hand, that since history evidences only hybrid races the progress of a civilization depends not on racial purity but on racial mixture.[79]

IV

Conclusions on Race and Politics

We may now draw together the various threads of our discussion. According to Grant, the factor of race determines as a matter of heredity the mental and political capabilities of a people and establishes the inherent superiority of one particular race, the Nordic, over all other races of mankind.

But on the basis of our foregoing analysis there would appear to be no warrant for this view. In the first place, the racial theorists have failed to isolate the environmental from the hereditary influences and consequently can affirm nothing concerning the respective roles of each. In the second place, they have failed to establish the innate superiority in intelligence of either a particular race or a particular racial type. In the third place, not only have they failed to demonstrate the superior cultural achievements of the Nordic type or of the white race, they have failed, even more, to establish that culture is a function of race. In the fourth place, though they have not always overlooked the heterogeneity of peoples, they have failed to perceive or to accept the necessary implications of this fact: that if races are not pure but mixed, then whatever intellectual or cultural attainments are attributed to a people must be the attainments not of a particular race or type but of a people racially mixed. In the fifth place, they have failed to appreciate or to reconcile the profound fact of individual variations or differences, so great and overlapping as to pale into virtual insignificance whatever slight differences have thus far been alleged to exist between the races. And in the sixth place, they have failed to realize that superiority is not general but specific, that the possession by an individual or a group of a "superior" trait is a particular possession that in no way establishes a general superiority in all traits.

When we add to these considerations the additional failure of the racial theorists to establish even the existence of a "Nordic race," then it becomes patently impossible to grant the validity of Grant's thesis.[80] There is neither a "Nordic race" nor a hierarchy within or among the races. There can, in consequence, be neither a superior Nordic intelligence nor a superior Nordic record of cultural attainment. Nor, most important of all, can there be an equation of race with particular social or mental qualities.

These reflections compel the further recognition that what the racial theorists have done has been, in effect, to confuse the concept of race, a legitimate field for scientific inquiry, with the concept of racism, the unwarranted "belief in the superiority of one race over another."[81] It is not race, that is to say, but racism, the falsification of race, which is the principle of politics affirmed by Grant and the several theorists of racial aristocracy. And racism has no warrant in anthropological science. The condemnation of democracy, therefore, on the ground that it refuses to grant constitutional recognition to a racial aristocracy by restricting to that aristocracy the exercise of political power, is a condemnation that can have no basis in race. More than that, the condemnation is revealed in the light of the evidence to be not a condemnation but rather a justification of the democratic principle; for if there is no superior race or racial group, there can be no legitimate exclusion from the political process of any segment of the population on racial grounds alone.

Thus democracy, in refusing to surrender political rule either to the white race or to any particular branch of the white race, and in insisting that a true political system purporting to rest on human dignity must include all races and all racial types on a basis of political equality, finds itself rooted in the verities of the science of man.

7

The Concept of Biological Aristocracy

I

THE PRINCIPLE OF BIOLOGICAL ARISTOCRACY

In the course of our discussion of race, it was pointed out that the differences *within* races are far greater and more significant than the differences *between* races. It is precisely in this distinction that the biological theory of politics differs from the racial theory. It builds not on the idea of a "chosen people" or a superior race but on the concept of superior individuals, and it attempts to do this in two ways: first, by denying to the allegedly unfit or inferior the right of political participation; and second, by achieving through the procreation and fertility of the "best" stocks, a race of superior men.

The Greek poet Theognis struck the keynote of this thesis as long ago as the sixth century B.C., when he wrote:

> "With Kine and Horses, Kurnus! we proceed
> By reasonable rules, and choose a breed
> For profit and increase, at any price;
> Of a sound stock, without defect or vice.
> But, in the daily matches that we make,
> The price is every thing; for money's sake,
> Men marry; Women are in marriage given:
> The Churl or Ruffian, that in wealth has thriven,

May match his offspring with the proudest race:
Thus every thing is mix'd, noble and base!
    If then in outward manner, form and mind,
You find us a degraded, motley kind,
Wonder no more, my friend! the cause is plain,
And to lament the consequence is vain." [1]

And it has been affirmed many times since, for example by Campanella, in whose ideal *City of the Sun* "men who are weak in intellect are sent to farms" and "male and female breeders of the best natures" are distributed "according to philosophical rules." [2] It was not until the work of Galton in the latter part of the nineteenth century, however, that the doctrine began to take modern and decisive shape and to rest on a basis of affirmed scientific truth.

The foundation of Galton's eugenical theory was his belief that "a man's natural abilities are derived by inheritance, under exactly the same limitations as are the form and physical features of the whole organic world." [3] But while we must turn to heredity if we would understand the nature of an individual, Galton argued, it is impossible at the same time to ignore the impact of environmental influences. In fact, Galton observed,

"Man is so educable an animal that it is difficult to distinguish between that part of his character which has been acquired through education and circumstance, and that which was in the original grain of his constitution. . . . The interaction of nature and circumstance is very close, and it is impossible to separate them with precision. . . . We need not, however, be hypercritical about distinctions; we know that the bulk of the respective provinces of nature and nurture are totally different, although the frontier between them may be uncertain, and we are perfectly justified in attempting to appraise their relative importance." [4]

In thus postulating a dichotomy between nature and nurture, and in affirming the possibility of their effective appraisement, Galton gave to the expounders of biological aristocracy the twin pillars of their doctrinal structure. More than that, Galton himself proceeded to attempt the delineation he had stated was measurable, and inquired, for this purpose, into the history of eminent families. Finding in that history what he thought was a consistent line of superiority in intellect and achievement, he concluded that nature and not nurture was the dominant force.[5] This view, he felt, was sustained by his investigations into the intelligence of twins. If the environment were dominant, he held, then identical twins should differ and dissimilar twins grow alike; but the evidence did not bear this out.[6] Even more, his findings that "the brains of the nation lie in the higher of our classes," together with his reading of "very many biographies," convinced him of the existence of a tendency among intellectual men and women to marry among themselves. "The possibility of improving the race of a nation," he therefore concluded, "depends on the power of increasing the productivity of the best stock." [7]

The fallacy in Galton in presupposing eminence to be adequate proof of ability when it was his very task to demonstrate that that eminence was the result of ability, did not deter his followers from accepting and extending his results. Of these the most notable was Karl Pearson, who declared:

"I will not dogmatically assert that environment matters not at all; phases of it may be discovered which produce more effect than any we have yet been able to deal with. But I think it quite safe to say that the influence of environment is not one-fifth that of heredity, and quite possibly not one-tenth of it. There is no real comparison between nature and nurture; it is essentially the man who makes his environment, and not the environment which makes the man." [8]

This specificity, unlike that of his somewhat more cautious teacher, enabled Pearson to claim for heredity all the qualities of man—physical, moral, and intellectual—and to insist that since a nation needs its best brains in positions of leadership, it must breed from the superior families and give ability its proper place. Otherwise, Pearson declared, he could see nothing in store for man but racial decline and national degeneracy.[9]

The doctrines of Galton and Pearson found ready acceptance in America, where men were all too ready to perceive in their application the alternative to democracy. If it is not the race but the individual that counts, and if "heredity is almost the entire cause for the mental achievements of [eminent] men and women," [10] then clearly it must be admitted, as with Professor East, that "our whole governmental system is out of harmony with genetic common sense. Would it not be better to revise it, to revise it radically" so as to give more power to the best? [11]

The affirmative answer given to this question by anti-democratic theorists furnished the theme to the debate which raged through the pages of the *Journal of Heredity* in 1918–19 and set the tone for the biological denunciation of democracy in the years to come. Initiated by Alleyne Ireland, who inveighed against democracy for its refusal to commit political rule to the able few rather than to the incompetent many—to the expert rather than to the inexpert, to "the rare man of high morality" rather than to "the common run of men"—and who dramatically argued the incompatibility of democracy and efficiency,[12] the proposition of democracy's inadequacy found many defenders.[13] Prominent among these were Paul Popenoe and R. H. Johnson, who drew heavily upon the findings of Galton to argue in a joint work for what they called an aristo-democracy—"a government by the people who are best qualified to govern." Their argument, somewhat confusedly set forth because of their attempt to reconcile rule by experts with democratically chosen legislatures, and to maintain the biological argument in conjunction with Madison Grant's Nordic thesis, may be summed up in these words:

"Too great democratization of a country is dangerous. The tendency is to ask, in regard to any measure, 'What do the people want?' while the question should be, 'What ought the people to want?' The *vox populi* may and often does want something that is in the long run quite detrimental to the welfare of the state. . . .

"This idea of the equality of human beings is, in every respect that can be tested, absolutely false, and any movement which depends on it will either be wrecked or, if successful, will wreck the state which it tries to operate. It will mean the penalization of real worth and the endowment of inferiority and incompetence. Eugenists can feel no sympathy for a doctrine which is so completely at variance with the facts of human nature. . . .

"The fundamental differences in man can not be due to anything that happens after they are born; and . . . these differences can not be due in an important degree to any influences acting on the child prior to birth. . . . They must be due to the ancestry of the individual." [14]

The insistence on heredity as the determinative force in human capabilities and the denunciation of democracy in these terms for its failure to construct a political system based on the natural inequalities ensuing from hereditary differences, have, in more recent years, been given effective restatement by a variety of anti-democratic theorists. From among these the exposition by Professor Sait may well serve as representative of the biological school.

II

E. M. Sait: Democracy in Decline

In the longest chapter of his major publication, Sait offers what is at once a defense of aristocracy and a denunciation of democracy, combining in the latter endeavor the most effective arguments of Ireland and N. J. Lennes. "We are not listening now," he tells us of the critical literature on democracy, "to the complaints of a dispossessed aristocracy. We hear the authentic voice of a new generation that bends its eager eyes upon the future." And this voice, Sait maintains, affirms that the belief in the permanence of democracy is in disharmony with the facts of history and the scientific attitude.[15]

It is not merely, in Sait's construction, that city life leads to the deterioration of the masses.[16] Nor is it simply the fact that the franchise has been given to all adults, women as well as men.[17] These deterrents are important, but they are not crucial. What is crucial, according to Sait, is democracy's disregard of the natural or biological differences in men. What we find in democracy, Sait observes, is that

"public opinion rules. Whether it rules well or badly depends upon the character of the people, and upon circumstance. . . . In view of the fact that government, nowadays, has to meet perplexing problems and that the problems tend steadily to become more intricate and more technical, the immediate future of democracy may well be found in the answer to two questions. Does the capacity of the people increase in proportion to the difficulty of their task? Does their interest in politics mount in like measure? The facts indicate a negative answer." [18]

The facts, indeed, indicate even more. They make plain, Sait says, that in our era of political democracy there is "a marked social fluidity, an absence of status and rigid class distinctions. The gates of opportunity are opened wide; and an able man finds it easy to rise in the social scale, perhaps from the humblest to the highest station." [19] But in the process of ascent there is a twofold consequence: the able, more intelligent, and successful elements have, in rising from the lower to the higher classes, been draining away from the lower classes all talent and genius and increasing the talent and genius of the upper classes. Talents, Sait argues, are hereditary; therefore the lower classes will find themselves unable to replenish their exhausted supply—not through intermarriage, for like inevitably mates with like, intelligence with intelligence, stupidity with stupidity. As a result, democracy finds itself with what Ireland has called "a constant upward and downward genetic pressure tending to produce an increasing difference between the two ends of the social spectrum." [20] This process of class differentiation, Sait insists, will go on, and increasingly become more evident. Eventually, therefore, Sait holds, if democracy is to survive, it must take formal cognizance of the variability in class abilities and give special talent and genius its superior place in the political system. And herein lies the dilemma of democracy: if it gives superior ability its place it ceases to be a democracy; while if it refuses to give superior ability its place it invites, nay, inevitably brings, destruction.

The refusal by democracy to pursue the first of these alternatives is, for Sait, all the more serious in the light of the added considerations adduced by Professor Lennes. These are, first, the rapid headway that democratic ideals have made in practice, tending to disregard social differences and equalize opportunity, thereby facilitating transfer from one occupational class to another; and second, the increasing complexity of our industrial organization, which has brought with it an increasing number of distinct occupations. This now makes it possible, according to Sait and Lennes, to identify the mental level of an individual by the highest point he has reached in the occupational scale; for each individual, it may safely be assumed, will endeavor to reach the highest point in that occupation best suited to his talents. We have, then, a homogeneity of traits within each occupational class, a homogeneity which, "fortified by the practice of assortive mating, ensures the formation of hereditary occupational castes."

This hypothesis, Sait holds, is confirmed by the data of the intelligence tests, which show "that intelligence grows distinctly higher as we go upward in the occupational scale and that the intelligence of children corresponds with that of their parents." The reliability of these tests as a measure of innate capacities is, for Sait, beyond dispute, attested as it is by the constancy of the intelligence quotient of an individual from early childhood on, by the variability of I.Q.'s in persons reared in the same environment, by the similarity or identity of I.Q.'s in persons reared in very different environments, and by the high correlation between a person's intelligence quotient and his academic and occupational success.[21]

To save ourselves from the "excesses" of democracy, Sait thereupon concludes, we must abandon a political system based on the fallacious principle of quantity and turn instead to an aristocracy based on quality; for only through rule by the most intelligent few can civilization hope to flourish and endure.

III

ANALYSIS AND CRITICISM OF THE BIOLOGICAL THEORY

These are formidable arguments, buttressed by the weight of an impressive authority. If their central proposition is to stand, that heredity and not environment is the dominant, the determinative force in the formation of individual differences, then the theory of democracy must fall; for no rational political thinker would urge that political power be given to the incompetent many if the inherently superior few were available and ready to exercise it. Conversely, if the theory of democracy is to be sustained, that central proposition must be disproved.

Our inquiry into the validity of the biological theory shall, in the light of these considerations, proceed on the following grounds: (*a*) the theory of the inheritance of mental characteristics, particularly as evidenced by the studies of family genealogies and of twins; (*b*) the correlation of intelligence with social and occupational achievement; and (*c*) the validity and significance of the intelligence test as a measure of intelligence and achievement. From the results secured by these inquiries, we may be able to draw relevant conclusions concerning the respective roles of heredity and environment, and their implications for politics.

A. THE INHERITANCE OF MENTAL CHARACTERISTICS

The apparent concentration of superior abilities and achievements in particular families has long documented for the exponent of biological aristocracy the thesis that the possession of mental as well as physical characteristics is predominantly a matter of heredity and not of environment. But when we examine more closely the family studies offered in evidence,[22] we note that they are all subject to at least five major objections: they indicate resemblance of ability in family strains but not the causes of the resemblance— either heredity or environment can be offered in explanation; they locate too few descendants; they fail to project their studies backwards; they do not adequately take into account the admixture of hereditary strains through marriage; and they employ inadequate tools and rest on questionable standards of measurement. A brief word in explanation may suffice to make each of these objections clear.

That these studies show a definite tendency for ability to run in families is not denied. But what these studies do not show is the relative impact of heredity and environment as isolated causal factors. Ward demonstrated, for example, that in the very cases cited by Galton to prove genius is a function of heredity, both opportunity and education were universally present;[23] and Bentley pointed up in an incisive discussion the failure of Woods in his evaluation of royalty to account for the vast influence of environmental factors.[24] As Klineberg observes:

"All of these studies . . . suffer from a fatal methodological defect, namely, that these families were relatively homogeneous not only in their heredity but also in their environment. Family histories of this type fail to separate the two factors and are of little help in this problem." [25]

In all of these studies the number of descendants actually traced is but a fraction of the total possible number. Thus it has been shown that of a possible 50,000 descendants of the Edwards family, only 1,394 were located; and of these less than half were considered eminent.[26] When it is borne in mind that the more eminent—and the more disreputable—are always the easiest to locate, the numerical sample finally adduced appears far too small to warrant conclusive generalization. For what were the descendants who were omitted; and how many were they? To these questions we are given no reply.

More important, however, is the failure of these studies to project their inquiries further into the past. Thus, while it is customary for delineators of the Edwards family to point with pride to the two American presidents, as well as to the many judges, clergymen, and university presidents descended from the "first" Edwards and his wife Elizabeth Tuttle, it is no less significant to record that this same Elizabeth Tuttle was herself divorced by her husband for "adultery and other immoralities," that one of her sisters murdered her own son, and that one of her brothers murdered a sister.[27] We are told, on inquiry, that the fathers of two great national poets—Shakespeare and Petöfi—were but humble butchers of the town; [28] that Pasteur was the son of a soldier himself descended from a long line of tanners, and Faraday of a blacksmith and a farmer's daughter; [29] that Rubens came of an adulterous father and Beethoven of a drunken and ill-tempered one; [30] and that Babbitt, himself a protagonist of the biological argument, could point to but one unusual ancestor, a gentleman "held up in his epitaph as a warning example of churlish miserliness." [31]

Indeed, Raymond Pearl showed in a painstaking study that of sixty-three philosophers eminent enough to earn at least a full page in the *Encyclopaedia Britannica* only two fathers and a mother were able to merit a separate article on their own account, and only five of the sixty-three produced gifted or distinguished children. He showed, further, that the eighty-five poets of eminence there listed were descended from fathers of such obscurity that only three merited special mention in the *Encyclopaedia* and thirteen could not be found at all.[32] This is, it may not unfairly be held, a somewhat less than conclusive demonstration of the evidence that is required to prove the biological theory; for if heredity were determinative the disclosure of genius anywhere should point to genius both in the ancestors and in the descendants. The fact that it frequently does not, indicates the play of other factors. It suggests, too, that if an investigation were pressed into the ancestries of many of our distinguished men or families, there would somewhere be uncovered an unsavory figure, one who, were he employed as the starting point for the family tree, would lead to the production of results difficult to explain in terms of the biological thesis alone.

The failure of genealogical studies adequately to take into account the admixture of new strains through marriage is a decisive condemnation of their procedure and applicability. As we trace our ancestry back we find that it will diverge as well as converge, that not only will it embrace the notables but that it will also include the mediocrities and the unknowns brought into the family through the ordinary processes of human production. Each generation, in consequence, is the product of a fresh hereditary admixture, and the proportion of blood we bear of a distinguished ancestor diminishes as the number of horizontal lines of generation increase. The mere fact of hereditary combinations, then, at once renders precise evaluation impossible, unless we include in the analysis the variegated blood streams of countless families and separate with some degree of accuracy the heredity of each from its environmental situation. This, however, the genealogists have failed to do.

It is only in relatively recent years that precise tools of measurement have been made available to the genealogical investigator. "The earlier 'family history studies' were handicapped in that their investigators had no means of actually measuring the qualities traced, but were forced to resort to opinions, ratings, character judgments, and other fallible devices."[33] Thus Woods, for example, explains that his basis for estimate is "the adjectives that are used by historians and biographers."[34] Now this, patently, is subject to criticism not merely on the ground of scientific inadequacy but equally on the ground that what adjectives are employed varies with the histories or biographies read. Nor is this all. It has been frequently observed by Harold Laski that men who live differently think differently. This is, as absolute generalization, a dangerous half-truth; but nowhere is its validity so effectively portrayed as in the evaluations men apply to other men. What is eminent for some is inconsequential for others. What is average in one group or situation is held superior in another. Standards differ, and the men who apply them differ both in the application and the regard. The affirmation, then, that some men or families are superior to others, is inexorably a relative and therefore scientifically questionable judgment.

It is difficult to escape the conclusion that for an understanding of the relative roles of heredity and environment in the transmission of mental characteristics little is to be gained from the genealogical studies offered to us. The failure clearly to isolate the hereditary from the environmental makes the facts vulnerable to either interpretation with equal legitimacy or, as MacIver emphasizes, illegitimacy. They tell us nothing directly about either heredity or environment; consequently they are not evidence for either position.

A more serious attempt has been made to measure the influence of the environment by the experimental method, particularly through the study of twins. Galton, it will be recalled, presented the simple argument that if the environment were dominant, then identical twins should differ and dissimilar twins grow alike. When his findings failed to sustain this hypothesis, he concluded that heredity rather than environment is the determinative factor. But it is, of course, logically possible to argue a contrary position: that if the environment were dominant, then identical twins may or may not differ, depending upon the specific impact of environmental conditions, and dissimilar twins may grow even more dissimilar; while if heredity were dominant both identical and dissimilar twins should grow alike. Galton's failure to take adequate account of such alternative possibilities renders his conclusions as false in logic as they are insufficient in fact.

More relevant are the studies of identical twins reared apart. These studies, however, are too few to have statistical significance, and demonstrate only that the twins show both great similarities and great differences, in some cases the differences in one pair becoming the similarities in another.[35] Even less conclusive for the biological thesis are the studies of children of different parentage reared together, for not only is it impossible for any two people to have the same environment in all respects—the same home, for example, may afford different environments for different children while different homes provide similar environments—it is essentially to shift the study from that of individual differences to the measurement of the effect of one or the other variable on group averages.[36]

What these cases do, in effect, is to offer evidence in support of the position that *both* heredity and environment operate; they do not measure the relative potency of either. If anything, Klineberg inclines to the belief that the evidence indicates environmental influences to be more important in the causation of individual differences; [37] but it is clearly safe to say that the studies do not establish the thesis that heredity is the decisive or dominant factor in the formation of mental characteristics.

Two observations may still be made before we leave this aspect of the problem. First, note should be taken of the frequent arguments advanced by exponents of biological aristocracy that mental traits are inherited not merely in the matter of intelligence but also in the matter of personality, of behavior. Thus we find in Ireland the insistence that "the character of the people is determined chiefly through the operation of biological law." [38] Examination of the evidence, however, does not tend to support this view. As the exhaustive analysis by Schwesinger shows, personality even more than intelligence is an expression of environmental rather than of hereditary influences. So great, in fact, are the complexity and variability of personality traits that they create in each individual an entirely different pattern from every other individual, and render psychologists actually engaged in the study unable even to agree on a central concept or definition of personality, much less to offer a binding scientific analysis or basis of personality.[39]

It is not unimportant, in the second place, when dealing with the inheritance of mental characteristics, to recognize that the influence of the environment is itself almost a form of heredity. Men "inherit" or acquire not alone a biological constitution but also—and from their environment alone—a social heritage, a tradition, a body of ideas.[40] This is not, let it be emphasized, an argument in defense of the discredited Lamarckian theory of the inheritance of acquired characteristics; nor is it in the proper biological sense an argument for inheritance at all; rather is it, in Pigou's terms, an argument that

"the environment of one generation *can* produce a lasting effect, because it can affect the environment of future generations. Environments, . . . as well as people, have children. Though education and so forth cannot influence new births in the physical world, they can influence them in the world of ideas; and ideas, once produced or once accepted by a particular generation, . . . may remodel from its very base the environment which succeeding generations enjoy. In this way a permanent change of environment is brought about, and, since environment is admitted to have an important influence on persons actually subjected to it, such a change may produce enduring consequences." [41]

B. THE CORRELATION OF INTELLIGENCE WITH ACHIEVEMENT

It is Sait's contention not only that intelligence is determined by heredity but that such determination is revealed by the social and occupational status of the individual. He arrives at this latter conclusion through the application of a single device and a series of assumptions. The device is the occupational scale of Professor Lennes, a pyramiding of occupational classes on the basis of the alleged units of intelligence required.[42] The assumptions, also those of Professor Lennes, are these: first, that men work in those occupations best suited to their talents; second, that men strive to attain the highest level within their particular occupation; third, that the social ladder permits men to rise to the highest level commensurate with their talents; fourth, that this process has so far progressed that it is now possible by looking at a man's occupational status to perceive both his talent and his mental capacity; and fifth, that this migration from one class to another has now largely ceased, leaving us with a series of occupational castes rather than fluid classes— castes because, through the principle of assortive mating, men will produce descendants who are like themselves in both talent and intellect. In final support of which Sait, with Lennes and McDougall and the other theorists of biological aristocracy, presents the evidence of intelligence test scores to show that those who are highest in the occupational scale are actually the most intelligent. Let us inquire into the validity of Sait's several assumptions.

That it is merely assumption and not fact that men work in occupations best suited to their talents is at least suggested by the failure of Sait to adduce evidence in its support. The further failure of anti-democratic theorists anywhere to delineate the relative significance of the factors of accident (such as geographic or social propinquity), of necessity (such as the acceptance by men in time of need of jobs irrespective of interest), and of opportunity (such as the exclusion or restriction of men from certain occupations because of irrelevant racial or religious considerations)—all these would appear to indicate that until specific evidence is brought forward to buttress the thesis it can receive no scientific acceptance. Nor can the argument be rhetorically salvaged by pointing to the indisputable fact that a certain occupation may contain men with a demonstrated talent for that occupation. This is only to evade through the illogic of circular reasoning the very issue of proving that those men of talent could not equally or better exercise their talents elsewhere, and that men whose talents fit them for a particular occupation are actually engaged in that occupation. In this connection, it is not without value to recall that men frequently pursue or attempt to pursue a particular occupation for reasons other than talent, such as interest or security or prestige, and that talent is itself a quality frequently discovered only in the course of an individual's development on the job.

It is to be observed that Sait is offering in his second assumption not a biological analysis but a theory of social, indeed of personal, motivation. No more delicate study commends itself than this inquiry into the minds of men, but in this we are dealing with a discipline where our knowledge is only now beginning to emerge. Yet Sait, in unhesitatingly assuming the reality of individual drives for attainment and position, does not consider at all that vocational choice and striving for advancement may be based on other psychological factors than the I.Q. alone. For example, the child who comes from a family which has convinced him that he is awkward, selfish, stupid, may be reluctant as an adult to apply for a job which another person with much the same "native" ability but a different family background may take in his stride. A young man studying for a professional career for which he is intellectually and emotionally well suited may fall in love and give up schooling to take a routine job and get married. A sick wife or a large number of children may keep a man from risking a steady though low income for a possibly more challenging job at better pay. Many psychological drives operate in the choice of an occupation and in the striving, or lack of striving, for position within that occupation. It is a gross and unwarranted simplification to attribute these drives to intelligence alone. This is particularly true when we bear in mind that some men are neither free to choose nor to dare to strive, as is the case with the Negro in the American South.

All that has been said up to this point applies with equal relevance to the concept of the social ladder. Setting these considerations temporarily aside, however, let us examine the evidence for the theory of accessibility. Does the social ladder really permit men of talent to rise?

In a penetrating analysis Schwesinger observes that so to phrase the question is to ignore the central difficulty of agreeing on the criteria of achievement, on what is meant by success, by rising on the social ladder. To this important fact, adds Schwesinger, we must join the realization that

"often what an individual actually achieves is out of proportion to what he could achieve, but for the interference or effect of certain variables, such as health, interest and ambition, motivation, economic drive, responsibility towards others, 'moral' support and encouragement by others, and personality thwartings—as timidity, sensitiveness, uncontrollable temper, and the like. On the other hand, certain dynamic qualities of aggressiveness and persistence often overcompensate for intellectual weaknesses." [43]

These observations are reinforced by the suggestive study of Morris Ginsberg, who, approaching the problem from a quite different point of view, sought an answer to the reality of the social ladder by inquiring into the degree of mobility between social classes of three generations in England.[44] His findings gave some evidence of upward mobility, but only enough to show that the ladder can lift but relatively small numbers. There was, on the other hand, little evidence of downward mobility, thus confirming Thomas Huxley's dictum more than half a century ago: "That which is to be lamented, I fancy, is not that society should do its utmost to help capacity ascend from the lower strata to the higher, but that it has no machinery to facilitate the descent of incapacity from the higher strata to the lower."[45]

This is not, of course, to argue that classes in America are no longer fluid, that we are a caste rather than a class society—though for a large portion of the population this is undeniably true.[46] It is merely to note that social mobility in America is not as absolute and as binding a principle as Sait and others would have us believe. The social ladder may not, in point of fact, be a greased pole; but its rungs are all too frequently dislodged, occupied, or otherwise rendered inaccessible. Considerable qualification, then, is required if the doctrine of social mobility is to stand.

Sait's further assumption that, in view of the increased rapidity of this supposed migration, the level of an individual's intelligence is now revealed by his occupational status is, therefore, equally unsupported by the hypothesis of the social ladder. Whatever a man's position may be, we have no right, in the absence of specific evidence, to infer that merit rather than accident put him there, that intelligence rather than wealth or influential connections enabled him to rise in the world. And thus far not only is such evidence still lacking; everyday experience abundantly illustrates the reverse truth.

We come, finally, to the last of Professor Sait's several assumptions—the theses of assortive mating and of occupational castes. That like mates like to beget like has always been a favorite theme of the eugenist school of anti-democratic thought. It is also a persuasive theme, for even a cursory glance would show that many people marry others of similar rather than different ability, that many who marry have much in common. But there are many factors aside from similar I.Q.'s that have their effect on mating. Interest, status, wealth, religion, occupation, physical attraction—are these irrelevant in man or woman's choice of a mate? While it may be true that a genius is not likely to marry a feeble-minded person, it is also true that a genius does not restrict his selection of a mate to other geniuses. Intellect is but one of several factors that enter into such a situation, as the numerous differences among marital couples attest.

Consider, for example, the important distinction between the phenotype or outward hereditary character and the genotype or actual hereditary character. Where is the evidence that men select their mates not on the basis of seeming appearance but on the basis of genealogical research in order to discover what those mates may contribute in a hereditary way to their joint progeny? Consider, again, such a factor as propinquity. While it is obviously true that people do not marry only because they are near each other, it is no less apparent that they do not marry if one spends his life in Australia and the other never leaves New York City—even if they are of like intellect.

These are pertinent considerations, yet still more significant is the evidence of genetical science itself. And here we find that, through the combination of genes, parents may and do produce children unlike themselves, that brown-eyed parents may and do produce both brown-eyed and blue-eyed children, just as superior parents may and do produce mediocre or inferior children and mediocre or inferior parents produce superior children. While it may be true, further, that the proportion of superior children emerging from superior parents may be greater than the proportion emerging from mediocre parents, it is equally if not more significant to note that, in absolute numbers, more superior children emerge from the mass of mediocre parents than emerge from the few superior parents. As Jennings says:

"From the higher many lower are produced; from the lower, many higher. From the great mediocre group are produced more of the higher than the higher group itself produces; and more of the lower than the lower group itself produces. . . . The 'classes' do not perpetuate themselves as such." [47]

Heredity, in a word, does not require likeness. Like does not necessarily produce like.

It is sometimes urged, however, in more moderate vein, that the thesis is not that like mates with like but that like *tends* to mate with like, not that like begets like but that like *tends* to beget like. Such propositions, of course, rest on far more reasonable ground; for "we have no more justification for denying the importance of heredity than some eugenists have when they deny the importance of environment." [48] Even here, however, certain cautionary remarks must be entered. In the first place, to argue that like tends to mate with like involves social as well as biological phenomena. This means that intellect may or may not be the crucial element of likeness. In the second place, like may tend to beget like, but the particular form of the likeness is never predetermined. Here again resemblances other than intellect may emerge.

These genetical conclusions suggest that the theory of assortive mating and of the production of like progeny is seriously open to question. And as we have already seen, there is little or no evidence to sustain the argument that occupational migration or social mobility has occurred in the open and free way that Lennes and Sait envision it, much less that it is now at an end. The concept of occupational castes, then, which rests on the conjunction of these hypotheses, must also be rejected as unsubstantiated; it has been given no warrant from the science of genetics.

It is highly significant to note that throughout his many assumptions Sait has made no real attempt to isolate the hereditary from the environmental influences, to distinguish the social from the biological. He has told us nothing as to the respective roles of the two factors in determining the status of an individual. On the basis of his argument, in consequence, there is equal warrant for asserting the operation not of hereditary but of socio-economic factors. Nor, again, does Sait explain how, if talent is hereditary, it managed to get into the lower classes in the first place. Nor, further, does Sait elaborate what he means by upward. True, he offers the occupational scale of Professor Lennes; but this is more a technological than it is an economic scale, and its minute refinements resting on a point by point difference in what Lennes holds to be an intelligence unit is meaningless when we consider that the normal variation in intelligence test scores, for example, is so great that "as much as five points from test to test can be looked for from the average individual" and "that a variation up to ten points in the average I.Q. of different groups may be caused by such environmental differences as normally exist between American homes today . . . , while differences as great as thirty points may be caused in extreme individual cases; or by extreme differences in environment (e.g., from the very poorest to the very best homes)." [49] Moreover, the individual differences within a particular occupational group are infinitely larger than the differences between the occupational groups, a fact which attests at once to the unreality of Lennes' occupational scale.[50]

In addition to this, it is pertinent to record the decisive twofold objection that confronts any attempt to set up a social pyramid on the basis of occupational classes alone. One is the oversimplification in equating the social with the occupational. The other is the relativity of the standard of measurement. That social classes do not rest on occupational distinctions alone is too evident to require elaboration here: the very fact that there are social classes within an occupation and social classes that include several occupations is sufficient to disprove Sait's all too ready equation. The second objection is equally apparent, for there has ever been great disagreement as to what constitutes an adequate measure of superiority, as to what makes it possible legitimately to say that one class is higher than another class. If we resort to the test of income, poorly paid teachers would rightly object to the higher status accorded, say, professional athletes or businessmen, and the able family practitioner with a moderate income rightly demur to being considered the inferior of the doctor who loses his professional competence in the lucrative practice of caring for the nerves and obesity of "upper-class" women. If we employ the test of service, who is to assess the relative contributions of the lawyer and the farmer, the poet and the engineer, the statesman and the priest? Whatever the decision, there can in this regard be no finality; for judgments are always relative, and always based on a degree rather than a fullness of knowledge. It is important, too, to avoid here the common confusion of difference with superiority: that there are differences is undeniable, but that differences always imply rank is legitimately open to challenge.

The argument of Professor Sait, therefore, that superior talent and mental capacity are demonstrated by social and occupational status, must be regarded as little more than a circular proposition. It assumes at the start the very thing it set out to prove—arguing in these terms that those who do the "best" are the "best," that the fact that the upper strata have talent is the consequence of talent ascending to the upper strata. The argument identifies correlation with causation, a serious if frequent logical confusion, and fails completely to illuminate the controversy as to the respective roles of heredity and environment.

C. THE VALIDITY AND SIGNIFICANCE OF THE INTELLIGENCE TEST

There is, however, one final bit of evidence that Sait and the several theorists of biological aristocracy offer in support of their general argument. This is the testimony of the intelligence tests. The results of these tests, they insist, conclusively demonstrate that the higher we go in the occupational scale the higher is the intelligence, and that there is a direct correspondence between the intelligence of children and that of their parents.

Let us put aside, for the moment, the definition of "higher" in this hypothetical occupational scale. Let us agree that, generally speaking, this is a correct statement of the facts, that there is such a relationship. But this, when stated, still leaves open the crucial matter of the interpretation of those facts. Here the explanation may take at least three forms: we may, with Professor Sait, contend that those in the upper strata are there precisely because of their superior intelligence; or, alternatively, we may argue that their superior intelligence is the result rather than the cause of their superior socio-economic position; or, finally, we may insist that both factors are operative. On the basis of the results alone, either of the first two interpretations could be advanced with equal legitimacy, or illegitimacy.[51] An analysis of the material may point the way to a solution.

If we turn, at the outset, to the meaning of "intelligence," we find, among careful students of the subject, a surprising degree of divergence.[52] And since there is great disagreement as to what intelligence is, there is equally great disagreement as to what it is that intelligence tests measure. Boas, for example, regards the test as a measure of a person's ability to perform the test.[53] Goldenweiser conceives it to be a measure of many things but not in any real sense a measure of intelligence.[54] Hooton looks upon it as a measure both of "the environment of the testees and the intelligence of the testers." [55] Klineberg holds it to be essentially "a measure of achievement into which both native and acquired factors enter." [56] And Schwesinger concludes it is best "to use the term 'test intelligence' to describe the characteristics measured by existing psychological tests." [57] Whatever the specific nature of the agreements and the disagreements, it is clear that there is today no generally acceptable theory of an intelligence test as a measure of intelligence.

The central reason for this is the fact of cultural diversity. It is impossible to measure in the same test people of diverse cultural backgrounds and conclude therefrom that the results are truly representative of innate capacity. This is obvious in so extreme a comparison as that between the primitive and the product of a modern civilization. It is no less a valid consideration when applied to a rural as against an urban child, or to urban children of dissimilar cultural backgrounds, such as those coming from homes where different languages are spoken, or those who vary in education and in occupational experience. It was the failure to make these distinctions that so largely discredited the tests given in the early twenties and before; yet it is on the basis of these "careless generalizations" that Lennes and Sait have advanced their postulates. It is today recognized that only within a relatively homogeneous culture can the intelligence test be applied with any degree of relevance or validity, that "the use of the same test upon individuals with a different cultural, social, educational, economic, or national background, does not give a reliable result." And this evidences beyond all serious objection that the intelligence tests "are highly charged with environmental content," that what they measure is not heredity alone but both heredity *and* environment.[58]

This view is sustained rather than repudiated by the fact that children of successful fathers obtain higher scores on the intelligence tests; for these superior children are the products not merely of superior endowments but also of superior environments. As Hankins observes:

"The more intelligent, energetic, self-controlled, and ambitious parents will not only contribute superior physical and mental endowments to their offspring, but will provide for them superior advantages for physical, mental, and moral development. . . . How much of the superiority of their children is, therefore, due to environment, it is impossible to say, largely because their superior environments are themselves to a very great extent a consequence of the superior inherited capacities of the stocks to which they belong." [59]

The correlation between intelligence, heredity, and achievement is undeniably present. But for the anti-democrat to establish correlation alone is not enough. He must establish, beyond this, the existence of a causal relationship. He must demonstrate that this superior status is the result rather than the concomitant of superior intelligence—and this, unless he achieves the impossible task of isolating the hereditary from the environmental influences, he cannot do. As Ginsberg points out, "examination of the tests employed shows that generally the children of the economically superior parents do better just in those matters in which their experience at home would help them." [60] Further and equally conclusive evidence of the pronounced impact of the environment on intelligence test scores is found in the twofold fact that test scores are improved by school training and that the placement of foster children in better homes not merely increases their scores but tends to produce in the foster children an occupational hierarchy similar to the foster fathers.[61] In fact, concludes Klineberg, not only is there "no necessary relation between economic status of the parents and the ability of the children," there is "nothing in the occupational hierarchy that cannot be explained on the basis of the environmental hypothesis." [62]

D. CONCLUSIONS ON HEREDITY AND ENVIRONMENT

What, then, are we to conclude of the respective roles of heredity and environment? The evidence that there are significant hereditary differences among individuals in capacity and aptitude is entirely conclusive. In no other way can we explain the variability of individuals within a single occupation or within similar environments. No less conclusive, however, is the evidence that environmental factors are both vital and everpresent. This makes unavoidable the conclusion that *both* factors must be embraced in any analysis of the situation: one cannot exist without the other. In MacIver's phrase, "Life and environment are *always* correlative." [63] Elsewhere he says:

"Every phenomenon of life is the product of both. Each is as *necessary* to the result as the other. Neither can ever be eliminated and neither can ever be isolated. Both are, in every particular situation, exceedingly complex. Both have been operative, to produce every particular situation, through unimaginable time. For these reasons it seems impossible even to conceive two situations involving precisely the same combination of hereditary and environmental factors. Every situation is in this respect unique, just as every human face is in some way different from every other. Where two or more factors are equally necessary for a given result, it is vain to inquire which in general is the more important." [64]

The crucial question, then, cannot be the issue, heredity *or* environment. This is to pose an entirely non-existent problem. Nor can it be an inquiry into the dominance of one as against the other. This is both to presuppose the separateness of the two factors and to postulate a general problem that is inapplicable to a specific situation. The only question that can legitimately be raised is that of the relative significance of the two variables in terms of a specific characteristic for a specific individual in a specific environment. This has been well stated by Schwesinger, whose words merit repetition here:

"It would appear . . . that each human trait possessed its own range of variability under the influence of environment, and a different susceptibility to environment; some characteristics varying widely with slight changes in environment, some varying widely but only with extreme changes in environment, and others varying within very narrow limits, and each with a different susceptibility. Looked at in this light, the problem of heredity and environment is not a general problem, but is specific to each characteristic and to each environmental factor." [65]

And because men so differ, both in the range and in the susceptibility of their different characteristics, "the problem of heredity and environment must . . . be thought of not only as specific to each characteristic and to each environment, but as specific to each individual in respect of each of his characteristics, and to each factor of his environment." [66]

In the light of these considerations we must refuse to accept as a legitimate issue the insistence by anti-democratic theorists that heredity and not environment is dominant in the formation of individual differences. Both their issue and their arguments move on fallacious ground: not only is there no proof of the predominance of one over the other, there is ample evidence to show that they are, in fact, inextricably intertwined and, in general terms, immeasurable.

IV

DEMOCRACY AND THE POLITICS OF BIOLOGICAL ARISTOCRACY

According to Alleyne Ireland, the balance of political power should be transferred "from numbers to intelligence," and the concept of "better voters" substituted for that of "more voters." [67] According to Sait, this intelligence and these better voters are to be found in the biological aristocracy, made up of rural rather than of urban folk, of men rather than of women, and of men who (a) have proven themselves to be superior by virtue of their social or occupational success, (b) possess a higher degree of intelligence as evidenced by their higher intelligence test scores, and (c) are the descendants of superior families.

But our analysis has shown that Sait's various categories of the best are without foundation. What evidence there is amply suggests that urban rather than rural life is conducive to superior intelligence as measured by standardized tests; and there is no evidence beyond the idle speculations of theorists to sustain the myth of male intellectual superiority. Beyond these considerations, it has been shown that social or occupational success is in no sense the consequence of hereditary influences alone, that higher intelligence test scores establish neither innate superiority of intelligence nor the exclusive genetic transmission of such superiority, and that existing studies of familial descent have established nothing concerning the respective roles of heredity and environment. To build, therefore, as Sait does, a concept of the best on hereditary factors alone is to construct not a workable principle of politics but a metaphysical abstraction.

Consider, in these terms, the necessary implication of Sait's doctrine. Consider what the consequences would be if we were to restrict political power to the currently "superior few" and to their descendants, assuming—but only for the moment—that the definition and identification of that "superior few" could be effected. In a few years we would find a subsequent generation exercising that political power not only over the mediocre but also over equals, and in some cases perhaps superiors, and in time over a numerically larger number of equals; for by the processes of reproduction, as we have seen, more superior people come from mediocre parents than come from superior parents. Nor is this all. The presumably aristocratic group would itself soon contain mediocrities, for by the evidence of biological inheritance not all superior parents produce superior progeny. Then we would be faced with the very real problem of effecting a redistribution of political power every few years in order to maintain inviolate the principle of rule by the biological best or deny that principle by maintaining in power one group of superiors and mediocrities as over against another group of superiors and mediocrities. Apart from the historically demonstrated reluctance of men in power readily to surrender their place to the claims of principle alone, there is the immense difficulty of determining who or what is superior even on the biological basis—whether it is, among other things, physical or mental excellence, or the imaginative or stolid mind, or even qualities of aggressiveness or humility, not all of which may operate in conjunction with each other. Heredity may be necessary, but it is clearly not sufficient.

For these several reasons, therefore, we must conclude that the principle of biological aristocracy has failed to establish its claim, either in biological fact or in logic.

We cannot forego the subject of biological aristocracy without entering comment on two corollary doctrines. One is the theory of democratic degeneracy and decline. The other is the theory of eugenics as state policy to improve the stock.

The anti-democratic thesis that democracy is effecting a decline in civilization through its failure (a) to breed heavily from the "superior few" and to restrict the procreation of the "inferior many," and (b) to give political power to that biologically "superior few," requires, in the light of our preceding discussion, no detailed refutation. Though there be a difference in the fertility of social classes, two things are nonetheless clear: first, that the "lower" classes are through their fertility contributing a vital part of the superior intelligence of the community; and second, that the improvement of the inferior cultural and other environmental conditions of the poor will in all probability remove their apparent inferiority.[68] The issue, that is to say, is a social rather than a biological one, a consideration which effectively removes the foundations from McDougall's tragic vision of democracy—"speeding gaily, with invincible optimism, down the road to destruction"—because of its failure to procreate the best.[69] Even more damaging to this view of racial decline and degeneracy is the fact that it has by no means been established that we *are* in the midst of racial decline and degeneracy. The restatement by East, Sait, and others of the McDougall thesis is but a re-echo of a theme that has survived through many centuries of Western civilization, at least from the time of Plato and Theognis, and which has still to be factually demonstrated.

The concept of eugenics as a political principle is immersed in controversy even among those who expound it. Thus, while Hooton and Freeman regard it essentially as a negative concept to prevent the procreation of the worst or the unfit,[70] others, like Stoddard, would employ it in a positive program for the betterment of the stock.[71] Quite apart from the general reluctance of people to lend themselves to a breeding program, the positive phase of eugenics suffers from the fact that men are not agreed as to what it is we should procreate. While some would urge breeding for physical excellence, others would insist on mental capacity, and still others on a variety of ideals that would find little general acceptance. More important is the consideration that such a program would impose on the future current conceptions of desirability, a highly relative and suspect undertaking. But the decisive consideration is that even when all these objections have been met there is still the fact that biology alone cannot accomplish the stated goals. It is not heredity, but heredity *and* environment, that determines the nature of man; and the eugenists fail precisely in the degree that they ignore the non-biological factors.[72]

On the negative side, the criticism by Klineberg warrants extended citation:

"In the first place, the determination of what is fit or unfit is difficult to make with any objectivity; in one society the physically defective, in another those who criticize their government, might seem to be the ones who should be eliminated. In any eugenics program, positive or negative, the community is at the mercy of those who establish the standards of fitness. It is obvious that this possibility leads into such serious danger that the greatest caution is necessary in its application. This danger becomes a real one when we think of the number of outstanding men of genius in our history who have defects which would lead to their inclusion among the unfit from certain points of view. In the second place, such individuals might not only have defects themselves, but come of families similarly defective. A eugenics program would have prevented their birth, and the loss would have been incalculably greater than any conceivable gain. Third and most important, the reduction in the amount of defect by this method is so small that it would take many generations to effect a perceptible movement. As Jennings and others have pointed out, although there may be rather more defective offspring proportionately among defective than among normal parents, the large majority of defectives come from parents who are perfectly normal as far as all our tests make it possible to determine. The distinction between phenotype and genotype is pertinent at this point. A great many persons who appear healthy may still be capable of breeding defective children, and since there is no way of determining this in advance, negative eugenics would be of little help in improving the population. Hogben has made a statistical study of the possibility of reducing defects in this manner, and he shows clearly that it is remote." [73]

One final point and we shall be done with the concept of biological aristocracy. It is sometimes argued that while the racial and biological theories alone are inadequate solutions to the political problem, a fusion of the two will give us the right and ultimate answer. Thus Lothrop Stoddard, for example, urges that we combine the two concepts to produce a racial-biological aristocracy.[74] This is clearly a spurious argument, however, which succeeds only in affirming the errors of both schools of thought. It fails, as with both the racial and biological theories, to explain or to incorporate the impact of cultural variations; and it fails to perceive the contradiction that arises when racial inferiority and biological superiority are fused in the same individual, as in a non-Nordic of superior intelligence and achievement.

For political democracy, then, there is no issue. Men must be accepted as political equals and given an equal opportunity to demonstrate whatever inequalities their heredity and environment have given them.

8

The Concept of Natural Aristocracy

I

DEMOCRACY AS DENIAL OF ORDER AND DEGREE

From that fountainhead of anti-democratic thought, Plato's *Republic*, there is to be derived still another of the several dissents from the democratic principle. This is the concept of natural aristocracy, the doctrine that men are by nature variously unequal and that a wise state—one that is founded on justice—will be so constituted as to reflect in its social and political order a hierarchy rooted in the natural inequalities of mankind. "Each individual," said Plato, "should be put to the use for which nature intended him." The shoemaker should be a shoemaker and not a pilot also; the soldier should be a soldier and not a trader also; and those only should be rulers whose natures "are fitted for the task of guarding the city." Each in his place, each performing his true and natural function—this, in Plato's view, is the just society, just because it conforms to the right order of nature.

Democracy, however, while undoubtedly "a charming form of government," is, according to Plato, a government "full of variety and disorder, and dispensing a sort of equality to equals and unequals alike." It fails to institutionalize the inequalities among men but seeks instead to·equalize those whom nature has diversely endowed. It neglects the true life of law and order for the false life of liberty and equality. It raises those who don't deserve to be raised and lowers those who do. And because it ignores in all these ways the just dictates of the natural order, it is, Plato concludes, an unwise and therefore undesirable system of government. Aristocracy and hierarchy alone, argues Plato, are the just and proper foundations of the state.[1]

In the literature of anti-democratic thought this doctrine has been given wide and varied expression. It was stressed, for example, by Harrington when he developed his thesis of "a natural aristocracy diffused by God throughout the whole body of mankind." [2] It was argued by Burke in his condemnation of Levellers who "only change and pervert the natural order of things." [3] Sorel invoked the doctrine in his plea that men "ought to be content with the place that nature and circumstances have assigned to each" of them; [4] and Treitschke, in his vehement denunciation of the democratic state, regarded as central what he termed democracy's false "fundamental idea [of] the natural equality of all mankind." [5] But nowhere has this concept of order and degree been more concisely and lucidly set forth than in the speech of Ulysses before the tent of Agamemnon, where, pointing to the fact that

> "The heavens themselves, the planets and this centre,
>   Observe degree, priority, and place,"

and to the evil consequences which ensue when this unity of hierarchy is disturbed, the Prince of Ithaca attributed to the denial and suffocation of degree the fever and the chaos that attend mankind:

> ". . . O, when degree is shak'd,
>   Which is the ladder to all high designs,
>   The enterprise is sick! How could communities,
>   . . . .
>   But by degree, stand in authentic place?
>   Take but degree away, untune that string,
>   And, hark, what discord follows! each thing meets
>   In mere oppugnancy." [6]

Of the many special forms that this doctrine has taken in recent years, the writings of such English theorists as W. H. Mallock and

A. M. Ludovici provide interesting illustration. In Mallock's view, democracy's basic error is that it aims at social even more than it does at political equality, in violation of what he conceives to be the elementary facts of human nature and of human progress.[7] Some men, Mallock argues, are "made giants by nature"; others are "condemned by nature to live and to die dwarfs." To attempt to equalize the natural inequalities of human capacity, to deny "the domination or the triumphant influence of the greatest," is, in consequence, not merely to contravene the facts of history as well as of nature; more important, it is to destroy "all that has hitherto been connected with high breeding, or with personal culture."[8]

A more distinctive position is that put forward by Nietzsche's translator and disciple, Ludovici, for whom aristocracy and democracy represent the choice between life and death.[9] The true natural aristocracy, says Ludovici, is the aristocracy of "taste," embodied in those men who—like Napoleon and Charles I—best represent the maximum of flourishing life. Put these men at the head of the state, Ludovici argues, and grade the rest of society according to their occupational capacities, and you will have formed a true hierarchy consonant with the dictates of nature, one that alone can save the nation from the false and unnatural dogmas of destructive democracy.[10]

These several indictments of the democratic principle on the general ground that democracy is a denial of the order of nature—of hierarchy, of degree—have been given extended expression in American as well as in European political thought. One of the earliest and in some respects still the most notable of these statements is the exposition by John Adams in his *Defence of the Constitutions*. Convinced of the superior influence and capacities of "the rich, the well-born, and the able," Adams labored long, if not always consistently, to produce a theory of government predicated on the natural hierarchy of orders and classes in society. Holding rank to be the unalterable foundation of mankind as of nature, Adams argued that without the acknowledgment of such gradations in the constitution of the state, "it will be found to be imperfect, unstable, and soon enslaved." In these terms democracy became, for Adams, a demonstrably false—because unnatural—theory of state.[11]

The views expressed by Adams were shared by many of his contemporaries, for example Hamilton, who postulated as a natural division of mankind the cleavage between "the rich and well-born" and "the mass of the people," and Gouverneur Morris, who argued for a constitutional recognition of what he considered to be the natural clash of interests between the aristocracy of the rich and the democracy of the poor.[12] They were shared, too, in some measure, by later scions of the Adams name, Brooks and Henry, who deplored in a joint work the leveling tendencies of democracy—"the democratic system of averages"—and who contrasted sadly the "elevated man" that was George Washington with the "level of degradation" that was Andrew Jackson.[13]

In more recent times, however, the systematic espousal of the concept of natural aristocracy has been most clearly and strongly made by two distinct though not always separate schools: the New England humanists, whose pre-eminent spokesmen have been Irving Babbitt [14] and Paul Elmer More; [15] and the conservative Catholics, whose general position has been argued by such lay and secular writers as Ralph Adams Cram, F. S. Campbell,[16] and Fulton J. Sheen.[17] That the two groups can in great measure be joined is indicated by the later writings of More [18] and particularly by the political essays of T. S. Eliot.[19] A brief account of each of these schools may serve to make clear the broad outlines of their criticisms of democracy.

In the conception of the new humanists, as More and Babbitt style themselves, "mankind is not capable of self-government," nor can equalitarianism be a right basis for political organization. Such "an unethical ideal," says More, ". . . slurs over the fact of human depravity" and ignores the natural inequalities that render some men able to rule and others capable of being controlled and directed.[20] The just man—he whose character is determined by "his truer self, which controls and checks and knows and pronounces judgment . . . of everlasting validity above the shifting valuations of the moment"—should, in the just state, have the privilege of imposing his will on those inferior to him; for only "when each division of society, . . . and each member of society, has a distinct place and responsibility, and is recognized and rewarded accordingly," can "the people be saved from themselves." The denial by democratic humanitarianism of the dualism of human nature, of "the law of just subordination" that compels a system of "obligation and command" in conformity with the dictates of the inner check (the standards of the higher self), can mean, More argues, only the denial of perfect and just government.[21] To secure this just government, he holds, we must return to the justice of Plato and the natural aristocracy of Burke, thereby to "bring the character of the few to bear in some effective way upon the impulses of the many; it would be an aristocracy of justice." [22]

The abstract and somewhat indefinite authority of the inner check to which the humanists appeal, is supplanted, in the construction of certain Catholic thinkers, by the laws of nature as derived from God. According to this view, for instance as expounded by Sheen, these laws give man insight into his own true nature and make plain to him not merely what he is but what he ought to be. In acting as he likes, therefore, man is not really free; for "true freedom" consists instead in his doing what he ought to do. As Sheen puts it, liberty, correctly understood, does not mean the right to choose wrongly, "to be indifferent to truth and to virtue, . . . to do what you *please*." Rather is it "the right to do whatever you *ought*," to go back to

"a Truth which is inseparable from the purpose of man; namely union with his final end, who is God. As man corresponds in his thinking and in his actions with that Purpose, he is free because he is true." [23]

And since it is the Church which is divinely ordained and therefore best able to discern the objective and absolute truths inherent in the nature and purpose of man, it is the business of the Church, of religion, "to give citizens a set of principles, a hierarchy of value, fundamental convictions and beliefs, and a set of moral standards." [24]

About these things, Sheen argues, there can be no tolerance, no dissent, for "tolerance does not apply to truth or principles." [25] The essence of the right state, therefore, is not freedom of speech, freedom of press, and the like. These, Sheen says, are merely the accompaniments, not the core, of democracy.[26] The just state is founded on traditions, on law and order, and more particularly on an order based on function, which implies duties and obligations, not rights. This means, according to Sheen, an order based on a hierarchy of occupational differences, a vocational stratification guarded by the state and assuring justice through the right principles of God.[27] The failure of modern democratic states, Sheen holds, is the fact that "they are ceasing to be republics and are beginning to be democracies, i.e., they are allowing the impulses and passions of citizens directly to influence government." Only by avoiding "arithmetic-democracy, mob rule, pressure-group government," and by adhering to a government of order, to a system of duties and responsibilities rooted in our occupational function, can we hope, Sheen says, to realize the just law and the right state.[28]

In T. S. Eliot we find a line of thought that attempts, even more than More, to fuse the new humanism with the conservative wing of Catholic thought. "A dogmatist in principle and in temper," [29] Eliot ridicules the supernaturalism of Babbitt for its independence from God and argues that it is necessary to have not merely high ideals but "*absolute* ideals," Catholic ideals. "As forms of government become more democratic, as the outer restraints of kingship, aristocracy and class disappear, so it becomes more and more necessary that the individual no longer controlled by authority or habitual respect should control himself." Through the exercise of this inner check, Eliot holds, appropriate application can be made of "the ideas of authority, of hierarchy, of discipline and order." These, and not the equalitarianism of the democratic theory, point the way to a correct social solution; for, says Eliot, "there is a fallacy in democracy . . . in assuming that a majority of natural and unregenerate men is likely to want the right things." [30]

In Plato and Burke, in More and Eliot and Sheen, in all these several and varied statements of the concept of natural aristocracy, there is contained a central and common indictment of democracy: that what democracy does is to treat as equals men who are by nature unequal, thereby ignoring or suppressing certain important social values. What unifies society, according to these theorists, is hierarchy, an ordered scheme of things resting on the natural gradation of position. In denying hierarchy, these writers say, democracy denies unity: its formlessness ensures only that the commonplace, average man rises to the top, and that the values attained under a proper hierarchical form are submerged.

In the philosophical thought of George Santayana these doctrines are put forth with a succinctness and a clarity that merit extended exploration, so it is, consequently, to his numerous writings that we now turn.[31]

II

THE NATURAL ARISTOCRACY OF GEORGE SANTAYANA

A self-styled "Tory in philosophy," a man who delighted in the works of Mallock and who early fell under the influence of Matthew Arnold, a Catholic "aesthetically and politically, though not theologically," [32] a humanist with a love for discipline and a dislike for disorder, an admirer of strong men such as Caesar and Mussolini,[33] a seeker after the "better things" in life, the refined, the beautiful, and the traditional, a cultivated gentleman whose love for ordinary men varies in ratio to his physical distance from them,[34] Santayana represents in consummate degree, both in his ideological beliefs and personal habits, the natural aristocrat disdainful of democracy. "I feel no great affection or even pity," Santayana has declared, "for this doctrine of democracy, which came to me not as my own child, nor even as a foundling left at my door, but as a figment of words or obsessions in a dream." [35] "This terrible levelling," this "uniformity in multiplicity," this "hollowness" of liberal politics and "tragedy of self-government"—for these doctrines, Santayana says, doctrines which deny the naturalness of natural inequality and put into positions of power "the instincts of the majority—the most cruel and unprogressive of masters," he can elicit not sympathy but horror.[36] For if the life of spirit is to endure, it must not be oppressed by the mob.[37]

The trouble with democracy, Santayana argues, is that it ignores the first principles of nature: order and inequality. "We count heads as if we paid out money by weight, without asking whether it was gold or silver." [38] But this surely, says Santayana, is an irrational and unjust thing.

"A government is not made representative or just by the mechanical expedient of electing its members by universal suffrage. It becomes representative only by embodying in its policy, whether by instinct or high intelligence, the people's conscious and unconscious interests."

And it can embody those interests only if it places its trust in men of natural eminence.

"The democratic theory is clearly wrong if it imagines that eminence is not naturally representative. . . . There is no greater stupidity or meanness than to take uniformity for an ideal, as if it were not a benefit and a joy to a man, being what he is, to know that many are, have been, and will be better than he." [39]

Is not this, indeed, Santayana asks, the reality that nature reveals everywhere about us? Look at the people, "the ignoble conglomerate beneath," the "comparatively level multitude," producing a public opinion "characterised by enormous inertia, incoherence, and blindness." [40] And compare with these the men of natural eminence, genuinely representative of the common interest, and embodying within themselves the qualities of progress, of discipline, and of harmony.

It is true, Santayana admits, that aristocracies have not in practice always reflected these natural inequalities; nor have they always radiated benefit and through the removal of suffering ensured happiness; and because of such failures they are indeed subject to rightful reproach. But this does not, for Santayana, justify condemnation of the aristocratic or theistic ideal; rather does it mean the substitution of natural for artificial inequalities and the establishment of the just state "where all are not equal, but where all are happy."

"Lucifer's fallacy consisted in thinking natural inequality artificial. His perversity lay in rebelling against himself and rejecting the happiness proper to his nature." [41]

After all, Santayana observes, where the same task is proposed to unequal strengths, the competition but emphasizes the inequality, a fact which at once renders incredible the ideal of social democracy which seeks to unite "all mankind into a society of equals." [42] The right state should instead capitalize on this natural inequality and institutionalize it into a form of government.

"This would be timocracy—a government by men of merit. . . . Such a timocracy (of which the Roman Church is a good example) would differ from the social aristocracy that now exists only by the removal of hereditary advantages. People would be born equal, but they would grow unequal, and the only equality subsisting would be equality of opportunity. If power remained in the people's hands, the government would be democratic; but a full development of timocracy would allow the proved leader to gain great ascendancy. The better security the law offered that the men at the top should be excellent, the less restraint would it need to put upon them when once in their places. Their eminence would indeed have been factitious and their station undeserved if they were not able to see and do what was requisite better than the community at large. An assembly has only the lights common to the majority of its members, far less, therefore, than its members have when added together and less even than the wiser part of them." [43]

In this way, Santayana argues, through the denial, on the one hand, of democratic uniformity, and the constitutional affirmation, on the other, of natural inequality, a just state founded on order and rooted in freedom will be secured. By freedom, of course, Santayana adds, is meant not simply the freedom to live, but what the ancient Greeks realized to be far more significant, the freedom "to live well"; "not freedom to wander at hazard or to let things slip, but on the contrary freedom to legislate more precisely, at least for oneself, and to discover and codify the means to true happiness." What we moderns regard as liberty—the liberty to do as we please, the "liberty to drift in the dark"—is in fact the very antithesis of liberty; it "is the most terrible negation of freedom." Forced and artificial as classic liberty was, limited in its application to "an ascetic aristocracy" as circumstances compelled it to be, there was nonetheless, Santayana insists, a profound and valid insight in the assumption of Greek philosophers and cities "that true liberty is bound up with an institution, a corporate scientific discipline, necessary to set free the perfect man, or the god, within us"; for "only the truth about God and happiness," if we somehow but find it, can make us free.[44] Real freedom, in consequence, being a product of knowledge, is secured only when man "obeys a force which, in the best sense of the word, *represents* him," and which, in coercing him to pursue the right direction, truly helps him to be himself. Without purpose, Santayana says, freedom is "nothing but frivolity." [45]

We are brought, then, to this: right government, which is good government, is a function of aristocratic society, of a world graded in value according to the several levels and degrees of excellence, and in which the timocratic man shall alone have ultimate possession of political power.[46] There is no injustice in this, in Santayana's view, to any man in any stage of the hierarchy. "On the contrary, by accepting that appointed place and that specific happiness, each servant of the universal harmony could feel its infinite value and could thrill the more profoundly to a music which he helped to intone." [47] The only conditions that must be maintained to justify this inequality and hierarchical order, Santayana says, are the avoidance of injury and the elimination of injustice. "So that an aristocratic or theistic system in order to deserve respect must discard its sinister apologies for evil and clearly propose such an order of existences, one superimposed upon the other, as should involve no suffering on any of its levels." [48]

In these terms, Santayana asserts, the democratic theory is clearly in the wrong. Instead of recognizing the true inequalities that set off man from man, it seeks to establish uniformity. Instead of acknowledging distinction, it endeavors to reduce "all things as far as possible to the common denominator of quantity." [49] Instead of good government, the government of self, it institutionalizes self-government, the government of each by all.[50] Instead of realizing that the good is not relative to opinion but is rooted in the nature of living beings, and that knowledge and tradition best reveal that nature and therefore that good, it repudiates the governance of the dead and trusts instead to the irrational judgment, "the apathy and vagueness of the million." [51]

"If a noble and civilised democracy is to subsist," Santayana observes, "the common citizen must be something of a saint and something of a hero." [52] That he is not, as nature and history are held to attest, is, for Santayana, the final and decisive refutation of the doctrine of democracy as ideal.

III

COMMENTARY: THE UNITY OUTSIDE OF DEGREE

There is, at first blush, in this naturalistic indictment of democracy, a strength and an impressiveness unmatched by any other doctrine in the realm of aristocratic thought. The sheer simplicity of its primary contention—that men are different merely because they are different; it is intrinsic to their natures and requires no explanation beyond the elementary fact of recognition—has an unaffected persuasiveness altogether lacking in such mythological constructions as the theories of racial and biological aristocracy. We see everywhere about us men who, for whatever cause, are superior or inferior in some quality or capacity to ourselves and to other men, and it is easy for us to conceive of these differences as inherent and natural to man.

We tend to accept this interpretation the more readily, moreover, when we conjoin with this first contention the second major argument advanced by the natural aristocrats: that as some superior cause or power (divine or natural) fashioned the very universe in which we have our being according to a definite pattern or order— one in which each element, each entity, has its given place and function, as Shakespeare said, its prescribed priority in degree—why should we, mere mortals cast but for a passing moment on the stage of eternal time, arrogate to ourselves the right to deny this same unity in human affairs? As there is order and degree in nature, these theorists hold, so there is order and degree in man. All that a right state need do, in consequence, is to reflect in its political structure a graduated order based on natural rank and station.

The failure of democracy to do this means, in the view of these critics, the denial and the loss of two central values. One is the denial of political rule to those most qualified to exercise it—those whom Santayana has called the naturally eminent, the "aristocracy of noble minds" [53]—and the elevation instead of the commonplace, average, inferior man to the top. This results, according to the natural aristocrat, in the loss of competence and of wisdom in the administration of the state. The other is the denial of unity itself. The formlessness of democracy, that is to say, the lack of any ordered scheme of things, is held, in this conception, to be a severe social loss when compared with the unity and the harmony that ensue from the hierarchical organization that is oligarchy.

These doctrines, as we have said, are at first surmise both attractive and plausible. On examination, however, both their virtues and their logic are revealed to be less self-evident and less formidable than this first cursory impression would allow. It is not necessary here to dwell on the invalidity of the first charge: that democracy is a leveling process in which political power is ultimately entrusted to the average rather than to the superior man, and that average men, the people, are, as John Adams and Santayana said, a mob. This we showed in an earlier chapter to be entirely without substance. Democracy, whatever else it may be or do, is in no sense rule by the average man or by the mob; nor does it, conversely, deny power to the superior man. The only direct and important charge in this indictment of the democratic principle that should command our attention, in consequence, is the second, the claim that what unifies society is hierarchy and that democracy's lack of hierarchy—its formlessness of structure—renders unity impossible.

To this paramount objection only two things need be said. First, with respect to the principle of hierarchy—the essence of "aristocracy"—it is plain that the argument suffers from the elementary truth that it offers no road to its attainment. We may agree that it would be desirable if the best (the aristocracy) governed; but such a position is irrelevant to the political problem unless (*a*) it is shown how a government of the best can be secured and maintained, and (*b*) that democracy prevents the attainment of such a government while some other *system* secures it.

Santayana asserts in reply to the first condition that the best will emerge as a consequence of the full and unfettered operation of equality of opportunity. But this, obviously, is to gloss over the fact that rarely, if ever, has there been a society in which complete equality of opportunity—one divorced from considerations of class, of economic advantage, of religion and race, and the like—has applied. Santayana would appear to recognize this limitation on his doctrine when he attacks actual "aristocracies" for their artificial as compared with natural eminence, but he offers no hope that such equality can ever in the real world come to be. After all, it was Santayana himself who said of the *Life of Reason* that it was a collection of "materials for a utopia." [54]

Nor does Santayana squarely face the issue of how such an aristocracy, assuming it can be selected, is to be maintained. It is the lesson of all history that every aristocracy sits unsteadily on the throne of power, for every aristocracy is challenged by rebellious subjects, whether they be rival pretenders to the aristocratic mantle or deniers of the legitimacy of that mantle itself. Every aristocracy, in consequence, is confronted with this simple yet defeating dilemma: if it employs force to maintain itself against such challenge, the aristocracy—through the principle of the corruption of power (as Mill and Acton made clear)—degenerates and thus ceases to be an aristocracy; if it abstains from force, it is unlikely long to retain power, in which case it also ceases to be an aristocracy.

Consider, for example, the illustration offered by the history of the Catholic Church. In its beginnings and for some time thereafter, the early bishops of the Church ruled primarily by spiritual example: by their precepts and by their behavior they sought to justify their claim to rightness and to superiority and thus to secure the allegiance of the people. Later, however, when the Church's position had solidified and it had become a strong and highly organized force, in conjunction with and under the aegis of the state, an attempt was made (as in the late Roman Empire after the death of Constantine the Great) to compel obedience through coercion; and with this change in the use of weapons came a change in the nature of the rulers. The medieval popes were no longer merely spiritual advisers, they were feudal monarchs; and by the time of the Renaissance the Church was governed by such corrupt pontiffs as Leo X and Alexander VI. Thus we see from a new standpoint the inherent instability of aristocratic rule and the general invalidity of the aristocratic thesis; for whether the aristocracy rejects force and surrenders power or uses force to maintain power, it must cease to be an aristocracy. The logic of the aristocratic principle, in brief, is the negation of the aristocratic state.[55]

Santayana fails similarly to meet with any degree of adequacy the second requirement of a valid aristocratic doctrine, namely, that democracy be shown to prevent a government of the best while some other form of state secures it. He refers, it is true, to the example of the Roman Church, but, quite apart from the special circumstances that surround so unique an institution, the blemishes of corrupt pontiffs such as Alexander VI and Leo X, and the record of contemporary bishops in Mussolini's Italy and Franco's Spain, are hardly calculated to render the illustration a conclusive one. Can we turn then to a system of hereditary monarchy? If so, we are reminded at once of the blunders of a George III of England and the imbecility of a Charles II of Spain, the ravages of a Leopold II of Belgium and the insipid frivolity of a Louis XVI of France. What of dictatorship? Do the best come to power under a Hitler, a Stalin, a Franco, a Mussolini? Only, we have seen, if they have also the "right" religion, the "right" race, the "right" political ideology, the "right" personal devotion, the "right" degree of servility and maneuverability. Can we then resort to the rule of a clique based on a particular class? Here too, however, history has shown that the first requisite has not been competence but membership in the ruling class. On the record, no non-democratic system selects its rulers on the single criterion of competence alone. No non-democratic system secures the "best."

This brings us to the second aspect of the major objection leveled against democracy by the theorists of natural aristocracy. This is the charge that democracy denies the principle of hierarchy and consequently makes impossible the unity assured by degree. In one respect this argument is correct: democracy does deny the hierarchical order of oligarchy. But it by no means follows that there is consequently no order in democracy. In advancing this claim Santayana —as Carlyle and Mallock—fails to perceive that unity can and does inhere in structures other than degree, that hierarchy is only one of the unifying forces in society, and that democracy, when properly understood and properly realized, can arrive at a structure that enduringly binds man to man. Democracy builds not on the denial of order but on another order—an order based not on the sense and formalization of degree but on the conception of a pervading common: not common in the sense of commonplace, but common in the sense of the fundamental human things that are universal in nature.

in the sense of basic interests and deeper loyalties that join rather than divide the members of the community.

This sense of the common, this conviction that men can be held together by common rather than dividing interests, by a "consensus about values cherished in common," is in a very profound way the heart of what Rousseau was trying to capture in his construction of the general will. It is what Jefferson was feeling for when he insisted, in opposition to Hamilton's doctrine that the way to get a right and stable order is to have certain interests organized one against the other, that the common interests of the nation make up the superior organizing force. In the democratic form of state it is not gradation of position, it is not station or rank, it is not birth or class or possession of some metaphysical quality such as Santayana's "natural eminence" or Ludovici's "taste," it is not the things that divide, that set off man from man, that are the central element of cohesion. In democracy it is the pervading common—the conception of a nation in which each man, each citizen, "is *equally* a member of it," quite apart from all the differences that mark him off from other men—that is the abiding unity.[56]

Here, indeed, in this very conception of nationality, we find a striking realization of this sense of the common. An American is not less an American because he is poor rather than rich, or because he is uneducated rather than educated, or even because he is conservative rather than liberal or radical. Nor, again, is he any the less an American because he is a tailor rather than a lawyer, or a teacher rather than an engineer, or a merchant rather than a soldier, or any of these rather than a professional politician. What makes him an American is a quality that transcends all such exclusive delineations; it is the quality of citizenship, of being equally a member of the great state. Where men are citizens, they are equally incorporated into this larger whole. And their unity as citizens—be they American or French or Russian—rests not on the features that divide but on the greater commonalty that joins them together. We see this sense of the common not only in such national emergencies as war, but in the pride with which men of all groups and all faiths acclaim their national heroes and revere their national symbols. And we see it, more profoundly, in the normal, everyday, even matter-of-fact pursuit of a common way of life by a people greatly divergent in interest and in background yet deeply and closely knit together by a greater unity, by "the sense of common interests to be sustained by common endeavor," a common which "over-rides the differences within the group but . . . does not abolish them." [57] For these reasons nationalism, within the territorial confines of the state, has a saving virtue. It brings men together in a unity independent of ladders of degree. It maintains men in an order founded on equality of citizenship, not inequality of status. It builds on the common rather than on the uniquely divergent in man. It unifies rather than divides a commonwealth.

We can see these truths the more clearly perhaps if we pause briefly to examine two dominant errors in the construction of Santayana's thought, errors central as well to the thinking of Plato, of Sheen, and of other theorists in this general aristocratic school. One is the over-simple interpretation of human nature, the view that the essence of a man is in the particular function he can or does perform, and that men differ, in consequence, as nature differs. The other is the assumption that certain fixed and known values or standards properly govern the habits and practices of men, that men can, for example, be driven to liberty through coercion.

A. THE NATURE OF NATURAL MAN

The obvious and immediate difficulty of any theory of nature and of natural man is the difficulty of definition. According to the theorists of natural aristocracy, each man in the right social order has his natural place and should observe it. As Plato said, it is not the business of the shoemaker to guide the affairs of the state. But what is man's natural place?

Consider Santayana's description of the nature of mankind:

"Their true nature is not adequately manifested in their condition at any moment, or in their words and thoughts vapidly flowing, or even in their prevalent habits. Their real nature is what they would discover themselves to be if they possessed self-knowledge or . . . if they became what they are." [58]

This, if taken literally, asserts that the true nature of man is not what he actually is at any one time but what he ought to be, in which event the shoemaker might well be held to be not *really* a shoemaker but only *seemingly* so; his real nature has yet to be revealed. If this is so, then the shoemaker's true nature may eventually turn out to be that of a warrior or a statesman or a minister of God. He can in no wise be judged on the basis of what he seemingly is, only on the basis of what he truly is. But how then is his true place to be determined? Santayana says by nature and the full and unrestrained operation of equality of opportunity. But this, as we have already seen, is to ignore the fact that history reveals no societies in which such a condition has prevailed. Nor does Santayana himself expect such a society to appear, at least not in a non-utopian world.

We are brought, then, back to the dictates of nature and to the fundamental question, who is to recognize and decide the true nature of man? The Church, as in the exposition by Sheen, argues its competence and its power to do so and invokes in support the authority of God. Clearly, for those who admit both the existence of the deity and the correct reading of his plans and execution by the Church, this claim is beyond refutation. But what if one were to deny that the Church had read correctly the mind of the deity, or that there is a deity who has a mind to be read, or if he has a mind to be read that man—even churchly or saintly man—rather than another deity can read it? Such denials—in effect shared, at least in part, by Santayana in his theological renunciation of Catholicism—leave no alternative but the reading of nature by nature itself or by man. The former, however, can never be more than a verbal evasion of the evident fact that nature, even when read by itself, must in fact be transcribed by man; and man, in the process of transcription, selects, arranges, and otherwise edits the revelations nature sets forth for him. It is thus not nature but man who is the ultimate judge, the final authority of that which is "truly" natural.[59]

We return, then, to the second and only logical alternative; man as determiner of the nature of natural man. Here, however, we find Santayana and other advocates of the doctrine restricting the process of determination to eminent man, naturally superior man, man governed by his higher and truer self. But such restrictions beg the very question to be answered, namely, who is to select these truly aristocratic, naturally eminent men? If they select themselves, there is obviously no assurance that the selection is based solely on the dictates of nature—dictates which they must still demonstrate their inherent capacity to read—or that theirs is a natural rather than an artificial eminence. And if, once selected, their qualities decline or are by others surpassed, or if what was considered man's nature is revealed at some future date to have been his apparent rather than his real nature, what reason is there to suppose that the "natural" aristocrats will, in accordance with nature's laws, voluntarily relinquish their place in the hierarchy? History, as Santayana admits, instructs us otherwise.

These reflections may serve to suggest some of the logical difficulties in this metaphysical doctrine. There are, however, three or four less abstract and somewhat more central considerations that even more effectively dispose of this aristocratic position.

First, there is the crucial consideration that no man is adequately defined in terms of a single aspect of his personality. To take but one of the many social relationships of man—say, his occupational function—and to equate this with the totality of his being is grossly to misconstrue and simplify his nature. One need not affirm what the nature of man is in order to point out what it is not. And it is surely not the quality of being a tailor or a soldier or a teacher or an engineer that is alone or even dominantly the essence of a man. This, important as it is for the impress it leaves on the individual, is only one of the several social relationships of man. He is also a member of a church, of a family, of a cultural or professional group, of a racial or national group, of a city and a state, and these too leave their marks as they contribute to the molding of his personality. Nor is he merely the sum of these particular relationships. It is not merely that it is impossible to foresee how these varied relationships will combine in a single man; more important is the fact that, however they combine, he is still something more than all of them—he is a person. And as a person his nature, his personality, is so complex and varied that no single formula of description can possibly include all the aspects of his being. The curtness with which a harried medical practitioner discharges his professional duties is in striking contrast to his warmth and sociability in the presence of his family or friends, and both are different from his behavior at professional meetings, as these vary in turn from his conduct at religious gatherings. Applied politically, this means that men act not simply as shoemakers or as lawyers and the like, but as citizens, and more than citizens, as people.

Thus we see that men become not merely something other than it is thought they ought to be but something other than it is frequently thought they are. Our central difficulty here is that we tend too easily to categorize, that we tend too much to think in types. As a contemporary thinker observed:

"The idea we form of another's personality is always generalised and imperfect, because we cannot fully conceive the elements of unlikeness to ourselves which it contains. How often do we dismiss a man as a member of a social type, especially if his activities lie in social spheres remote from our own, as a grocer or a priest or a concierge or a member of parliament or whatever it might be, who, if we knew him better, would appear less and less the type, the mere member of an occupation or a class, more and more the person, a being with the richness and elusiveness and incompleteness—and seeming contradictoriness—of personality. . . . We can never form a completely true idea of a personality because its revelation is itself fragmentary, not integral. 'We are all fragments, not only of humanity, but of ourselves.' " [60]

And since we are but fragments, how unnatural and irrational it is to select a part and try to make that part the whole. In doing this, the theorists of natural aristocracy themselves deny one of the signal truths of man's nature: his quest for unity. It is the record of all history that man has refused to be delineated by a particular segment of his activities. It is equally that record that he has insisted on his right, indeed, in these terms his "natural" right, to be regarded as a person beyond any mere one of his social relationships.[61]

There is a second consideration which merits our attention here, one which stems in part from our earlier discussion on the difficulty of definition. This is the fact that, since the determination of what is natural is always relative to man, "men are tempted from a variety of motives to draw up different sets of principles to indicate the true nature of man." [62] To speak of man's true nature or self—in contradistinction to his actual self—as being somehow the true fulfillment of his life is thus to open wide the gates of conflict; for what that fulfillment is depends obviously on who is doing the conceiving. In such terms, Dorothy Fosdick notes,

"One's true nature becomes nothing less than a state of being good, according to a variety of interpretations of the good. Being one's true self means being an improved self, with no end to the definitions of what improved shall signify. We find we have embarked on the limitless quest of how to be a perfect person, and there is no hope of agreement on the nature of perfection." [63]

There is, third, the very real and pervasive difficulty inherent in the fact that men all too frequently refuse or do not desire to become even what they may know they ought to become. It is one thing, that is to say, to set forth a series of ideals which men may acknowledge to be noble and just. It is not always the same thing to effect the coincidence of those ideals with the practices and habits of those same men.[64] The example of the sinner who refuses to become saint, of, say, the perennial drunkard who repeatedly offers eternal vows never to drink again, is a sufficient instance in point. What the theorists of natural aristocracy ignore, in this connection, is that political societies can be constructed only on what men are, not on what they ought to be, and what men are is rarely what utopian thinkers prefer. It is not without significance that every major utopia penned by man—from Plato to Santayana—has been an undemocratic one, for every major utopia has been constructed on a principle of ideal rather than of actual men.

One final point still remains to be made. This is the not unimportant consideration that reason no less than nature is and should be a guiding element in the conduct of human affairs. What the theorists of natural aristocracy do is to build on one central factor to the diminution and at times almost the exclusion of the other. Thus for Santayana the life of reason is conceived as a harmony in accordance with nature. But there is still the alternative of the use of reason to modify or control nature in accordance with human ideas. Not everything in nature is good and desirable for man, not everything pursues a clear and consistent pattern or order. If reason is a natural attribute of man, there can be no natural objection to man's employment of that attribute to effect a congenial modification in his environment; and in this endeavor the natural, while it must be respected, should not be sacrosanct.[65] To argue, therefore, that the social order should conform to the natural order, is to postulate a narrow unilateral relationship which foregoes in no small detail the great and imaginative capacities of the human intellect.

These several considerations underscore the undue simplification with which Santayana and the theorists of this school approach the nature of "natural" man and help us to see the invalidity of their central view—that function alone is the key to man's nature. Function is important, to be sure, and as a segment of that nature it has its vital and necessary place. But as an inclusive interpretation it distorts and perverts that nature into binding channels which in no way explain the totality that is man. To hold, moreover, that men should or do differ as nature differs is not merely to yield the rational constructs of man to the restrictions of a previously prescribed order; it is to argue that nature has one rather than many orders, that the particular order described is *the* natural order, and that this natural order is, *ipso facto*, a desirable and just order. These, it is plain, are propositions immersed not only in faith but even more in human values. And values, as the diversity of eternal truths entombed in the vaults of history attest, are always relative.

B. TRADITIONAL VALUES AND "TRUE FREEDOM"

This brings us to the second dominant error of the theorists of natural aristocracy. This is the view that certain standards or values rightly govern the behavior of men, and that knowledge of these standards—with consequent adherence thereto—will lead the individual to freedom: not, to be sure, the illusory freedom that is his when he does as he likes, but the "true freedom" that comes from self-fulfillment in accordance with the highest dictates of nature. And since, in this construction, only the superior few possess the self-knowledge and the self-control to recognize and to conform to these truths, it is their particular responsibility to instruct, to guide, and if need be to compel, obedience on the part of the many. This, of course, implies hierarchy, a system in which the natural aristocracy commands and the natural multitude obeys. Such a system, according to these critics of democracy, is amply justified by its exaltation of those superior values which nature alone reveals. For as one commentator tersely remarked: "What is the right direction is a question of fact and not a question of opinion." [66]

Now values, whatever else they may imply, exist only for the particular individuals who seek them. They do not inhere in the state, as Hegel would have us believe, for the state is itself but the vehicle through which those who at any one time dominate the state pursue the particular values they deem worthwhile. Nor do they inhere in the collectivity—group, class, or nation—for the collectivity is either an abstraction incapable as such of experiencing values or an organization through which men pursue in common values they can experience only in their immediate and personal lives.[67] Values are uniquely a matter of the individual being, and as individuals differ, values differ. Democracy, therefore, as a form of state which men desire, is itself both a value and a means to other values.[68] The validity of the attack on democracy in this context, in consequence, can only be sustained if it is shown that democracy denies specific individual values that are superior to those it allows.

There are, in these terms, two such specific values democracy is held by these theorists to deny. One is its denial of, its failure to adhere to, traditional standards. Quite apart from the difficulty of delineating the nature of these traditional standards, especially in view of the cleavages that exist among rival proponents of various absolute and eternal claims, there is one central and sufficient objection to this argument that can be made. This is the fact that traditional standards, when imposed, may interfere with the growth of individual personality and coerce the community into a straitjacket. It is, of course, entirely legitimate for a man to follow traditional standards if he so desires, whether or not those standards are the creed of a particular group or church. Where that pursuit is unfettered, no man need join if he feels himself disinclined. But to ask the state to impose that particular creed on all men is to deny the right of withdrawal by any. Here is the prime reason why there are certain limits beyond which the state, far more than any other association, should not go; for if it does it denies the creativeness and the healthy challenge that ensue from the free clash of a variety of values, and it molds into a uniform pattern—to an extent unimagined even by those who charge democracy with a leveling tendency—the many diversities of the human personality. To ask the state to coerce those whom the particular creed cannot persuade, moreover, is to admit to the weakness of its own moral powers, a strong indication in itself that the creed does not truly reflect the dictates of nature.[69]

When we conjoin with these several factors the final recognition that there is no one universal standard of behavior, that men vary as their beliefs and ideals vary, and that conflicts of values cannot be resolved in terms of some external standard for the standard is itself part of the conflict—when we perceive and appreciate these things, then can we know that the absolutism of particular values, traditional or insurgent, is a denial rather than a fulfillment of the nature of man. For it seeks to make both universal and eternal the moral particularism of a temporary few. In denying this, and in recognizing that the greatest, the most profound, the most crucial of all values is the value to choose values, democracy achieves its supreme justification.[70]

The other value democracy is held in this context to deny is the realization of "true freedom." Only through the coercion of men into the right paths of behavior as determined by traditional values, the theorists of natural aristocracy hold, can men truly be free. That democracy fails so to coerce men is, for these critics, the basis of its undesirability. As we have just shown, however, the doctrine that traditional values can in any final or complete sense determine the right way of life for all men is without validity. The inability of these theorists to assure the real conditions for the just selection and full development of the naturally eminent, moreover, raises grave and in fact conclusive doubts as to whether those who represent themselves as the natural and proper rulers of the state are in actuality what they profess to be. These considerations strongly support democracy's refusal to impose as true that which is debatable. They render equally questionable the realization of "true freedom" even by the supposedly aristocratic state.

There is another factor, however, which refutes still more decisively the allegation of the critics, and that is the invalidity of their term "true freedom." Freedom can only be true to itself, not to a value conjoined to it. We can force men to do good or we can force men to do evil. We can force men to follow paths we conceive to be right or we can force them to follow paths we conceive to be wrong. But we do not thereby force them to be free. Freedom, it has been rightly said, is the absence of chains, the removal of restraints. And we do not render men "truly" free by imposing limitations on them. Through certain limitations, to be sure, we maximize or assure certain freedoms, certain specific liberties which otherwise might improperly be interfered with. But what we thereby do is to select from among a variety of freedoms those we particularly esteem. We restrict some liberties to gain others. To the man who is restricted, however, there is no gain in freedom. Coercion does not make him "truly" free, though it may provide the conditions under which other men may be more largely free. Freedom, in a word, is not the quality of being true or false but simply the quality of being free. Those who, therefore, as Santayana and Sheen, speak of man's fulfillment in "true liberty" entirely misconstrue the nature of the problem with which they are dealing.

IV

DEMOCRACY AND THE THEORY OF NATURAL ARISTOCRACY

The essence of the indictment of democracy by Plato, Mallock, Santayana, and other theorists of this school, is the charge that democracy treats as equals men who are by nature unequal, suppressing or denying thereby two central values: the rise of natural eminence to the top and the unity that follows from degree.

That men are variously unequal is too evident to admit disputation. That they are "naturally" unequal, however, is one of those partial truths that obscure rather than make plain the full explanation. If, as Santayana insists, aristocracies have in practice been built largely on artificial rather than on natural eminence, and if the full freedom and equality of opportunity necessary to the growth and emergence of true eminence can exist but in the utopias of the *Republic* and the *Life of Reason*, then rarely if ever can we equate the inequalities that actually exist among men with the inequalities that would naturally exist were the proper conditions assured. And since there is no precise standard by which such natural inequalities as do exist can be determined, it is patently impossible for any state to treat with the right degree of inequality those who are "truly" by nature unequal.

This practical consideration goes a long way toward being the sufficient justification of democracy's refusal to attempt the institutionalization of the impossible. But there is yet another consideration which renders invalid the aristocratic indictment on this count. This is the fact that the respect in which democracy attempts to treat its citizens as equals—by affording them equal political rights and equal opportunities—is precisely the respect which alone makes possible the rise of true eminence to the top. Where equality of citizenship and of opportunity are assured, the inequalities that are inherent in men's natures or personalities are given free rein to exert an unequal impact on political and social affairs. Unequal men are enabled to hold unequal political office, exercise an unequal influence, and enjoy unequal social status, all in accordance with their varying abilities. The principle of merit, far from being denied, is molded into the very fabric of the state. Oligarchy, on the other hand, by excluding from the channels of ascension those who are not already members of the favored class, limits the rise of political ability or talent and thus denies the principle of eminence. It is not democracy but oligarchy, therefore, which is to be condemned on this score.

We are left, then, with the criticism that democracy, through its refusal to adhere to a hierarchical structure founded on degree, denies the supreme value of order and unity. This is the central charge on which the aristocratic criticism must stand or fall, and in its favor one important acknowledgment must be made. This is the recognition that there are great differences in the applicability of the argument according to the unique or special circumstances of the moment, according to such factors as time, place, national development, the state of the masses, and the like. At certain stages in a people's evolution, history has made clear, democracy may indeed become unduly difficult if not impossible of operation. Where, for example, the great masses of the people are illiterate and impoverished, where they have been without contact with the larger affairs of government and have no habituation with it, where their normal pattern of political existence has been a series of steps from one crisis to another, from one dictator to another—where such conditions prevail, as in so many of the Latin American states, it may well be that democracy will find itself unable to operate and to survive. If the critics of democracy were to point to such situations and say that under those conditions democracy is not likely to maintain unity and order, they would be stating a fact whose truth experience might not infrequently uphold. But when they generalize this fact into a principle of politics, they tread on completely unjustifiable ground.

It is unjustifiable in that it ignores the fact that unity lies also in a structure outside of degree, in a structure and an order knit together by a sense of the common rather than a sense of the divergent. It is the conception that co-operation, not subservience, is the greater and stronger force, that people can be united on the broader basis of a common way of life far more than they can on the reflected glory that comes to them through the prestige of a "higher" but narrow class. It is not the denial of structure, though to be sure it is the denial of aristocratic structure—of order based on respect for station and rank. It is rather the affirmation that forms of state can be constructed on a different kind of structure, on a system of order and of unity based on respect for the individual and on the abiding interests that inhere in the pervading common.

This conviction that the truly sound bond of unity inheres in the common rather than in the divergent is strongly reinforced by an examination of the nature of man himself. According to the theorists of natural aristocracy, a single aspect of man's nature—his function—is sufficient to define his essence. But no one factor, as we have seen, can adequately encompass the totality that is the nature of a man. He is always more than the segment that is his occupational pursuit, always more than any of the particular segments that define his miscellaneous activities. He is or seeks to be fundamentally a unity of his own, and it is a unity not of degree but of cohesion. As it is within himself, so it is within the greater unity that is society. He moves and has his being not merely as a carpenter or a father or a Negro or an Episcopalian. These delineate aspects of his being; they do not encompass the whole. They affect his place in the community but they do not separately define it. When the theorists of natural aristocracy argue, therefore, that ladders of humanity should be constructed on the steps of occupational function, they ignore and thereby distort the very unity that is the nature of man. It was no accident that he who spoke of a brotherhood of man made no reference to such ladders of humanity; rather did he urge with profound insight the commonalty of equals.

Similar considerations help to explain the inadequacy of Santayana's argument that a right order consists in adherence to traditional standards. We are faced at the outset with the twofold difficulty of determining what standards are traditional and of selecting from such traditional and often conflicting standards those which are right from those which are wrong. In this it is not tradition but reason that alone can be the ultimate guide. More important, however, is the recognition that such standards, however determined, when applied absolutely so as to fit all the varieties of individual personality into a single and pre-established pattern cannot but stunt the growth of a large portion of humanity. They force the totality that is man to conform to values which are not his own and which may appeal to only a fragment of that totality, and by thus ignoring the fullness of his nature they limit and distort the infinite possibilities of his development. When we add to these reflections the presumptuous assumption that any special few contain in themselves possession of complete and final truth, and by virtue of that possession have the authoritarian duty of imposing that truth on all mankind—on the pretense that men through such coercion will thereby be rendered "truly" free—we see with striking clarity the injustice and invalidity of their claim.

Once again, therefore, we are led to the reaffirmation of our primary principle, that unity inheres in the common, not in degree. This is the structure on which democracy builds, a structure in which there is no assumption of eternal and absolute truths— unless it be the assumption that there may not be any eternal and absolute truths—and in which there is no permanent universalization of a particular set of values, unless it be the value to select values. It is a structure in which values are left free so that diverse groups and diverse individuals may pursue in common or alone those special values they deem desirable, and in which traditional values or standards may freely be modified in accordance with changing concepts of truth and of value. In building on this structure, on this order that unifies men through their sense of commonalty, democracy justifies in full measure its repudiation of the aristocratic doctrine of degree.

9

Authority and the Restrictive Way of Life

It is the peculiar dilemma of the aristocratic theory that those who espouse it must embrace authoritarianism or abandon aristocracy. This is so because no aristocracy is long permitted to sit unchallenged. It is confronted, on a small scale, by rival pretenders to the "aristocratic" throne. And it is faced, on a broader scale, by those who deny that it—or any other allegedly superior few—truly comprises the political best.

In the democratic state such conflicts are resolved through the free organization of conflicting opinions. But in the oligarchic state the resolution is arbitrarily imposed: the fusion of power with what is considered to be rule by theoretical right renders opposition inconceivable to the rulers. Indeed, it makes the suppression of that opposition the first business of the state. In consequence, as Toynbee and others have shown, the "aristocracy" degenerates. What was once creative becomes coercive. And those who coerce seek to rationalize their domination in terms of their original ideals. Thus the cycle of overlapping categories is completed: aristocratic theories breed authoritarian practices and authoritarian practitioners evolve aristocratic ideas. It is the old story of the Janus-faced god: on the one side the resplendent face of aristocracy, pleading, as with Santayana, the desirability of order; on the other the grim and shadowed but ever pervasive countenance of authority, ready to compel, if necessary even by force, at least outward obeisance to the strictures of command.

The authoritarian principle is not, however, simply an obscure or incidental appendage to the aristocratic ideal. It stands also in its own and independent right as a doctrine of no mean significance, a doctrine which asserts its capacity—through strength and the right of imposition—to maintain the order and the authority essential to the operation and survival of the state.

What democracy does, in the construction of the authoritarian theorists, is to permit freedom of political action, which means, inescapably, political conflict. But this very tolerance of conflict, they say, is what guarantees political disunity. It makes for division, which is weakness, and for disorder, which disrupts authority. It immerses government in the petty rivalries and squabbles that disturb the harmony and stability of the state, and, by basing government on the changing whims of the people—with consequent vacillations and shifts in policy—renders impossible the maintenance of coherence, continuity, and indeed authority itself. If that coherence and that stability are to be assured, they argue, it is imperative to institute strong and authoritative government: government not merely independent of the fluctuations of dissident opinions but, more important, government characterized by a firm central will—a will that is at once constant and assured, a will that imposes a single organization, a single discipline, a single creed, a will that brooks no deviation and no challenge. Only in this way, these critics of democracy insist, can the authority essential to the integrity of the state and the peace and order of the commonwealth be maintained.

Apt and incisive articulation was given to these views in the very passage in which Shakespeare's Ulysses inveighs against the alleged consequences of the denial of degree. It thus reveals not merely the nexus which binds the aristocratic to the authoritarian doctrine but the heart of the authoritarian principle itself.

> "Strength [Ulysses said] should be lord of imbecility,
> . . . .
> Force should be right; or rather, right and wrong,
> Between whose endless jar justice resides,
> Should lose their names, and so should justice too.
> Then everything includes itself in power." [1]

I

THE DOCTRINES OF AUTHORITARIAN THOUGHT

Various doctrines have been put forth in amplification of this authoritarian theory, but they are in no sense easy to discriminate. Common to them all is the idea that someone or something embodies the right will of the state and that this will should thereupon be imposed as the universal pattern of thought and behavior. For some theorists this will is contained in a single person, the right man, who by some intrinsic quality or superior power is truly the embodiment or the representative of the right way of life. For others it is not the man but the class that somehow embodies the right principles of conduct. And for still others it is neither man nor class but idea, principle; it is government as the incarnation of the right abstraction, that is the true guide for political behavior. None of these categories, of course, can be held to be exclusive: man and class, for example, are always overlapping configurations, and both frequently resort to an ideological abstraction in support of their claim. Then too within each category the various shades of delineation remain always to be weighed. But when all these considerations have been taken into account, there is still a kind of distinction that can be drawn from the emphasis placed on these respective elements. It is a distinction which not only permits a convenient if rough classification; it provides an acute insight into the nature of authoritarian thought. For these reasons a brief inquiry into the content of these doctrines is in order.

Government predominantly in the name of, or under the banner of, a single person. In this doctrine are included those theories that lay greatest emphasis on the role of the right man, the leader, and argue that into his hands alone should be entrusted the reins of authority. It is the category of personal absolutism, totalitarian and non-totalitarian alike, but it is the personal absolutism essential to dictatorship. Despite the extravagant claims of James I, it is not necessarily that of monarchy. It resembles monarchy, to be sure, and most vividly in the obvious fact of single-man rule. But it is not technically to be identified with monarchy, for it lacks the legitimacy both of accession and of succession. The distinction between dictator and monarch can be seen quite clearly, by way of illustration, in the examples of Caesar and Napoleon, each of whom, though a dictator. yet insisted on becoming king. Our immediate concern, then, is with the dictatorial form of personal rule, and here there are two central ideas which command our attention.

One is the simple, prosaic, peculiarly non-mythical, and non-totalitarian theory that power concentrated in the right man, the dictator, will, by its singleness of direction and authority, best secure the welfare of the state: not merely from the dangers of disunity and disorder within but from the exactions imposed by otherwise stronger states without. This doctrine invokes no ethereal incantations of ideology; it does not endeavor to embrace within a single orbit all the manifold activities of individual and community. It pleads only the simple ground of necessity, the requirement of a strong hand to prevent the emergence or to curtail the prolongation of crisis.[2] This is the argument on which men have normally rested the justification of personal rule throughout history: from Greek tyrants like Pisistratus and Roman dictators like Caesar to the variety of unconstitutional despots or *caudillos* who have controlled the destinies of the modern Latin American states—men like Francia in Paraguay, Rosas in Argentina, Díaz in Mexico, Gómez in Venezuela, and numerous others.

The important feature of this argument to be noticed here is that it makes the claim of personal authority superior to that of ideology. The dictator rules not because he is the embodiment of an idea, a principle, for the idea is superfluous. Nor does he rule because he has some supernatural mission to fulfill. If he has a mission at all, it is the much less mysterious one of maintaining himself and his supporters in power. It is—and this is particularly true of the Latin American dictatorships—not the program but the person that is central. Consequently, as an acute observer has reminded us, parties in Latin America have been "as much the expression of personal loyalties as of political principles. The dictators themselves were personal rulers; there was not, and could not be, that regimentation which has been the foundation of the modern totalitarian state."[3]

Markedly different is the second theory which seeks to justify the absolutism of dictatorial rule. It is personal, as the ancient tyrants and modern *caudillos* were and are personal, but in a very

special way. Now the dictator rules as the embodiment of an ideology. He is the prophet sent to lead his people to their divinely
ordained mission. He is the mystical essence of the unity of state
and people, in the Germanic concept, of state and the spirit of the
folk. He is the Leader, who knows, unlike the people, what the
people want. "That," said the Nazi apologist Wilhelm Stapel, "is
what makes him a Leader." [4] As the Pope is infallible in matters
of faith and morals, so, for Goering, "the Leader is in all political
and other respects concerning the national and social interests of
the people simply infallible." [5] In the Italian construction he is
infallible not because he is God but because he is great almost like
a God, as is evidenced by the following passage taken from a fascist
secondary school text:

"Religious dogmas are not discussed because they are truths revealed by God. Fascist principles are not discussed because they
come from the mind of a Genius: Benito Mussolini." [6]

The modesty that permitted Il Duce to differentiate between
himself and God was thrust aside, however, by Nazi theorists who
saw no such distinction between the Führer and the agent or representative of the deity. The approach to this charismatic identity
can be seen in such statements as those of the Reichs-Minister of
Justice, Hans Frank, who perceived in Hitler the Messiah newly
sent by God:

"Formerly, we were in the habit of saying: *this is right or wrong;*
to-day, we must put the question accordingly: *What would the
'Führer' say?* This attitude towards the 'Führer' as well as his own
person, are the Categorical Imperative to which German life must
henceforward conform. We are under the great obligation of recognizing as a holy work of our Volk's spirit the laws signed by Adolf
Hitler's name. Hitler has received his authority from God. Therefore
he is a champion, sent by God, for German Right in the world." [7]

But it is in such pronouncements as the famous prayer written by
Baldur von Schirach for the Hitler Youth that we find the identity
made direct and complete:

"Adolf Hitler, we believe in Thee. Without Thee we would be alone. Through Thee we are a people. Thou hast given us the great experience of our youth, comradeship. Thou hast laid upon us the task, the duty, and the responsibility. Thou hast given us Thy Name [*Hitler Jugend*], the most beloved Name that Germany has ever possessed. We speak it with reverence, we bear it with faith and loyalty. Thou canst depend upon us, Adolf Hitler, Leader and Standard-Bearer. The Youth is Thy Name. Thy name is the Youth. Thou and the young millions can never be sundered." [8]

Government predominantly in the name of, or under the banner of, a class. In both the foregoing constructions it is the argument of the authoritarians that only through a concentration of power in the right man can the stability and order of the commonwealth be secured. There is, however, a body of theory which places greatest emphasis not on the man but on the class. It is the argument we find expressed, for example, in the *Republic*, where Plato urges the transfer of political power to his philosopher-kings, the guardian class. It is the argument advanced, in somewhat different form, by Calhoun in his plea for the dominance of the Southern slavocracy. And it is the argument which, in the contemporary era, has been restated in still other forms by doctrinaire reactionary theorists of the extreme right and doctrinaire proletarian theorists of the extreme left.

All are anti-democratic in their common attempt to stratify society into absolute and mutually exclusive social classes and then to organize the state on a basis of class subordination. Instead of admitting into the political process the will of all classes in the community, as democracy insists, they would make dominant only the will of their own, permanently excluding—through annihilation or suppression—those dissident groups on the wrong side of their particular dichotomy. They would return to the feudal or create the absolute state, which are always class states. They would make real Spengler's insistence that "class-States . . . are the *only* States," institutionalizing thereby the political supremacy of one sector of the populace over all other sectors. They would impose an order expressive of class differences and of class interests. And they would integrate society through the principle of might, for those who "know" the right way of life must, if necessary even by violence, see that all pursue that right way. This is the class theory of the state, the conjunction of authority with a doctrine of class superiority.[9]

The manner in which this class theory has been applied is strikingly illustrated in Franco's Spain, where the new trinity of army, church, and Falange share political domination by supporting the personal absolutism of the Caudillo.[10] And it is illustrated too in the class rule of the Soviet Union, where the dictatorship of the proletariat is revealed in practice to be the dictatorship of the party in the name of the proletariat.

Government predominantly in the name of, or under the banner of, a principle. From the stern righteousness of John Calvin and the turgid rhetoric of Georg Wilhelm Friedrich Hegel, we derive our third broad category of authoritarian thought. This is the doctrine which admits the relevance, indeed stresses the importance, of the right man and the right class, but which conceives of both as instruments in the attainment or effectuation of a greater goal, the idea. It is the conception of government as the incarnation of an abstraction, a principle, in which men realize both themselves and the higher purpose for which they exist: this higher purpose being, as with Calvin, the will of God, or, as with Hegel, the fulfillment of the Ideal. Both are absolute, totalitarian concepts. Both are intolerant of dissent and opposition. Both abhor the principle of majority will. Both deny democracy.

In the Hegelian totalitarian construction, the state is conceived to be an organic unity with a will and a personality of its own. It is more than just the sum total of its members, more than just an association delineating a part of communal life. The state is, for Hegel, the very whole itself, a being in which the individual resides and for which he lives, a mystical absolute in which the ideal is embodied and the good attained. It is "the rich inward articulation of ethical life, . . . the architectonic of that life's rationality," [11] and as such its actual will is always the absolutely rational will. It is not, therefore, Hegel argues, the business of the individual to oppose his will to that of the state; for it is only through the surrender of his false and fallible individual will to the real and right state will that he can realize his true fulfillment, his true destiny, his true freedom. Man is not free, Hegel insists, when he is unrestrained. He is free only when he is self-determined, when, that is, the rational will of the higher self, the state, controls and directs the will of the individual self. "Only that will which obeys law, is free; for it obeys itself." [12]

In thus surrendering himself to the state, Hegel says, man not merely identifies himself with the state; he identifies himself with the universal that is the state. For "the State," in Hegel's conception, "is the Divine Idea as it exists on Earth." [13] As he elsewhere expressed it:

"The state is the actuality of the ethical Idea. It is ethical mind *qua* the substantial will manifest and revealed to itself, knowing and thinking itself, accomplishing what it knows and in so far as it knows it. . . . The state is absolutely rational inasmuch as it is the actuality of the substantial will which it possesses in the particular self-consciousness once that consciousness has been raised to consciousness of its universality. This substantial unity is an absolute unmoved end in itself, in which freedom comes into its supreme right. On the other hand this final end has supreme right against the individual, whose supreme duty is to be a member of the state. . . . Since the state is mind objectified, it is only as one of its members that the individual himself has objectivity, genuine individuality, and an ethical life." [14]

This complete surrender of the individual to the ideal mystically incarnated in the organic unity that is the Hegelian state is equally emphasized in the even greater absolutism of the theocratic state, as was pre-eminently exampled by the rigid theocracy of the early Puritans and by the doctrines of their dominant figures, the cleric John Cotton and the magistrate John Winthrop. Here, in the very beginnings of the American commonwealth, was applied that Calvinistic philosophy which, in the name of divine sanction, repudiated democracy and established the extreme authoritarian state. The Puritan leaders were men who loved power, even as they loved God, "and accounting themselves God's stewards they reckoned it sin not to use it in his name." [15] It was not for them, as Puritans, to consider the will of the majority, for did not God himself speak in the Scriptures through a chosen minority? Cotton expressed their antagonism to democracy full well when he declared:

"It is better that the commonwealth be fashioned to the setting forth of God's house, which is his church: than to accommodate the church frame to the civill state. Democracy, I do not conceyve that ever God did ordeyne as a fit government eyther for church or commonwealth. If the people be governors, who shall be governed? As for monarchy, and aristocracy, they are both of them clearly approoved, and directed in scripture, yet so as referreth the soveraigntie to himselfe, and setteth up Theocracy in both, as the best forme of government in the commonwealth, as well as in the church." [16]

Indeed, Parrington points out in his summation of this theocratic absolutism, popular enactments were held by the Puritan leaders not merely to be prompted by the carnal desires of natural men; they were veritably conceived as no better than an insult to God, implying, as they did, the insufficiency of the Scriptures to every temporal need. In Parrington's words:

"Granted the conception on which the theocratic experiment went forward, namely, that Jehovah was the sole lawgiver and the Bible the sufficient statute-book; granted also that these priests and magistrates were stewards of God's will; and the centralization of power in the commonwealth becomes invested with a higher sanction than the terms of the charter. It was an oligarchy of Christian grace. The minister was the trained and consecrated interpreter of the divine law, and the magistrate was its trained and consecrated administrator; and both were chosen by free election of the Saints. If unfortunately the Saints were few and the sinners many, was not that a special reason for safeguarding the Ark of the Covenant from the touch of profane hands? . . . Unregenerate and sinful men must have no share in God's work. The Saints must not have their hands tied by majority votes. This explains, quite as much as mere love of power, the persistent hostility of the leaders to every democratic tendency." [17]

These, then, are the doctrines of authoritarianism, doctrines which have moved men and influenced in no small measure the course of human history. Powerful as they are, however, they have never—with the partial exception of the Puritan theocracy already noted—taken firm root in American thought. But while these doctrines are not advanced today in their extreme form, they are implied and indeed are inherent in many of the arguments of aristocratic theorists. In fact, strands of these concepts appear repeatedly in nearly all the pleas of aristocratic thinkers for the right of the "best" to impose on the community their particular conception of the best, though these same writers, it should be added, are not infrequently unaware of the logic and the implications of their own argument.

An outstanding example of this tendency is Irving Babbitt, leader of the American humanists, whose work illustrates in profound degree the conjunction of the aristocratic ideal with the authoritarian principle.[18]

II

THE RESTRICTIVE AUTHORITARIANISM OF IRVING BABBITT

The essence of Babbitt's political thought is a non-theological puritanism. A dour, uncompromising thinker, he early found congenial the stern asceticism of Buddhist doctrine and the harsh, rigorous spirit of Puritan ethics. He distrusted human nature and sought to curb what he called the expansion of its natural impulse. He revered the principle of authority and emphasized the obligations and the duties rather than the satisfactions and fulfillments of men. He looked to the supernatural (which he defined as insight and control *within* man) for the key to human understanding; but the superhuman (which he regarded as "dogmatic and revealed religion" imposed from *outside* of man)—and particularly the Church as an institution of the superhuman—he held in deep distaste.[19] His concern lay with the traditions of the past; he cared little or nothing for the prospect even of a glorious future.

Out of these habits and these beliefs he evolved a theory of aristocracy which blended into a framework of authoritarianism: with

its repudiation of the doctrine of the rights of man and its acceptance of the doctrine of the "right man," the leader, the man of
standards; with its scorn for the masses and its respect for and
reliance on the classes, and particularly the "right class"—the class
of wealth, of property, of character; with its invocation of the
"right principle," the higher self, embodied not alone in the individual but in the abstraction that is the state, and through the
state in those bodies least subject to majority influence or control—
the Senate, and paramountly the Supreme Court. Democracy he
held to be a reflection of the baser nature in man; consequently he
could say: "Puritanism, our national principle of concentration,
is the indispensable check on democracy, our national principle of
expansion." [20]

To perceive the nature of his anti-democratic argument, and
the manner in which he fused aristocratic values with the principle
of authoritarianism, let us pause to consider the structure of his
argument in somewhat greater detail.

It is important to understand, Babbitt begins, that no man

"has got the Truth tucked away in a set of formulae. . . . But
though the truth cannot be finally formulated, man cannot dispense
with formulae. The truth will always overflow his categories, yet
he needs categories. He should therefore have formulae and categories, but hold them fluidly; in other words, he must have standards, but they must be flexible." [21]

This recognition, however, Babbitt holds, is subject to one major
qualification. It cannot apply to questions of truth and error. "The
essence of humanism," he says, "is moderation," but one can properly
begin to mediate only *after* he has disposed of the issue of truth.
One should not, for example, assume a moderate attitude toward
murder. Nor should one betray his first principles in order to
compromise with error. "When it comes to first principles, the
issue raised is not one of moderation, but of truth or error." And
here, in this most basic of all realms, while one does well to open
one's mind, he should do so "only as a preliminary to closing it,
only as a preparation, in short, for the supreme act of judgment
and selection." This is the case with the issues now at hand.

"The differences of doctrine I debate [says Babbitt of his *Democracy and Leadership*] . . . are of a primary nature and so not subject to mediation. . . . The opposition is one of first principles. . . . In general I commit myself to the position that we are living in a world that in certain important respects has gone wrong on first principles; . . . we are living in a world that has been betrayed by its leaders. On the appearance of leaders who have recovered in some form the truths of the inner life . . . may depend the very survival of Western civilization." [22]

What are these first principles, these truths of the inner life? First, according to Babbitt, the duality of human nature, the dichotomy within man into a higher and a lower self. "If man is to become human he must not let impulse and desire run wild, but must oppose to everything excessive in his ordinary self, whether in thought or deed or emotion, the law of measure." This law of measure is the higher or ethical will, the principle of control in human nature, the *frein vital*, "which is the true voice of man's higher self." It is "felt as a power of control over the natural man and his expansive desires. Deny this ethical will and the inner life disappears." [23] Is it not written in the book of Buddha: "Self is the lord of self, who else could be the lord?" [24]

Consider, on the other hand, says Babbitt, what has actually happened in the world today. Instead of adhering to the nobler and restrictive dictates of the higher self, we have surrendered to the baser and expansive impulses of the lower or natural self. We have left the teachings of Burke for the doctrines of Rousseau, and the world of Rousseau "is a world without degree and subordination; a world in which no one looks up to any one else or expects any one to look up to him; a world in which no one . . . has either to command or to obey." [25] We have abandoned the good of aristocracy for the evils of unlimited democracy, sacrificing thereby "a truly human hierarchy and scale of values to the principle of equality" and the cult of the common man, which is, Babbitt insists, "hard to distinguish from the cult of commonness." [26] We have denied, through our lack of interest in the perfection of the individual, the quality of genuine leadership, and produced, through our "sickly sentimentalizing over the lot of the underdog, . . .

an inferior and even insane type of leadership." [27] We are, as a consequence, "in danger of producing in the name of democracy one of the most trifling brands of the human species that the world has yet seen, . . . a huge mass of standardized mediocrity" utterly incapable of maintaining the standards necessary to the preservation of the race.[28]

What we do in democracy, Babbitt holds, is to entrust our destinies to man, ordinary man, which is an absurdity when we realize that "the only thing that approaches the absolute in man is his ignorance."

"The notion in particular that a substitute for leadership will be found in numerical majorities that are supposed to reflect the 'general will' is only a pernicious conceit. In the long run democracy will be judged . . . by the qualities of its leaders, a quality that will depend in turn on the quality of their vision." [29]

But it is precisely this vision, Babbitt insists, that a democracy lacks. "One should, therefore, in the interests of democracy itself seek to substitute the doctrine of the right man for the doctrine of the rights of man." [30]

Here, in Babbitt's construction, is the proper alternative to democracy. "What counts practically," he tells us, "is not justice in the abstract, but the just man, . . . he whose various capacities (including the intellect) are acting in right relation to one another under the hegemony of the higher will." This true leader, this man of character, is the man with an allegiance to standards—like Burke, that "splendidly imaginative Whig," rather than Rousseau, he "who invented nothing, but set everything on fire"; like Washington and Hamilton rather than Jefferson; like Marshall and Webster rather than Jackson.[31] He is the man who has "earned the right to have an opinion." He is the man who has established his true mark of excellence by "his power to harmonize in himself opposite virtues and to occupy all the space between them." [32] He and others like him make up that saving remnant which is in opposition to the divine average, an opposition "that is one of first principles and is not therefore subject to mediation or compromise." [33]

In this saving remnant, this true aristocracy, we have, Babbitt holds, "the hope of civilization." It is not an aristocracy of intellect, scientific or otherwise; for such an aristocracy places mere pride above humility. Nor is it an aristocracy of artists or of Nietzschean supermen, for the one leads to rule by the senses and the other to violence and death.[34] It is rather an "aristocracy of character and intelligence," an enlightened minority characterized above all by its recognition of and adherence to the highest principle, the higher will.

There is, says Babbitt, no great mystery about this higher will. It is simply "the higher immediacy that is known in its relation to the lower immediacy—the merely temperamental man with his impressions and emotions and expansive desires—as a power of vital control (*frein vital*)."[35] Exercised within man, it serves as a check on the ordinary or impulsive will of the people.

"The Jeffersonian liberal has faith in the goodness of the natural man, and so tends to overlook the need of a veto power either in the individual or in the State. The liberals of whom I have taken Washington to be the type are less expansive in their attitude towards the natural man. Just as man has a higher self that acts restrictively on his ordinary self, so, they hold, the State should have a higher or permanent self, appropriately embodied in institutions, that should set bounds to its ordinary self as expressed by the popular will at any moment."[36]

This permanent or higher self of the state that is to act as a veto power upon its ordinary self is embodied, according to Babbitt, more than any other institution in the Supreme Court; for it is with the fortunes of the Court, he argues, that "personal liberty and the security of private property . . . are closely bound up."[37] It is liberty, not democracy, justice, not universal suffrage, that are, for Babbitt, the higher ideals; and in his conception of these terms we find fully expressed the authoritarian nature of Babbitt's thought.[38]

"True liberty," he declares, "is not liberty to do what one likes, but liberty to adjust oneself . . . to law." It "involves an inner working with reference to standards, the right subordination, in other words, of man's ordinary will to a higher will." It requires a hierarchy as well as a subordination, for "there must be something central in a state to which final appeal must be made in case of conflict." The greatest, in fact "the only true freedom," says Babbitt, "is freedom to work."

"One is free to work and not to idle. Only when liberty is properly defined according not merely to the degree, but to the quality of one's working, is it possible to achieve a sound definition of justice (To every man according to his works). . . . It is in fact the quality of a man's work that should determine his place in the hierarchy that every civilized society requires." [39]

This recognition, Babbitt argues, is the basis both of genuine liberty and of right (Platonic) justice. To avoid weakening the sense of obligation to these values, he insists, we must abandon our false trust in democracy and return to traditional standards, to a sense of duties rather than rights, to a humanistic discipline. "In the last analysis," Babbitt concludes, "the only check to the evils of an unlimited democracy will be found to be the recognition in some form of the aristocratic principle, . . . the need of standards and discipline." [40]

III

COMMENTARY ON THE PRINCIPLE OF AUTHORITY AS THE BASIS OF A RESTRICTIVE ORDER

There are, it is plain, many resemblances between the Santayana and the Babbitt types of political argumentation, at least in the conclusions that follow from their respective ideas. Both share, for example, a profound faith in aristocracy, the concept of the best. Both believe that political power should rest on the principle of hierarchy and subordination. Both regard democracy as a system of decadence, of domination by the common—and for both, of course, the common is the vulgar and the inferior, not the universal. Both oppose to the alleged disorder of democracy the order of the authoritarian state; both, indeed, stress the paramountcy of this order.

Despite these and other similarities, however, there is one note

of difference that sharply and critically distinguishes the two doctrines. This is the fact that in the one case order is conceived as a
means of fulfillment, of expansion; in the other case it is regarded
as a means of restriction. When, to take an extreme comparison,
Mussolini argues for order, he has in mind an order which allows
for exuberant adventures on the part of the elite. When, to return
to the comparison at hand, Santayana argues for order, he thinks
of it as the basis of all the pleasurable higher joys in man; he
enjoys the amenities of fine living and wants to assure his continued
satisfaction in them. But when Babbitt argues for order, there is
no exuberance, no joy; there is only sobriety and restraint. His
concern is with the factor of tidiness, with the maintenance of the
status quo, and in his endeavor to secure these he tends to find
almost a virtue in restriction as such. His is that variety of puritanism which, in the words of Ralph Barton Perry,

"consists of a narrow preoccupation with morality, to the exclusion
of the graciousness and the beauty of life; a pharisaical emphasis
on the letter of the rule at the expense of its spirit; evil imagination,
prudishness, and canting humility; a hard repression of all spon-
taneities and natural impulses . . . a morbid habit of introspection;
censoriousness; hardness, intolerance, and an aversion to joy,
especially the joy of other people; obsequious submission to a cruel
and despotic God [or supernatural higher self], and through preoccupation with the moral law a neglect of those aspects which
nature and the universe present to the senses, the affections, and
the reason." [41]

His, in short, is an ethical, indeed political, puritanism which
promises only fewer joys of things to come.[42]

Here we see the central facet of Babbitt's thought. He pro-
pounds, with the other authoritarian theorists, the vague yet fundamental charge that democracy fails to maintain authority and order,
that democracy, because it permits a challenge to the assumption of
superiority, makes it impossible for authority to maintain itself. But
he is primarily concerned with a special kind of authority, an
authority that will serve as the basis of a restrictive, puritanical
order. He wants not merely order but a special kind of order, not

merely authority but a special kind of authority. And here, in this very distinction that he makes so vital—the distinction between authority and restrictive authority—we find the key that exposes the invalidity of his more general charge, that democracy is incompatible with authority itself.

For authority is not one but several. It is not something peculiar to oligarchy or even, in fact, to forms of government. It pervades every sphere of social life and every manner of social organization. It is found in the groups that form among boys in the street and in the groups that vie for political and economic power. It exists in the churches and in the schools, in business and in the arts. And it is in democracy as it is in dictatorship. Authority exists everywhere and for many purposes. It regulates the sale of drink and of drugs and the movement of vehicular traffic. It compels unwilling parents to send their children to school and taxes recalcitrant citizens for funds to make the school possible. And it achieves, through its regulation of the more important external relationships of men in society, through the granting of liberties and the imposition of restraints, what it is the primary business of every state to achieve— a system of order and control.

Authority exists, moreover, in many forms, and as there are many types of authority so there are many corresponding types of order that authority sustains. One would be hard pressed, indeed, to uncover a state lacking in some kind of authority and some kind of order, for these are the very bone and marrow of every politically organized community. Under certain circumstances, it is true, as in periods of crisis or collapse, authority may indeed be lacking; but this is a condition common to all types of government and to all forms of state. It is a possibility inherent in the very concept of government, democratic and authoritarian alike, and is therefore not a criterion of discrimination. Without order and authority operating in the normal course of events, no state could survive. And without that order and authority peculiarly congenial to its special form, neither dictatorship nor democracy could survive.[43]

When Babbitt argues, therefore, that democracy is a denial of authority, that Rousseau—who was for Babbitt the very incarnation of democracy—"headed the most powerful insurrection the world has ever known *against every kind of authority*," [44] he misconstrues the nature of democracy as he misconstrues the thought of Rousseau. Democracy no less than other forms of state rests upon the principle of authority, and as we have just seen inevitably so. And Rousseau, far from denying the principle of authority, was so determined to secure it that, along with his doctrine of democracy, he developed in his theory of the general will a doctrine that is in a very real and profound sense parent to modern totalitarian theories.[45] Every state, including the democratic state, has an order and an authority that sustains it; and every political theorist, including the brilliant if perverse Rousseau, builds a theory that creates an order and rests upon an authority. Without that order, without that authority, there could be neither a state nor an intelligible theory of the state.

We come, then, to the real issue in the case. This is the charge, not that democracy fails to maintain authority, but that it fails to maintain Babbitt's particular kind of authority—authority as the basis of a restrictive, puritanical order. To this latter construct, however, at least three crucial objections can and should be made. In the first place, it presupposes not only the existence of men qualified to prescribe that particular order; it assumes the existence of a state that will give these men the power to establish and maintain that order. Now everybody might agree that the most qualified *should* rule, if we take *should* as an ideal, an ethical principle. But if we condemn democracy we imply that another practicable system embodies the ideal, the "authority," that democracy rejects, that another practicable system selects these men and elevates them to positions of power. This, however, Babbitt nowhere demonstrates. Nor, if our analysis to this point is to have any meaning, could he possibly do so. As a result, Babbitt (like the "aristocratic" theorists) is simply talking in the air without reference to political realities. Indeed, he is constantly making false assumptions as to what those realities are.

In the second place, not everyone shares Babbitt's affection for the restrictive way of life. It is one thing to argue for a form of state in which each individual is left relatively free to follow the restrictive *or any other* way of life. This, the pattern of democracy, removes from the purview of state regimentation the broad individual pursuits of men. It allows each individual to select and to follow that particular path he deems most noble or most wise. whether it be a restrictive or an expansive path. It denies to no man the right to adhere to his particular moral code, to his sense of standards, to his revered traditions. It is a way of life that tolerates, constitutionally, every way of life. It is, to revert to our discussion in the previous chapter, a principle of government in which unity is attained through the free play of diversity.

It is quite another thing, however, to argue, as Babbitt does, for a form of state in which no individual is left free but in which all must conform to a prescribed pattern of existence. This, whatever the form it takes, has consequences of the direst nature. It stifles individual initiative. It frustrates the development of individual personality. It strait-jackets the community into narrow and unalterable channels of endeavor. It makes permanent and universal values and standards that are normally temporary and personal. And it does all these things, in Babbitt's particular construction, for a way of life the virtues of which are almost purely negative. Gone are the zest and the joy in living, gone the idle pleasures of play and lilting song. Now the age of piety is forced upon us. Now one is compelled to regard with full and unabated severity his place and his duties in the world. Now one can only say, as John Winthrop said: "I must keepe a better watch over my heart, & keepe my thoughts close to good things, & not suffer a vaine or worldly thought to enter, . . . least it drawe the heart to delight in it."[46] This is the authority of the restrictive way of life. This is the concept of order based on the principle of uniformity, on the denial of differences and of the right of the individual to pursue an alternative path, to pursue, above all, the path of expansiveness.

Here we come to the third crucial objection to Babbitt's argument. According to his doctrine, man should not have, because he does not require, a choice of values. Since the true way is already delineated, it is neither necessary nor desirable to look for another. It is not man's right to select; it is simply his duty to follow.[47] But for so drastic a regimentation of the human mind, for so severe an authority as to refuse to the individual the right to follow any but the prescribed way of life, there can, it is clear, be none but the highest justification. And it is this justification that the democrat rejects, arguing in his turn the lack of any infallible assurance that the restrictive way is the true, the necessary, or even the best way of life.

If, for example, authority sustains the order, the way of life, that Babbitt portrays, the question emerges: whose authority, by whom and for what? Not, surely, by the people, for they, in Babbitt's view, are but "the inert and unorganized mass." Nor can it be for purposes of democracy, or of pleasure, or of opportunity for all, or for that ideal known as social justice. These, according to Babbitt, are the wrong purposes. They are wrong because democracies are, as Mirabeau said, "more the slaves of their passions than the most absolute autocracies"; because it is not pleasure but work that defines happiness; because opportunity is excellent only if it means "that everybody is to have a chance to measure up to high standards"; and because "every form of social justice . . . undermines moral standards." [48] No, for Babbitt the answer to the questions, "by whom and for what?" is to be found in two words: "leadership" and "order," this order, of course, being the restrictive order based on puritanical standards. It is on the quality of the leadership, he argues, that everything ultimately depends; and where that leadership has a true allegiance to standards, "a right feeling for the past," it is the proper possessor of authority.[49]

In these terms, Babbitt holds, the restrictive order is the right and best order because it is in accord with the dictates of right leadership —the right man, the right class, the right principle. And it is the right and the best way because it is equally in accord with the right purpose—adherence to right standards and the right tradition. In both these cases, it is important to add, the authority and order envisaged find their center and their justification not in the many but in the few, not in the whole of the community but in a small minority thereof.

These postulates, it seems hardly necessary to add, the democratic theory denies. It is not merely that democracy is concerned with all rather than with only a part of the people. It is equally the fact that, in the democratic view, no leadership, not even the "right" leadership, can be presumed permanently to possess and to enunciate final truth; and no exclusive order, not even an order based on the "right" standards, can be held universally and eternally to embrace the right way of life. Democracy, to be sure, recognizes and employs the fact of leadership, but it does not attempt to institutionalize a particular leadership as the right and permanent leadership. Nor does democracy seek to impose on all the order and the standards of a few. It endeavors instead to assure the conditions on the basis of which a variety of standards may survive. Democracy denies neither leadership nor order nor standards; it merely refuses to make absolute and totalitarian any particular one. Here is the issue joined. Here is the core of the doctrinal conflict, the age-old struggle, in a political form, between absolutism and relativism. And to see the invalidity of Babbitt's absolutist position we have only to consider the nature and the implications of his two supporting doctrines: the theory of the "right" leadership and the theory of the "right" order.

A. THE THEORY OF THE "RIGHT" LEADERSHIP

The effectiveness of Babbitt's argument here lies in the simplicity of its construction. Each man, Babbitt holds, is torn within himself. On the one hand he is tempted to unimaginative, "common" action by the natural impulses of his lower self. On the other hand he is driven by the inner check, the *frein vital*, to control those baser inclinations in the greater service of his higher self. It is a test of man's capacity to discipline himself, and he who emerges from this test with full command of his higher faculties, with a firm grasp of and allegiance to the right standards, is, for Babbitt, the right man, the man fit for leadership. Since only a few will so emerge, these few comprise—by the very fact that they have shown themselves "capable of the more difficult stages of self-conquest" [50]—the small minority that is the right class, the class fit for leadership. And it is the distinguishing characteristic, indeed the virtue, of this right man and this right class that they act in subservience to the right principle, the dictates of the higher will. Thus we have, in Babbitt's view, the components of right leadership, that leadership to which alone should be entrusted the destinies of the state.

The simplicity that renders this interpretation so facile, however, is its own undoing; for it ignores in the process a variety of complicating factors that conclusively establishes its invalidity. Consider, for example, this concept of the right man. We are not dealing now, to be sure, with the charisma of the totalitarian leader, though in Babbitt's insistence on the principles of inner determination and inner restraint, and on the *duty* of those to whom the right man addresses his mission to recognize him as their qualified leader, we approach dangerously close to this dogma of spiritual belief, this faith or mystery impervious to, as it is outside, the realm of human reason.[51] Nor are we confronted with that mystical identity of the leader with God, an identity which at once both asserts and denies the existence of God and of the leader.[52] What we have here is the concept of a leader who is right in policy because he is right in character, and who should therefore be politically unaccountable to the people, who are wrong.

Foregoing for the moment the problem of right character, we see at once the plain truth that no man, not even the man of right character, can always be right in policy. No man is infallible and man in power least of all. History, depending on which textbooks one reads, teaches many things, but if there is any one universal lesson that can be derived from the record of the past it is this: that power, as Lord Acton said, corrupts, and absolute power corrupts absolutely. No one has put this more emphatically than Mill:

"The moment a man, or a class of men, find themselves with power in their hands, the man's individual interest, or the class's separate interest, acquires an entirely new degree of importance in their eyes. Finding themselves worshipped by others, they become worshippers of themselves, and think themselves entitled to be counted at a hundred times the value of other people; while the facility they acquire of doing as they like without regard to consequences insensibly weakens the habits which make men look forward even to such consequences as affect themselves. This is the meaning of the universal tradition, grounded on universal experience, of men's being corrupted by power." [53]

If, then, no man is infallible, and man in power is particularly prone to corruption, who or what is there to correct or redress the right man's lapse into error? Not, in these terms, another man, for who can be more right than the right man? Nor can it be a power or a will outside the right man, for this would shift the locus of authority to a source outside its proper place. No, in the theory of the right man there can be no one beyond the right man. Nor, even, can there be a thing within man, what Babbitt calls "law for man"; for, whatever be the nature of this thing or law or other self, it has already, by the very fact of its error, established its inability rightly to control man. More than that, such a thing or law or other self must, if it is to move out of the realm of abstraction into the world of reality, be expressed through the person, through the activities, of a particular man. So once again we are confined by the logic of the doctrine to the limits of the individual man. There can be no organized authority to appeal to, no agency of correction. And the internal authority has proved, by its misdeeds, its incapacity. Yet the trust, for Babbitt, is completely in the right man. Should the right man prove to be wrong the world has no alternative but to sit, to suffer, and perhaps to pray for his enlightenment. Such a concept of political irresponsibility democracy wisely and most properly rejects.

Much the same considerations apply to the concept of the right class. Just as it is easy to refuse to ascribe infallibility to others once we are persuaded of our own fallibility, so it is easy to see why no single class in the community can with justice claim infallibility for itself. And just as the concept of the right man wrongly permits no appeal to an authority outside that right man, so the concept of the right class wrongly excludes correction from sources outside itself. Both concepts, moreover, assume in these terms not only infallibility and absolutism but possession of or capacity to recognize and accept all present and future truths, an assumption as alien to the reason and the experience of mankind as it is necessary to the maintenance of the authoritarian claim.

To these considerations we may add a further reflection that even more incisively exposes the invalidity of Babbitt's argument. This is the realization that Babbitt's interpretation of the right class rests on a division of classes dichotomized by the presence or absence of, or, more accurately, adherence or non-adherence to, the higher will. It postulates a class theory of the state in which the ruling class is or, more precisely, ought to be—since it nowhere *is* (and indeed, in the absence of a practicable alternative to democracy, cannot come to be)—that class made up of an aggregate of right men. Now such an interpretation might conceivably have some validity in the construction of a utopia, but in the real world it can have none; for in the real world classes rest not on some mystical abstraction such as the higher will but on the more immediate and pervasive factor of like and unlike interests. Men come together for purposes of collective action and association because they want, broadly speaking, the same things. And there is no historical or contemporary evidence that interest and character inexorably coincide. Indeed, what evidence we have overwhelmingly attests to the very opposite: that men of character, even of Babbitt's "right" character, differ in interests and in class alignments.

Take, for example, the composition of Babbitt's ruling class. He defines it, strikingly, only by such vague and indecisive phrases as "that small minority"; "the saving remnant"; "the class of character," and the like. Nowhere does he actually venture to identify these abstractions. He evinces a deep respect for men of wealth and of property and would have us believe, apparently, that these comprise his favored class.[54] But nowhere, again, does he show that only those who have wealth and property have the right character, and that all who have the right character have wealth and property. Nor does he take into account the differences and the conflicts that prevail between men of wealth or between men of property. Nor, further, does he consider what these differences strongly indicate: that where men of character possess diverse values, even the strictest compliance with the dictates of the higher will cannot assure unity of action but will elicit a variety of response. Since the higher will is only a negative will, a will to refrain, men will refrain from doing only what their particular values reject as undesirable; and where values differ, notions of undesirability are bound to differ. The class existence and the class cohesiveness that Babbitt assumes, in consequence, can only be maintained if one is prepared to ignore the logical and practical considerations that render it meaningless.

These reflections make plain the tautological nature of Babbitt's argument up to this point. He argues that government should be in the hands of a man or class with the right character. But if no objective test exists to determine the innate quality of "rightness" on which his theory rests, then the logic of his argument leads merely to this: that the "right" man or class is that man or class which follows the "right" policies; and the "right" policies can only be followed by the "right" man or class. All of which, it seems hardly necessary to add, is an example of circular reasoning that leaves us completely in the dark.

We come, then, to the third concept on which hinges the theory of right leadership. This is the doctrine of the right principle, the idea, in Babbitt's construction, that where men act in accordance with their higher selves they are truly acting in the interests of right justice. Here we have Babbitt's substitute for the Hegelian ideal and the theocratic absolute. He accepts, with Hegel, the idea that the higher self is contained in the state, but he finds the locus of this higher self of the state not, as Hegel does, in a monarch, but in a judicial aristocracy, the Supreme Court.

Now to postulate that the state has a higher self is to advance the thoroughly discredited theory that the state is an organism, a mystical body that has a unity and a purpose and indeed a mind of its own. It is to describe an aggregate of bodies as a body and an aggregate of minds as a mind, just as one might describe an aggregate of trees as a tree or an aggregate of stars as a star. It is to visualize what a noted philosopher has called a "communal ghost," [55] and it is to endow this metaphysical abstraction with human attributes, even, as Bluntschli did, with sex.[56] It is to make an association into a person, a collective person whose mind and self are held to act independently of the individuals who comprise it. It is to equate this person with the whole of society, identifying the state with the community and leaving no room for the individual outside the orbit of the state. The individual becomes simply an ingredient, a means to the end that is the state. And the state is conceived as a mystical totality acting in the best interests of all.[57]

This, however, is as fanciful a doctrine as it is ingenious. The state is far less mysterious than this construction would have us believe. If it can be held to have a will, it is never more than the dominating will, the will of those who at any one time control the government. It is not a universal will; it is always a particular will, of one or of some who momentarily rule. Nor can we admit the complete absorption of the individual into the state. Man is always a member of a plurality of associations, not merely of the great political association that is the state. And as a member of many associations he seeks and finds values in realms outside as well as within the state. Thus the state, far from being the end for which he exists, is but an instrument itself, and by no means the only instrument, through which the individual may secure his particular goals. The state can never be morally absolute; it can never be the highest authority, the final end. There is always the individual, who is not merely the highest but in fact the only possible ideal. In him alone reside the values that make life meaningful.[58]

These considerations help us to see the invalidity of Babbitt's further localization of this higher self of the state in the Supreme Court, that body which a recent conservative writer has in somewhat similar vein called "the Conscience of Americanism." [59] In the first place, if the Court is the incarnation of the higher self, how can the Court itself divide? Plainly some of the justices in this event are not acting in conformity with the dictates of the higher will, and the question immediately emerges—and remains unanswered—whether it is the majority or the minority of the Court that is thus derelict. In the second place, how can the Court as the true embodiment of the higher self reverse an earlier decision? If the earlier ruling is wrong, the Court obviously had not then acted in accordance with the higher will. If the ruling now is wrong, the present Court is acting in defiance of the higher will. One of the two possibilities must apply. If, in either case, the fault is held to be in the judges, then clearly the Court cannot be the right expression of the higher self, for then it includes men lacking in the right character. If, on the other hand, the fault is not in the judges but somewhere outside them, then the communal ghost is not paying strict attention to its duty. However we approach it, the inconsistencies of judicial behavior lend no credence to Babbitt's deification of the Court as a higher self.[60]

Reflections such as these make plain the primary difficulty involved in this concept of a mystical higher self, and that is the logical as well as the practical impossibility of locating or even identifying it. It is not, as we have seen, in the right man or the right class or the right abstraction, state or Supreme Court. Can it then be in the individual, every individual, as an operating principle for each man to employ? According to Babbitt's argument it is, but only a very few are held to employ it. This, however, merely returns us to the central question: Who is to recognize the man who acts in accordance with his higher will? Almost every man has standards, a moral code, of one kind or another, and almost every man at some time in his life refuses to pursue a course of action or do a certain thing because it violates his own sense of justice or of honor. Does he then become a right man, only to cease being so when at another time he ignores that code? If so, rightness is a relative matter, both to the individual and to the situation of the moment. For Babbitt, however, this is not enough. He can be the right man only if he adheres to the right standards. But Babbitt fails to tell us how these right standards are to be discovered.

If they are to be discovered merely by the application of the inner check, then, as T. S. Eliot himself observed, "there is nothing left for the individual to check himself but by his own private notions and his judgments, which is pretty precarious." [61] If, on the other hand, they are to be discovered through enthusiasm rather than reason, intuition rather than historical convention,[62] then not only do we move into the realm of mysticism but we proceed illogically from the consequent to the antecedent—arguing, in these terms, that where the results happen to coincide with the particular standards of one's conception of the higher self, then self-control, intuition, enthusiasm, or the like has been exercised.

To these thoughts should be added the further observation that an analysis of the various theories based on the idea of a true self has led but "to a number of irreducible and contradictory conceptions of self, each of which has claims to existential validity for itself and for itself alone." [63] Thus we have a situation in which there are not one but many authorities, each affirming itself to be the only true self. From this welter of confusion only unquestioning faith, not reason, can extricate a particular self as the true self. And this, as one of Babbitt's disciples admits, is the ultimate recourse of the humanist: the identity of faith with truth.[64]

In the light of the foregoing considerations it is clear that the authoritarian theory of a "right" leadership cannot be sustained. Truth and justice are a monopoly of no one man, no one class, no one principle. To invest any one of these with absolute power, therefore, is to deny man's only safeguard against tyranny, the right and the power of appeal to a greater authority, the people.

B. THE THEORY OF THE "RIGHT" ORDER

It is a necessary implication of our argument to this point that a particular order cannot be justified as the right order simply on the ground that it accords with the right will of the right leadership, for if there is no right leadership there can be no such right will. Can it then be justified on the ground that it accords with the right purpose? Only, it is clear, if we can agree on who shall determine that purpose. But here we run into the patent difficulty that no such agreement can be secured. The authoritarian insistence that some one segment of the population shall permanently make that determination obviously cannot, as it should not, obtain the acquiescence of all. Nor have the authoritarian theorists themselves been able to agree on the particulars of that determination. Thus the doctrine, once again, cannot stand. It is Babbitt's view, however, that the right order justifies itself not merely in terms of its proper sanction but in the very fact that it is an *order*; that it, unlike democracy, maintains inviolate the principle of authority; and that it is, beyond this, a restrictive order, loyal to those eternal truths and values of the Puritan ethic.

Now if order as such were the only or paramount end of living, there would be an element of validity in this construction. But at least from the time that Locke opposed to this narrow Hobbesian concept of mere order the demand for a decent order, men have perceived the insufficiency of order for order's sake. Order, and the authority which sustains that order, is always a means to some other end, never the end itself. Otherwise men could not object to life in a prison, or in a slave gang, or in the modern totalitarian state. These have order, yet we scorn to imitate them in our daily living; for we perceive that certain conditions of order may also be conditions of servitude. We seek not simply law and order but, even as Babbitt, a kind of law and order that will enable us to lead a happy and satisfying life. We seek an order that will respect, not use or exploit men. We seek an order that will minimize the hazards of life and maximize the conditions for the development of the human personality. We seek an order that will in some way reflect the community's conception of justice, of liberty, and of the common weal. We seek not the whip but the helping hand.

To assign to government, in these terms, merely the negative task of suppression, of restraint, is surely the most shallow and ignoble of political ideals, and for three cardinal reasons. It leaves unanswered the purposes for which that order, that system of control, is to be imposed. It ignores the central fact that government is an instrument, not the master, of man, and as such it can and should be employed by him as a positive means to the attainment of his goals. And it fails to realize that the authoritarian state is less, not more, likely to assure the maintenance of that very order and stability it so highly regards.

This last reflection requires a word in comment. We are not concerned here, it should be noted, with the necessary instability of every government, every power-system, in a world of change. Our concern is rather with that special consideration which renders the authoritarian rather than the democratic form of state the more unlikely to endure. This is the authoritarian intolerance of plural allegiances, the refusal on the part of the authoritarian state to permit a diversity of faiths. Here, of course, we have the reaffirmation of the old absolutist position of Thomas Hobbes: that at all times and under all circumstances the citizen must obey the dictates of the state, that unless there is one unified authority there can be no unified allegiance, and that if this exclusive and all-embracive allegiance to the state is broken at any point then at that point social dissolution results.

History, however, has amply belied this view. Men are held together by bonds other than those of the state alone: there is the family, the church, and the variety of social groups into which men form and whose traditions they observe. Men have many loyalties and many beliefs, and their refusal to surrender all unto the great Leviathan has not, as the growth and development of the democratic state attests, disrupted their *political* allegiance to the state. Indeed, where men have been free to maintain their separate differences and to pursue their separate loyalties, they have been attached the more strongly to the greater unity which makes this possible. They have accepted, voluntarily and in a law-abiding spirit, that order which leaves them most widely free, that authority which wisely rejects the identification of order with co-ordination, that political rule which conjoins power with consent.

Where, on the other hand, obedience is made a function of command, where discipline and subordination are the core of social order, where loyalty is ordained rather than invited, resentment and rebellion quickly follow. No more politically dangerous practice exists than to keep the future in one's own possession: the frustration of the desires of the many, the indifference to the willing support of the ruled, these heighten rather than assuage the tensions and the instability of the authoritarian state. Where, moreover, those who crave the power and the authority of the coercive state find themselves the subjects rather than the agents of coercion—where, that is to say, the seekers of compulsion find they have (as in Hitler's Germany and in Stalin's Russia and in Franco's Spain they have) established the wrong dictator, the wrong ruling clique, in power—then that unpleasant reality consolidates the opposition and further aggravates the instability of the oligarchy. There is no way to evade this simple yet overwhelming truth: dictation breeds resentment and resentment breeds revolution. Only where government is responsive to the wishes of the people, only where there is a constitutionally recognized mode of appeal beyond the government to the community, only where leadership is recognized as an aspect of fellowship in ideas and ideals rather than the master-slave relationship of autocracy—only where these factors apply, can men hope to secure the stability and the order of the state.[65]

These considerations underscore once again the nature of the real issue at stake. It is not that of order *versus* disorder, of authority *versus* the lack of authority. Both democracy and oligarchy have the one, and even, no doubt, degrees of the other. The issue is that of a choice of orders, and of the basis on which the selected order is founded: whether it is to rest on the principle of consent, on a concept of unity through diversity, or on the principle of command, the concept of unity through uniformity. And here Babbitt leaves no doubt as to the kind of order he projects. His order, his right order, is an order rooted in discipline, in the habituation of all men—and indeed of all children—to those precepts of behavior that accord with the restrictive way of life.[66]

We have already seen some of the dangers inherent in this construction. And we have already noted, in our discussion of the problem of traditional standards, the impossibility of determining which standards are traditional and, where traditional, which are "rightly" traditional. What has been said in this regard of the expansive standards of Santayana applies equally, *mutatis mutandis*, to the restrictive standards of Babbitt. When, moreover, we bear in mind the failure of Babbitt's interpretation to establish either infallibility of sanction or rationality of content, we see that the choice of orders is removed from the ethereal realm of eternal truths to the less intangible and more realistic realm of individual preferences.

Here, it is plain, the order one prefers is peculiarly contingent on one's prejudices no less than on one's reason. If one has had, as for example Santayana has always had, by tradition, upbringing, and philosophical sympathy, an aloofness from the common; and if one has tended to equate this common only with the vulgar, to look upon democracy as the reflection of something untidy and aggressive; and if one has long believed that the wisdom and the good of the universe are contained but in a small minority (always, be it perceived, a minority of which one is himself a part); then clearly it is idle to seek to persuade such a one of the superior virtues of the democratic order. If, on the other hand, one rejects the idea that knowledge and political wisdom have been delegated only to a select and permanent few; and if one conceives of the common not as the vulgar but as the universal, as something fundamental and similar in each and every man; and if, above all, one denies the concept of a state organized solely or primarily for the benefit of a particular few; then clearly it is useless to preach the special virtues of the aristocratic-authoritarian order.

We need not, however, rest our argument simply on this individual choice of values. There is a further and more specific consideration that should be noted, one that goes beyond either and both of these alternatives, one that makes plain the unique reason why the restrictive perhaps more than any other authoritarian order cannot lay legitimate claim to being the right and exclusive order. This is the fact that the restrictive order, while it might create Sparta, can never give us Athens.[67] The humanism of Babbitt, it ought never to be forgotten, is not the humanism of the Renaissance, of men like

Lorenzo Valla and Aeneas Silvius in Italy, Rabelais and Montaigne in France, Colet in England, Erasmus, son of Rotterdam and man of Europe, of these and other great figures who sought to emancipate and enrich life rather than to delimit it. It is instead a humanism that seeks to build the whole man by making him the embodiment only of what was, not what is or what might be. It would put a halt to the earth and dwell only in the shadow of the past. It would stultify not only the ruled but eventually the rulers as well; for without diversity, without challenge, without flow, the ultimate in stability—stagnation—must follow.

This is why discipline, when so emphasized and exaggerated that it ceases to be contained within the society as but an aspect of the social order and becomes instead the containing body itself, is in the authoritarian state no longer discipline but, as Croce said, "a general process of fostering universal stupidity." [68] This is why progress, born, as Laski perceived, "from the selection of variations, not from the preservation of uniformities," [69] in the authoritarian state quickly disappears. This is why, indeed, the restrictive way of life is the very denial of all that life implies, why it enslaves those who profess it no less than those who are ruled by it. This is why the reason that is in man opposes with all its strength an imposition that can mean but death.

IV

DEMOCRACY AND THE PROBLEM OF AUTHORITY

The doctrines of authoritarian thought are too broad and too various ever to be encompassed within the ideology of a particular mind. He who would argue the supremacy of the state as ideal cannot at the same time argue *both* the concept of the leader as Messiah and the concept of the leader as expedient, *both* the rightful rule of the classes of the left and the legitimacy of the claims of the right, *both* the state as abstract principle and the state as the instrument or incarnation of God. Thus no man, least of all Irving Babbitt, can be held to be the embodiment or even the culmination of all authoritarian ideas. What we have in Babbitt, instead, is but a single slant, a particular and in some ways indeed a unique expression, of this general attitude opposed to democracy; he is in no sense the central exponent of authoritarianism. From another point of view, however, Babbitt fittingly concludes our series of expressions of authoritarian thought: not only because his argument affirms a particular and significant aspect of the authoritarian principle, but because (a) it contains strands of several authoritarian doctrines, and (b) it stands forth as a representative example of the necessary coincidence of aristocratic and authoritarian ideas.

This necessary coincidence with the authoritarian principle emphasizes again the peculiar difficulty of the aristocratic theory, namely, that it is a self-negating doctrine. As we have had occasion to point out earlier in this work, every aristocracy is confronted by a simple yet defeating dilemma: if it employs force to maintain itself against the challenge of rebellious subjects, the aristocracy degenerates and ceases to be an aristocracy; if it abstains from force, it is unlikely long to remain in power, in which event it again ceases to be an aristocracy.

Our concern in this chapter has been with those doctrines which seize the authoritarian rather than the suicidal horn of the aristocratic dilemma, as well as with those interpretations which scorn the aristocratic refuge and bluntly espouse the principle of the authoritarian state. According to these concepts the crucial weakness of democracy is its inability to maintain order and authority, and in Babbitt's particular construction a kind of authority that will serve as the basis of a restrictive order. But our analysis has clearly shown the invalidity of this first and more general allegation. Authority is not confined to the oligarchical state any more than it is confined to a form of state at all. It is the sanction for all forms of social power—from the family to the neighborhood club to the great political association that is the state. Wherever there is social organization, there is authority. And wherever there is authority, there is some kind of social order. Thus democracy and oligarchy are both founded on the idea of order and on the principle of authority as the basis of that order. What is different is the kind of order that is maintained and the nature of the authority which sustains it.

In the one case, for example, it is an authority rooted in consensus, in the general and freely given consent of a people to maintain a particular order and a particular way of life. In the other case it is an authority rooted in command, in a system of "subordination, obedience, and silence" imposed and maintained by a rigid application of discipline and might.[70] In the one case it rests on the intelligence and the interest of the people; in the other it deprecates and discourages both. In democracy the authority is derived and is therefore responsible; in oligarchy it is held to exist in its own and therefore irresponsible right, or, where the wielder further dissembles, "by virtue of a natural or intrinsic superiority . . . which entitles him to demand obedience apart from the interest of the subject." [71] In democracy, again, it is held the business of the government not only to maintain laws but equally to change them; in oligarchy, once the desired order is attained, change is no longer the concern of the state. In democracy, to anticipate a point, the reconciliation is that of order with freedom; in oligarchy there is but the master and the slave. These are the distinguishing characteristics of democracy and the authoritarian state; it is not the fact of order and authority itself.

Whether one prefers the features of the democratic order or the features of the authoritarian order is not, at the moment, the issue here. The significant, indeed only, consideration that requires emphasis at this point is that both do have an order and both do have an authority. The error of the authoritarian theorists is to confuse authority with authoritarianism. Authority is a prerequisite of order; it is relevant to democracy and oligarchy alike. Authoritarianism is a particular way—a prescriptive and arbitrary way—of meeting the requirement of authority. Authoritarianism is not a characteristic of the democratic state; but authority always is.[72] Thus the charge of the authoritarian theorists that democracy is undesirable because it alone fails to maintain order and authority cannot stand.

Quite different in many respects is the more specific and, at least in part, more accurate charge leveled by Babbitt. His objection to democracy is the fact that it fails to maintain that particular order he values—a restrictive, puritanical order. (It might be mentioned, parenthetically, that even the expansive order envisaged by a Mussolini or a Santayana is in a very real sense also a restrictive order, for the expansiveness they picture is one limited but to their own aristocracy or elite. For the masses there is still only exclusion and restriction, though not, to be sure, the puritanical restriction of Babbitt.) The accuracy of this charge inheres in the refusal by democracy to institutionalize as a pattern of existence for all the restrictive way of life. But this is no more than a partially valid criticism, as becomes apparent when we bear in mind that democracy does permit this restrictive pattern to be followed by those who would do so. Democracy denies the puritanical way of life to none; it merely refuses to extend it—as a compulsory measure—to all.

Here we have a profound insight into the nature of democracy as well as an important rebuttal to Babbitt's claim. The democratic order, unlike the authoritarian order, does not imply that all truth is known and in the hands of the rulers of the state. Therefore democracy leaves its people most largely free to pursue each in his own way that particular way of life he most values and respects. In these terms the puritan no less than the aesthete, the somber no less than the gay, the religious no less than the agnostic—each is left free to decide and to follow his own special values. Whereas the authoritarian state would secure not only the restrictive way of life for those who want it, but would go beyond this to deny any other way of life for others.

Now this, patently, rests upon a series of assumptions impossible to sustain. It assumes, in the first place, that those who do not prefer the restrictive way of life are ignorant of the truths inherent within us and would, if they but perceived and respected those truths, abandon their own false and peculiar ways. Truth, to be sure, does not depend on majority rule; yet what Jefferson termed "a decent respect for the opinions of mankind," when conjoined with the infinitesimal number of those who have ever perceived in puritanism the incarnation of all final and absolute truths, should warrant at the very least a reserve of doubt that the incarnation has taken place, and in the manner indicated. To this should be added the reflection that what we are here dealing with is not so much truth as values, individual preferences, which are no more reducible to logical argumentation than one's liking for chocolate as compared with strawberry ice cream.

The argument assumes, in the second place, that there is, however, a superior and even infallible warrant for the restrictive way of life in that it is sanctioned by the right leadership and the right purpose. But the theory of the right leadership, as we have seen, whether approached from the viewpoint of the right man, the right class, or the right principle, is a mystical rather than a rational conception, alien not only to the reason but equally to the experience of mankind. And to invoke the theory of a right purpose or order is to beg the question at issue by assuming at the start the very conclusion to be proved. So that the restrictive order can in no way lay legitimate claim to being the only true and just order or way of life. Babbitt's particular objection to democracy, then, must, equally with the more general authoritarian objection, be set aside.

Before concluding this discussion of the authoritarian concept, however, we must return to a point previously mentioned, and one that can never be stressed too strongly: this is the democratic endeavor to unite order with freedom. The reconciliation of these aspects of man's being has long, if not always, been the most delicate and difficult of the several tasks of state, and it is hard indeed to conceive of a task more fundamental and important to man; for how this question is resolved will determine the very nature of man's existence on earth. The authoritarian state resolves this problem simply enough—by cutting out half of it. We are given order but not freedom, authority but not the right to challenge it, control but not the voice to share in the formulation of the purposes for which that control is to be exercised.

The democratic state, on the other hand, attempts to assure both. It begins with the premise that order and freedom are not necessarily opposed one to the other but may be and indeed are complementary halves in the service of a greater whole: the welfare and the happiness of the community of man. It reduces order, accordingly, to a system of orders, a variety of patterns in which individual behavior follows no universally prescribed course. In this sense democracy may, perhaps, be held to be an absolute too; but it is an absolute only in its insistence that no one exclusive order can be absolute, that the most just order is that which tolerates many orders. And it reduces liberty to a system of liberties and restraints, trusting to the wisdom and the justice of the community to determine which particular liberties shall be restrained so that others may be free. The only liberty democracy makes absolute and inviolate here is the liberty of opinion, the freedom of men to hold and to profess their several opinions and faiths so that truth, as Justice Holmes said, may be left to the free competition of the market.

In this conjunction of order with freedom democracy most sharply breaks with all oligarchical governments, and in this conjunction democracy most completely commends itself both to the reason and the hearts of men.[73]

Conclusion

We have now seen why the various and successive attacks on democracy have failed to validate themselves. Here only one thing more needs to be said. This is that democracy, alone of the forms of state, provides the necessary mechanism for its own correction. Since men are fallible and problems many and diverse, judgments are bound at times to be erroneous. Since the exercise of power is dangerous and the possession of power corrupts, abuses are certain to follow. These are consequences common to all government, democratic and oligarchic alike. But in the one case there is no recourse short of revolution. In the other there is the constant and free play of critical opinion which, not at the grace of the ruler but as an indispensable constitutional device, shapes *and is free to correct* the policies of the state, installs *and is able to remove* the temporary governors of men. In this way men become not the tools of others but the masters of themselves. What they think and say and do matters, and matters profoundly. It is not, as in oligarchy, cause for suppression or neglect. In this way the unhampered organization of conflicting ideas, far from weakening the democratic state, strengthens it; for it ensures that each man is given both the opportunity to influence the making of decisions and the freedom to press for their recall, a freedom which enlists rather than rebuffs the sentiments and loyalties of men.

In oligarchy there are two cities: the city of the rulers and the city of the ruled. But the rulers may be ignoble and the rulers may err. Yet the city of the ruled stays ruled. In democracy the line between the cities is never completely drawn: who rules today may be ruled tomorrow; who is ruled now yet leaves his impress on the policies of the state. Here is the essence of the democratic achievement, here the failure of the anti-democratic promise.

NOTES

CHAPTER 1

1. Albert Weisbord, *The Conquest of Power* (New York, 1937), I, 15.
2. Gerhard Leibholz, "The Nature and Various Forms of Democracy," *Social Research,* V (1928), 91.
3. Arthur Rosenberg, *Democracy and Socialism* (trans. Rosen, New York, 1939), p. 355.
4. Here we see why such definitions of democracy as identify it with a particular purpose (e.g., M. J. Adler and Walter Farrell, "The Theory of Democracy," *The Thomist,* III [1941], 422), or a particular institutional form (e.g., G. D. H. Cole, *Social Theory* [New York, 1920], chap. vi), or which relate it to certain spiritual attributes (e.g., Thomas Mann, *The Coming Victory of Democracy* [New York, 1938], pp. 17–19), or which speak of it in such abstruse terms as "the government of all by all for the benefit of all" (e.g., N. M. Butler, *True and False Democracy* [New York, 1940 ed.], p. xi), serve only to confuse rather than to clarify our understanding of the term. For an analysis of similar and other inaccurate or inconclusive definitions, see R. M. MacIver, *Leviathan and the People* (Louisiana State University Press, 1939), pp. 63–70 and 142–68.
5. MacIver, *The Web of Government* (New York, 1947), p. 198.
6. Cf. *ibid.,* pp. 192 ff., and the same author's *Community* (2d ed., London, 1920), pp. 28–38, 232–37, 421–29.
7. Hermann Rauschning, *The Revolution of Nihilism* (trans. Dickes, New York, 1939).

CHAPTER 2

1. *The Prince* (trans. Marriott, Everyman's ed., 1908), chap. xv, p. 121.
2. Robert Michels, *Political Parties* (trans. Paul, New York, 1915), pp. 32, 205, 390, 400; and see his later article, "Some Reflections on the Sociological Character of Political Parties," *American Political Science Review,* XXI (1927), 761.
3. Gaetano Mosca, *The Ruling Class* (ed. Livingston, New York, 1939), especially chaps. ii, xii, xv, and xvi.
4. Vilfredo Pareto, *The Mind and Society* (ed. Livingston, New York, 1935), IV, chap. xii.
5. See his *Contribution to the Critique of Political Economy* (trans. Stone, New York, 1904), pp. 11–12.

6. A. F. Bentley, *The Process of Government* (Chicago, 1908), chap. ii and pp. 452–58.

7. Cf. P. A. Sorokin, *Contemporary Sociological Theories* (New York, 1928), p. 28 note 52 and p. 644.

8. *The Process of Government*, pp. 314, 455–57.

9. F. R. Kent, *The Great Game of Politics* (New York, 1924), pp. 322, 320, 182. It is important to emphasize that the organizational argument described here reflects only the thesis of this one book, not, for example, that of his later work, *Political Behavior* (New York, 1928), which rests predominantly on a psychological interpretation.

10. *The Great Game of Politics*, pp. 321, 72.

11. The role of pressure groups in a democracy, for example, is an obvious instance in point. See further R. M. MacIver, *The Modern State* (London, 1926), pp. 197–99.

12. *The Passing of Politics* (New York, 1924), p. 7.

13. *The Managerial Revolution* (New York, 1941).

14. *The Passing of Politics*, p. 24.

15. The anti-democratic argument is elaborated, with considerable rhetorical deviation, in Burnham's article, "Is Democracy Possible?" in *Whose Revolution?* (ed. Talmadge, New York, 1941), pp. 187–217. The argument for the managerial society is summarily restated in "The Theory of the Managerial Revolution," *Partisan Review*, VIII (1941), 181–97, and "Coming Rulers of the U.S.," *Fortune*, XXIV (November, 1941), 100 ff. Both arguments are treated, the latter with drastic modification, in *The Machiavellians* (New York, 1943). For what is almost a complete reversal of the managerial hypothesis and its several postulates, see his more recent work, *The Struggle for the World* (New York, 1947).

For Burnham's political thought prior to *The Managerial Revolution*, see his pamphlet, *The People's Front* (New York, 1937), where he offers the orthodox Marx-Trotsky interpretation of the state, democracy, and the class struggle; his polemic, "Science and Style," in the appendix to Leon Trotsky, *In Defense of Marxism* (New York, 1942), pp. 187–206, where he qualifies but still accepts those views; and his letter of resignation from the Workers party (May 21, 1940; in *ibid.*, pp. 207–11), where he repudiates Marxism and adopts the theory of the managerial society. In the analysis of Burnham's *Managerial Revolution* to follow herein, relevant passages from his other writings will be appropriately drawn upon.

16. For the doctrines of Waclaw Machajski, see Max Nomad, *Rebels and Renegades* (New York, 1932) and *Apostles of Revolution* (Boston, 1939); also Nomad's article on Machajski in *Encyclopaedia of the Social Sciences*, IX, 654–55, and his essay, "Masters—Old and New," in *The Making of Society* (ed. Calverton, New York, 1937), pp. 882–93. Excerpts from Machajski, who wrote under the pen name of A. Wolski, are available in the Calverton anthology, pp. 427–36.

17. In addition to Marx, Machajski, Nomad, and the authors cited in the remainder of the paragraph in the text, the primary sources of Burnham's

thought are the following: Lucien Laurat, *Marxism and Democracy* (trans. Fitzgerald, London, 1940)—see especially the last sixty pages of this important work, the French edition of which appeared early in 1939; Lawrence Dennis, *The Coming American Fascism* (New York, 1936) and *The Dynamics of War and Revolution* (2d ed., New York, 1940)—see below, chap. iii, note 36, for some illustrations of Burnham's indebtedness to these books; Bruno R., *La Bureaucratization du monde* (Paris, 1939)—see J. M. Fenwick, "The Mysterious Bruno R.," *New International*, XIV (1948), 215–18, and the review by Josef Soudek in *Studies in Philosophy and Social Science*, IX (1941), 338–39, for brief but incisive commentaries; and Lewis Corey, "Marxism Reconsidered," *The Nation*, CL (1940), 245–48, 272–75, 305–7.

18. See particularly *The Engineers and the Price System* (New York, 1921).

19. *Finanzkapital* (Vienna, 1910). For this and other references to Rudolf Hilferding I am indebted to Morris Watnick, whose forthcoming translation of Hilferding's book will make available to American students one of the seminal works of our time.

20. *The Modern Corporation and Private Property* (New York, 1932), especially Part I.

21. *The Managerial Revolution*, pp. 8, 273.

22. *The Machiavellians*, pp. 88, 236. See also *The Managerial Revolution*, p. 119, and his article "Is Democracy Possible?" in Talmadge, *op. cit.*, p. 190.

23. *The Managerial Revolution*, pp. 28, 59.

24. *Ibid.*, p. 63.

25. *Ibid.*, pp. 154–60.

26. *Ibid.*, pp. 166–70 and chap. x.

27. *The Struggle for the World*, p. 10.

28. *The Managerial Revolution*, p. 148 and chap. x.

29. *The Machiavellians*, p. 236. See also his "Is Democracy Possible?" in Talmadge, *op. cit.*, p. 190.

30. *Ibid.*, p. 217.

31. *The Managerial Revolution*, p. 119; *The Machiavellians*, p. 224.

32. *The Managerial Revolution*, p. 162.

33. See his argument in *ibid.*, pp. 283 ff. Note, however, the equally disingenuous argument he employs to uphold the reverse position in *The Struggle for the World*, pp. 144 ff.

34. See Sidney Hook, *The Hero in History* (New York, 1943), especially chaps. vi and x, and David Shub, *Lenin* (Garden City, N. Y., 1948), chaps. ix–xx.

35. See, for various aspects of this argument, F. J. Teggart, *The Processes of History* (New Haven, 1918), chaps. iii and iv; John Dewey, *Freedom and Culture* (New York, 1939), pp. 98 ff.; and M. R. Cohen, *The Meaning of Human History* (La Salle, Ill., 1947).

36. Hook, *op. cit.*, pp. 85 and 92.

37. Cf. *ibid.*, pp. 73–74 and chaps. v and vii; also Bertrand Russell, *Freedom versus Organization, 1814–1914* (New York, 1934), pp. 198–99.

38. For Peirce, see his representative statement on law and chance in the

Collected Papers of Charles Sanders Peirce (ed. Hartshorne and Weiss, Cambridge, 1931), I, 222–23. For Boas, see his *Anthropology and Modern Life* (New York, 1928), pp. 207–11. For Tolstoy, see his famous chapter on Napoleon's dispositions for the battle of Borodino in his *War and Peace* (trans. Maude, New York, 1942), Bk. X, chap. xxvii, pp. 871–74; also his epilogue on chance in *ibid.*, pp. 1253–58.

39. M. R. Cohen, "Causation and its Applicability to History," *Journal of the History of Ideas*, III (1942), 15.

40. See, for example, Karl Mannheim, *Ideology and Utopia* (London, 1936), pp. 74–83; E. P. Cheyney, *Law in History and Other Essays* (New York, 1927), p. 27; Allan Nevins, *The Gateway to History* (Boston, 1938), chap. ix; John Dewey, *The Public and Its Problems* (New York, 1927), p. 6; and MacIver, *Community*, pp. 15–16.

41. *The Managerial Revolution*, pp. 78, 110, 59.

42. See, for example, R. A. Gordon, *Business Leadership in the Large Corporation* (Washington, 1945).

43. Cf. N. W. Chamberlain, *The Union Challenge to Management Control* (New York, 1948), pp. 20 ff.

44. Cf. Gordon, *op. cit.*, pp. 6–7, 255–58, 267, and chap. vi, and T. C. Cochran and W. Miller, *The Age of Enterprise* (New York, 1942), p. 307.

45. *The Managerial Revolution*, p. 97; and see further pp. 126–27.

46. Cf. MacIver, *The Web of Government*, pp. 434–35.

47. See S. B. Mathewson, *Restriction of Output among Unorganized Workers* (New York, 1931). Mathewson's conclusions have been sustained by the further studies of F. J. Roethlisberger and W. J. Dickson, *Management and the Worker* (Cambridge, 1939) and Elton Mayo, *The Human Problems of an Industrial Civilization* (New York, 1933), whose investigations are summarized by G. C. Homans in his report to the National Research Council, *Fatigue of Workers* (New York, 1941), pp. 56–99.

48. See the comments on sabotage in his *Engineers and the Price System*, chap. i and pp. 108 ff., 146–50.

49. William Haber, *Industrial Relations in the Building Industry* (Cambridge, 1930), p. 215.

50. *Ibid.*, pp. 197 and 215.

51. See, for the industries mentioned, the following: Jacob Loft, *The Printing Trades* (New York, 1944); Joel Seidman, *The Needle Trades* (New York, 1942); McAlister Coleman, *Men and Coal* (New York, 1943). For a broad survey see the encyclopaedic *How Collective Bargaining Works* (New York, 1942), and, more pointedly, N. W. Chamberlain, *op. cit.*, especially chap. iv and appendices.

52. Seidman, *op. cit.*, p. 6 and chap. x.

53. *Ibid.*, p. 172.

54. Cf. Jack Barbash, "Ideology and the Unions," *American Economic Review*, XXXIII (1943), 868–76.

55. Cf. N. W. Chamberlain, *op. cit.*, and E. W. Bakke, *Mutual Survival* (New York, 1946).

56. See the summary treatments in R. E. Cushman, *The Independent Regulatory Commission* (New York, 1941); F. P. Hall, *Government and Business* (2d ed., New York, 1939); and M. W. Watkins, *Public Regulation of Competitive Practices in Business Enterprise* (New York, 1940), especially chaps. iv, v, vi, and viii.

57. *The Managerial Revolution,* pp. 150 and 259–60.

58. Aspects of this argument are more fully delineated in the discussion of the managers as a social class (immediately following) and in the discussion of sovereignty (sec. III, D below).

59. Apart from this crucial objection to Burnham's argument, there is a minor yet not unimportant consideration that merits attention here. This is the curious and fallacious way in which Burnham attempts to establish the managers as the dominant economic class by relating to them his twofold criterion of power: control of access to the instruments of production and preferential treatment in the distribution of its products. These two rights, he repeatedly insists, are fundamental to and determinative of the ruling class; yet they are not, he says, equally determinative. The one (preferential treatment) is incidental to the other. (*The Managerial Revolution,* pp. 214, 93–94.) If this is so, the question arises as to why Burnham employs preferential treatment as a central element in his criteria. If control of access is not merely essential but determinative, then those who possess such control have by that very fact the means whereby to assure themselves preference in treatment; while in point of fact no less than in logic those who derive preferential treatment may not themselves have such control.

The explanation of this confusion of power and privilege is suggested if we observe carefully the uses Burnham makes of this factor of preferential treatment. Throughout the book, wherever he is unable clearly to identify his ruling class on the basis of his decisive test—control of access to the instruments of production—he shifts his ground and attempts to identify men as members of the ruling class on the ground that they receive the most of what there is to get, arguing therefrom that since they get the most they must be those who control the instruments that produce the goods from which they get the most. (*Ibid.,* pp. 60 and 159.) But this is an inference based on circular reasoning, a process that permits Burnham to assume the very thing he set out to prove. Such a "demonstration" can be of little value in clarifying the problem of managerial power or control.

60. *Ibid.,* pp. 77 ff. and *passim.*

61. See, for example, Katherine Archibald, *Wartime Shipyard* (Berkeley, 1947), especially pp. 6 and 151–84.

62. Cf. Lionel Robbins, *The Economic Basis of Class Conflict* (London, 1939), pp. 17 ff., and Lewis Corey, *The Unfinished Task* (New York, 1942), pp. 191 and 199–204.

63. See in this connection the important point stressed by Karl Polanyi, *The Great Transformation* (New York, 1944), chap. xiii, that while the social structure may, under certain conditions, affect and indeed determine

the composition and the alignment of classes, that social structure may itself, under other conditions, be altered by the classes within it.

64. See, for example, C. A. Beard, *The Economic Basis of Politics* (New York, 1922).

65. See in particular Rudolf Hilferding, "State Capitalism or Totalitarian State Economy," *Modern Review*, I (1947), 267–69, and "The Modern Totalitarian State," *ibid.*, 597–605; also Gregory Bienstock, S. M. Schwarz, and Aaron Yugow, *Management in Russian Industry and Agriculture* (New York, 1944), especially pp. 8–31 and 152–57, and Julian Towster, *Political Power in the U.S.S.R.* (New York, 1948), especially chaps. viii, xiii, and xiv. This, indeed, is the thesis Burnham himself puts forward in his later work, *The Struggle for the World*, p. 124.

66. Cf. Franz Neumann, *Behemoth* (New York, 1942), especially pp. 288–92 and 385–92.

67. Goering, for example, amassed a huge industrial empire only *after* he had come to political power and was able to employ law and force to effect his economic purposes. Similarly, Lenin was able to dictate economic policy only *after* he had seized the power and machinery of the state, not before. See Kurt Lachman, "The Herman Göring Works," *Social Research*, VIII (1941), 24–40, and Emil Lederer, "Government Control in Russia," in *Government Control of the Economic Order* (ed. Lippincott, Minneapolis, 1935), p. 33. On the politicos as the new ruling class, see Dwight Macdonald, "The Burnhamian Revolution," *Partisan Review*, IX (1942), 76–84.

68. "State Capitalism or Totalitarian State Economy," p. 269.

69. Stammler's key work, his *Wirtschaft und Recht nach der materialistischen Geschichtsauffassung* [Economy and Law According to the Materialistic Conception of History] (Leipzig, 1896), is, unfortunately, not available in an English translation. For restatements of his doctrine, see the appendices in Stammler's *Theory of Justice* (trans. Husik, New York, 1925); also Fritz Berolzheimer, *The World's Legal Philosophies* (trans. Jastrow, New York, 1929), pp. 398 ff., and Rupert Emerson, *State and Sovereignty in Modern Germany* (New Haven, 1928), pp. 160–67.

70. See his *Economic Foundations of Society* (trans. Keasbey, London, 1899), Part III, chap. v.

71. *The Web of Government*, p. 126.

72. Cf. M. M. Laserson, *Russia and the Western World* (New York, 1945), chap. iv.

73. Cf. Roscoe Pound, *Interpretations of Legal History* (Cambridge, 1923), pp. 92–115; J. R. Commons, *Legal Foundations of Capitalism* (New York, 1924); and Walter Sulzbach, " 'Class' and Class Struggle," *Journal of Social Philosophy*, VI (1940), 29.

74. *Anti-Dühring*; quoted with approval by Lenin in his *State and Revolution* (rev. trans., New York, 1932), chap. i, sec. 4. My italics.

75. Cf. Hans Delbrück, *Government and the Will of the People* (trans. MacElwee, New York, 1923), pp. 91–92; Commons, *op. cit.*, pp. 214–19; and MacIver, *The Modern State*, pp. 303–5.

76. See A. C. Flick, *The Decline of the Medieval Church* (London, 1930), especially II, 279–304, 432–53, 466–75; also J. S. Schapiro, *Social Reform and the Reformation* (New York, 1909).

77. See Burnham's recognition of the importance of military power in history in *The Machiavellians*, p. 233, where he cited the "great, perhaps sometimes the decisive, influence" of the military on the social equilibrium, an admission which alone destroys his managerial thesis.

78. *Ibid.*, p. 137.

79. Cf. E. F. M. Durbin, *The Politics of Democratic Socialism* (London, 1940), pp. 175–76, and MacIver, *Social Causation* (Boston, 1942), pp. 113–20.

80. Cf. Reinhold Niebuhr, *The Children of Light and the Children of Darkness* (New York, 1944), pp. 104 and 147, and MacIver, *The Web of Government*, pp. 134–35.

81. *The Managerial Revolution*, pp. 169 and 156–58.

82. *Ibid.*, p. 74.

83. But see A. H. Hansen, "The Technological Interpretation of History," *Quarterly Journal of Economics*, XXXVI (1921), 72–83, in which the Marxian interpretation is held to be not so much economic as it is technological. For a converse view, see MacIver, *Society* (New York, 1937), pp. 444–59, and the same author's *Social Causation*, chap. x.

84. *The Managerial Revolution*, pp. 74–75; also "The Theory of the Managerial Revolution," p. 189.

85. MacIver, *Society*, pp. 451–52.

86. *Ibid.*, p. 452.

87. *Anthropology and Modern Life*, pp. 232–35.

88. Cf. Karl Polanyi, "Our Obsolete Market Mentality," *Commentary*, III (1947), 109–17.

89. *The Machiavellians*, p. 84.

90. It is to be observed that Burnham excludes completely the element of agricultural power, for in modern society, he holds, "the decisive sectors of economy are not agricultural but mercantile, industrial, and financial." (*The Managerial Revolution*, p. 61.) Politically considered, however, the rural element continues, even in modern American society, to be a very real and significant force. See A. N. Holcombe, *The Middle Classes in American Politics* (Cambridge, 1940), pp. 99–104 and 158–93, and P. H. Odegard and E. A. Helms, *American Politics* (2d ed., New York, 1947), pp. 224–45.

91. Cf. Eduard Heimann, "Industrial Society and Democracy," *Social Research*, XII (1945), 43–59, and A. D. Lindsay, *The Modern Democratic State* (London, 1943), pp. 183–90.

92. In *The Machiavellians* (p. 36) Burnham argues that the economic organization of the Italian cities in the medieval period required their expansion to nation-states, yet they failed to take that necessary step. Why? Burnham says it was a matter of choice, and that they chose wrongly. But how could those cities *choose* if economic imperatives alone decide? To this there is no answer. Burnham effects a similar contradiction to his economic determinism

in his article, "Stalin and the Junkers," *Commonweal*, XL (1944), 514, where he argues that the Bolsheviks in 1917 were men who attained power not through the imperatives of economic organization but through "their ideas, their will, and their discipline."

93. Cf. Karl Mannheim, *Diagnosis of Our Time* (New York, 1944), p. 159.

94. Cf. Dewey, *Freedom and Culture*, chap. iv, and Russell, *Power* (New York, 1938), chap. viii.

95. Pp. 163–64 and 171.

96. *Ibid.*, p. 162.

97. For an extreme statement of this view, see his *Machiavellians*, p. 236; and compare Mosca, *op. cit.*, p. 326.

98. *The Machiavellians*, p. 247.

99. *The Managerial Revolution*, p. 163.

100. Hans Speier, "Social Stratification," in *Political and Economic Democracy* (ed. Ascoli and Lehmann, New York, 1937), p. 259.

101. For the classic statement, see F. J. Goodnow, *Politics and Administration* (New York, 1900). For the limits of administrative power in a democracy, see Herman Finer, "Administrative Responsibility in Democratic Government," *Public Administration Review*, I (1941), 335–50, and P. H. Appleby, *Big Democracy* (New York, 1945).

102. See MacIver, *Leviathan and the People*, pp. 68–70, and Léon Blum, *For All Mankind* (trans. Pickles, New York, 1946), pp. 60–63.

103. *The Machiavellians*, p. 145.

104. *The Managerial Revolution*, pp. 169–70.

105. One has but to read the twoscore predictions advanced in *The Managerial Revolution* and *The Machiavellians* to perceive the disastrous nature of Burnham's venture in this regard. It may be enough here to recall his picture of the destruction of the Soviet Union and the British Empire as a consequence of the Second World War, and his description of managerial society triumphant in the United States, with "the 1940 presidential election . . . the last regular presidential election in the history of this country, or, at most, the next to last" (*The Managerial Revolution*, p. 261), to see that history, like man, does not always respond to "iron laws."

106. For an analysis of this aspect of the democratic problem, see Corey, *The Unfinished Task*, especially pp. 204–13 and 303–5.

107. "Some Reflections on the Sociological Character of Political Parties," p. 768.

108. Cf. MacIver, *The Modern State*, p. 425, and the same author's *Society*, pp. 438 ff.

109. "Marxism Reconsidered," p. 247.

110. MacIver, *Society*, pp. 441 and 452.

CHAPTER 3

1. *The Republic*, Bk. I, 338. All references to Plato's writings are to the Jowett translation, *The Dialogues of Plato* (3d ed., Oxford University Press, 1892).

2. Plato, *Gorgias*, 491–92, 483.

3. *Ibid.*, 488. See also the *Protagoras*, 350.

4. Russell, for example, holds that Plato unfairly caricatured and vilified his Sophist adversaries, imputing to them doctrines not at all characteristic of their beliefs. See his *History of Western Philosophy* (New York, 1945), pp. 75, 79.

5. The quotation is from chap. xiv, p. 115.

6. *Leviathan* (ed. of 1651, Oxford, 1929), Part I, chap. xi, p. 75.

7. As in his book, *The Outlines of Sociology* (trans. Moore, Philadelphia, 1899), pp. 116 ff.

8. *The State* (trans. Gitterman, Indianapolis, 1914), pp. 14–15, 68.

9. See *Beyond Good and Evil* (trans. Zimmern) and *The Will to Power* (trans. Ludovici), in *The Complete Works of Friedrich Nietzsche* (ed. Levy, Edinburgh, 1909), Vols. XII, XIV, and XV.

10. *The Decline of the West* (trans. Atkinson, New York, 1926–28), especially II, 452, 507.

11. *Politics* (trans. Dugdale and de Bille, New York, 1916), I, 15–16, 22.

12. *The Philosophical Theory of the State* (London, 1899), chap. vi, p. 152.

13. Pareto, *op. cit.*, IV, secs. 2178, 2179, 2190, 2174, 2183, 2253.

14. Benito Mussolini, *The Political and Social Doctrine of Fascism* (International Conciliation pamphlets, January, 1935, No. 306), p. 9. See also the writings of Il Duce's foremost apologists: Giovanni Gentile, "The Philosophic Basis of Fascism," *Foreign Affairs,* VI (1928), 290–304; and Alfredo Rocco, *The Political Doctrine of Fascism* (International Conciliation pamphlets, October, 1926, No. 223).

15. *Apostles of Revolution*, p. 6.

16. *Pareto's General Sociology* (Cambridge, 1935), pp. 7, 57, 59, 64–69.

17. *The Machiavellians,* especially Part VII.

18. *The Invisible Government* (New York, 1928).

19. *Ibid.*, pp. 33, 45–46.

20. *Ibid.*, pp. 16–17, 47.

21. The main items in Dennis' political writings are his two volumes, *The Coming American Fascism* and *The Dynamics of War and Revolution*. Of his many contributions to periodical literature, the following are of particular relevance: "Fascism for America," *Annals of the American Academy of Political and Social Science,* CLXXX (July, 1935), 62–73; "Portrait of American Fascism," *American Mercury,* XXXVI (1935), 404–13; "The Highly Moral Causes of War," *ibid.*, XXXVIII (1936), 299–310; "The Class War Comes to America," *ibid.*, XLV (1938), 385–93; "After the Peace of Munich," *ibid.*, XLVI (1939), 12–21; and "Can Democracy Put Men Back to Work?" *Current History,* L (1939), 35, 61–62. Reference should also be made to the exchange of letters between Dennis, F. L. Schuman, and Max Lerner, published under the collective title, "Who Owns the Future?" *The Nation,* CLII (1941), 36–44, and the addenda to this exchange in *ibid.*, pp. 111–12; also the exchange between Dennis ("The Dynamics of War and Revolution") and Paul Mattick ("Fascism Made in U. S. A.") in *Living*

Marxism, V (Winter, 1941), 1–36.   See also, for a more restricted economic analysis, Dennis' book, *Is Capitalism Doomed?* (New York, 1932), and for random but revealing insights his joint polemic with Maximilian St. George, *A Trial on Trial* (National Civil Rights Committee, 1946).

22. *Is Capitalism Doomed?* p. vii; *The Dynamics of War and Revolution,* p. viii; "Fascism for America," p. 62.

23. *The Dynamics of War and Revolution,* pp. 23, 25, viii.

24. *The Coming American Fascism,* pp. 226, 244; *The Dynamics of War and Revolution,* p. 186.

25. *The Coming American Fascism,* pp. 226, 233; "The Class War Comes to America," p. 388.

26. *The Dynamics of War and Revolution,* p. 186; *The Coming American Fascism,* p. 140.

27. "The Class War Comes to America," p. 389.

28. *The Coming American Fascism,* pp. 139, 146.

29. *Ibid.,* pp. 147, 299, and *passim; The Dynamics of War and Revolution,* p. xxviii.

30. "Can Democracy Put Men Back to Work?" p. 61; "After the Peace of Munich," p. 21.

31. *A Trial on Trial,* p. 42.

32. *The Coming American Fascism,* pp. 242, 224.

33. *Ibid.,* pp. 242, 239.

34. *Ibid.,* pp. 116, 143–44; see further pp. 122–23 and 213–14.

35. "Fascism for America," pp. 62–63, 72.

36. See, for example, the discussion of managerial supremacy in terms of the technical demands of the process of production (*The Coming American Fascism,* p. 239); the permanence of the new revolution, of ruling class, of war (*The Dynamics of War and Revolution,* p. 245; *The Coming American Fascism,* pp. 244, 142); the identification of Russia as a "dictatorship of management" (*The Coming American Fascism,* p. 10); the technology of unemployment (*The Dynamics of War and Revolution,* pp. 216, 240); the function of ideology and the replacement of "rights" by the "duties" of man (*ibid.,* pp. 245, 250); the end of American democracy and of capitalism in World War II (*ibid.,* pp. 129, 244); the revolution by structural necessity, not human aspiration (*ibid.,* p. ix; *The Coming American Fascism,* p. 209); the dating of the revolution and the revolution as unitary and world-wide (*The Dynamics of War and Revolution,* pp. 135, xxvi–xxvii, 236); the super-states and the dissolution of the British Empire (*ibid.,* pp. 210, 149); and more. But in this respect Dennis, with Burnham, owes an equal indebtedness to Max Nomad and others.

37. "The Dynamics of War and Revolution," *Living Marxism,* p. 31.

38. *The Dynamics of War and Revolution,* p. 125. See also *The Coming American Fascism,* p. 105, where he denies the applicability of absolute and eternal truths.

39. *The Coming American Fascism,* pp. 7, 115, 229, 230–31, 237; *The*

Dynamics of War and Revolution, p. 241; "Portrait of American Fascism," p. 412.

40. *The Coming American Fascism,* p. 224.

41. As M. C. Beardsley has effectively shown. "Mr. Burnham on the Elite," *Journal of Philosophy,* XL (1943), 435–41.

42. "Portrait of American Fascism," p. 412.

43. *The Dynamics of War and Revolution,* p. xxviii.

44. See the survey by F. G. Wilson in *Twentieth Century Political Thought* (ed. Roucek, New York, 1946), pp. 245–59.

45. Cf. Paul Pigors, *Leadership or Domination* (Boston, 1935), pp. 204–6, and C. J. Friedrich, "Oligarchy," *Encyclopaedia of the Social Sciences,* XI, 463–64.

46. Quoted in Russell, *Power,* p. 87.

47. See, for example, the studies of the Zuni by Ruth Benedict, *Patterns of Culture* (New York, 1934), chap. iv, and Irving Goldman, "The Zuni Indians of New Mexico," in *Cooperation and Competition Among Primitive Peoples* (ed. Mead, New York, 1937), chap. x; and the studies of the Arapesh of New Guinea by Margaret Mead in *ibid.,* chap. i, and her *Sex and Temperament in Three Primitive Societies* (New York, 1935), Part I.

48. As argued, for example, by William McDougall, *An Introduction to Social Psychology* (14th ed., Boston, 1921), chap. xi, and A. H. Maslow, "The Rôle of Dominance in the Social and Sexual Behavior of Infra-Human Primates," *Pedagogical Seminary and Journal of Genetic Psychology,* XLVIII (1936), 261–338.

49. See Alfred Adler, *Understanding Human Nature* (trans. Wolfe, New York, 1946), pp. 72–80 and 191 ff., and *The Practice and Theory of Individual Psychology* (trans. Radin, New York, 1932), chap. i. See also John Dollard *et al., Frustration and Aggression* (London, 1944), where the thesis is developed that "aggression is always a consequence of frustration."

50. Cf. Otto Klineberg, *Social Psychology* (New York, 1940), pp. 104 ff. See further Eduard Spranger, *Types of Men* (trans. Pigors, Halle, 1928), Part II, chap. v; G. W. Thomson, *The Grammar of Power* (London, 1924), chap. i; and H. J. Morgenthau, *Scientific Man vs. Power Politics* (Chicago, 1946), pp. 191–203.

51. Georges Sorel, *Reflections on Violence* (trans. Hulme, New York, 1941), p. 168.

52. Pigors, *op. cit.,* pp. 66–67.

53. *Ideas Are Weapons* (New York, 1939), p. 505.

54. E. Y. Melekian, "Nietzsche and the Problem of Democracy," *The Monist,* XLII (1932), 438–39.

55. Berle and Means, *op. cit.,* p. 353.

56. *Politics* (trans. Ellis, Everyman's ed., 1912), Bk. V, chaps. x and xi.

57. From the more significant of these clashing currents three may briefly be noted. First, there is the conflict within man himself. As such diverse figures as Spencer and Kropotkin both made plain, altruism no less than egoism has its place; and it is a simple psychology indeed that would rest the resolu-

tion of this conflict on the mere will to power (egoism) alone. Second, there are the conflicts between the several holders of power: power divided as to kind (political, economic, military, religious, etc.), as to level or grade (national, regional, local; superior, inferior; and the like), and as to form (executive, legislative, judicial, administrative; personal, institutional; and so on). This division or multiplicity of powers not only makes for the concentration—or deconcentration—of will in several centers; it also permits the appeasement of the passion for power in many men without at the same time yielding control of all power to any one or few. Third, there is the crucial question of the direction to be taken by the holders of power: power for what? Men seek power not alone for the sake of power but also because power is the medium through which they hope to secure any one or several of a variety of specific goals, as even so egotistical and glory-impassioned a man as Napoleon made clear. And if power is means as well as end, the will-to-power interpretation can by itself be but a partial one.

For aspects of these problems see C. E. Merriam, *Political Power* (New York, 1934), pp. 231–46, and C. C. Josey, *The Psychological Battlefront of Democracy* (Indianapolis, 1944), pp. 60–72 and chap. iii.

58. Cf. Helen Jennings, "Structure of Leadership—Development and Sphere of Influence," *Sociometry*, I (1937), 99–143, and F. M. Thrasher, *The Gang* (2d ed., Chicago, 1936), chap. xviii.

59. *The Coming American Fascism*, p. 147, and *The Dynamics of War and Revolution*, p. 33.

60. Speech of March 7, 1921. Quoted in W. Y. Elliott, *The Pragmatic Revolt in Politics* (New York, 1928), pp. 340–41.

61. *The Beggar's Opera*, Act. II, sc. i.

62. *The Art of Being Ruled* (New York, 1926), p. 102.

63. *Lectures on the Principles of Political Obligation* (New York, 1924 ed.), sec. 124.

64. John Stuart Mill, *Representative Government* (Everyman's ed., 1910), p. 183.

65. W. H. R. Rivers, *Social Organization* (ed. Perry, London, 1924), chap. ix, and W. I. Thomas, *Primitive Behavior* (New York, 1937), chap. xiv.

66. Cf. MacIver, *The Modern State*, pp. 227–28, and *The Web of Government*, chaps. x and xi.

67. *The Coming American Fascism*, pp. 116–17.

68. Ernest Barker, *Nietzsche and Treitschke* (Oxford pamphlets, 1914), p. 19.

69. Lionel Curtis (ed), *The Commonwealth of Nations* (London, 1916), p. 8.

70. W. R. Inge, *The Philosophy of Plotinus* (3d ed., London, 1929), II, 225.

71. Cf. A. D. Lindsay, *The Essentials of Democracy* (Philadelphia, 1929), pp. 61–63; MacIver, *The Modern State*, p. 151 and Bk. II, chap. vii; and W. E. Hocking, *Man and the State* (New Haven, 1926), chap. v.

72. See Green, *op. cit.*, Lecture G.

73. *The Essentials of Democracy,* p. 62; and see further the same author's *Modern Democratic State,* pp. 197–207.

74. Woodrow Wilson, *The State* (rev. ed., Boston, 1918), pp. 26 ff.

75. Cf. G. E. G. Catlin, *A Study of the Principles of Politics* (New York, 1930), chap. iv, and MacIver, *The Web of Government,* pp. 16–17 and chap. iii.

76. Lippmann, "Why Should the Majority Rule?" *Harper's,* CLII (1926), 403 ff., and Treitschke, *op. cit.,* II, 277–78.

77. Cf. Lindsay, *The Essentials of Democracy,* Lecture IV, and MacIver, *The Modern State,* p. 225.

78. Cf. Merriam, *Political Power,* pp. 180, 220–26.

79. MacIver, *Leviathan and the People,* pp. 27–28.

80. *The Social Contract* (trans. Cole, Everyman's ed., 1913), Bk. I, chap. iii.

81. MacIver, *Community,* p. 323.

82. Cf. MacIver, *The Web of Government,* p. 205.

83. This is the argument put forward, for example, by James Burnham in *The Machiavellians.*

84. T. B. Macaulay, *Machiavelli* (Girard, Kansas, 192–? [reprinted from the *Edinburgh Review* of March, 1827]), p. 54.

85. Quoted in Herbert Butterfield, *The Statecraft of Machiavelli* (London, 1940), pp. 22–23.

CHAPTER 4

1. Polybius, *The Histories* (Loeb ed., New York, 1922–27), Bk. VI, sec. 57.

2. For summary statements of this criticism, see F. W. Coker, *Recent Political Thought* (New York, 1934), pp. 309–14, and F. J. C. Hearnshaw, *Democracy at the Crossways* (London, 1919), pp. 53–68.

3. *Hegel's Philosophy of Right* (trans. Knox, Oxford, 1942), sec. 301, p. 196.

4. *The Decline of the West,* II, 358; and see further pp. 455–64.

5. See his *Institutes of the Christian Religion* (trans. Allen, 7th Amer. ed., Philadelphia, 1936), Bks. I, chap. iv, II, chaps. ii and iii, and IV, chap. xx.

6. See, for example, the contemptuous passages in his *Reflections on the Revolution in France* (Everyman's ed., 1910), pp. 49, 57–58.

7. As in his *Revolt of the Masses* (New York, 1932), pp. 18–19.

8. Gustave Le Bon, *The Crowd* (Eng. trans., London, 1896).

9. Emile Faguet, *The Cult of Incompetence* (trans. Barstow, London, 1911).

10. See, for example, his *Reflections on Violence,* p. 78.

11. See the analysis in B. E. Lippincott, *Victorian Critics of Democracy* (Minneapolis, 1938), pp. 6–53.

12. H. S. Maine, *Popular Government* (5th ed., London, 1897).

13. As in his typical comment to the members of the Constitutional Convention that "the people are turbulent and changing, they seldom judge or determine right." *The Records of the Federal Convention of 1787* (ed. Farrand, New Haven, 1911), I, 299.

14. See his *A Defence of the Constitutions of Government of the United States of America*, III, chap. iii, in *The Works of John Adams* (ed. C. F. Adams, Boston, 1851), VI, 161–216.

15. Most notably in "The Dangers of American Liberty," in the *Works of Fisher Ames* (ed. Seth Ames, Boston, 1854), II.

16. *Ibid.*, p. 394.

17. H. L. Mencken, *Notes on Democracy* (New York, 1926), pp. 101, 21. See further his attack on democracy and the common man in R. R. LaMonte and H. L. Mencken, *Men versus the Man* (New York, 1910), pp. 152 ff.

18. *The Passing of Politics*, p. 271.

19. Harry Atwood, *Back to the Republic* (10th ed., Chicago, 1934), pp. 34, 37.

20. *The Behavior of Crowds* (New York, 1920), chap. ix; *Liberty* (New York, 1930), especially chap. viii; and *The Conflict of the Individual and the Mass in the Modern World* (New York, 1932), pp. 152 and 20 ff.

21. *History and Social Intelligence* (New York, 1926), pp. 574–75 and chap. xix.

22. "Democracy and Heredity—a Reply," *Journal of Heredity*, X (1919), 367.

23. *Memoirs of a Superfluous Man* (New York, 1943), pp. 152, 17, 136–37, 262–63. See further his earlier work, *Our Enemy, the State* (New York, 1935), pp. 148–49.

24. W. W. Willoughby, *The Nature of the State* (New York, 1896), p. 413.

25. J. A. Schumpeter, *Capitalism, Socialism, and Democracy* (New York, 1942), pp. 162, 290–91.

26. See, for example, his *Political Behavior*, pp. 76–80, 148–52, 304–17.

27. *Intelligence in Politics* (New York, 1936), chap. viii.

28. Walter Lippmann, *Public Opinion* (New York, 1922) and *The Phantom Public* (New York, 1925).

29. *The Phantom Public*, pp. 39, 52, 197, 199.

30. From among Cram's many writings, the following are representative and embody the essence of his thought: *The Nemesis of Mediocrity* (Boston, 1917), *Convictions and Controversies* (Boston, 1935), and *The End of Democracy* (Boston, 1937). Perceptive revelations are contained in his autobiographical work, *My Life in Architecture* (Boston, 1936), and there are significant relevant passages in his *The Sins of the Fathers* (Boston, 1919) and *Towards the Great Peace* (Boston, 1922).

31. *My Life in Architecture*, p. 95; *Towards the Great Peace*, pp. 126–27; *The End of Democracy*, p. 14.

32. *The Sins of the Fathers*, p. 45.

33. *The End of Democracy*, pp. 6–7, 212; *The Nemesis of Mediocrity*, p. 46.

34. *Convictions and Controversies*, pp. 148–50, 184.

35. *Ibid.*, p. 192; also p. 196.

36. *My Life in Architecture*, p. 294.

37. *Convictions and Controversies*, pp. 156–57, 175, 149, 161.

38. *Towards the Great Peace,* p. 130.

39. *The Nemesis of Mediocrity,* pp. 30, 21–22, 46.

40. *My Life in Architecture,* p. 296; and cf. his chapter "The Quantitative Standard," in *The Sins of the Fathers.*

41. *The Nemesis of Mediocrity,* pp. 30–35, 46.

42. *Ibid.,* pp. 21–22; *Convictions and Controversies,* p. 161.

43. *The End of Democracy,* p. 35; *Convictions and Controversies,* p. 174.

44. *Towards the Great Peace,* p. 135.

45. *Ibid.,* p. 76; *The End of Democracy,* p. 19.

46. *Convictions and Controversies,* pp. 199–200.

47. *My Life in Architecture,* p. 20. See his proposal in later years that the president be made a lifetime king with the title, "His Highness the Regent of the Republic of the United States: a good title and significant." *The End of Democracy,* p. 187.

48. *The Phantom Public,* pp. 52, 25.

49. *Ibid.,* pp. 185, 61–62.

50. Cf. MacIver, *Leviathan and the People,* pp. 65–66, and Lindsay, *The Essentials of Democracy.*

51. *Convictions and Controversies,* p. 260.

52. See Lippmann, "Why Should the Majority Rule?"

53. *The History of Herodotus* (trans. Rawlinson, Everyman's ed., 1910), Bk. III, chap. lxxxi, p. 251.

54. Cf. MacIver, *Leviathan and the People,* pp. 67–68, and J. W. Hudson, *Why Democracy* (New York, 1936), pp. 159–60.

55. Cf. MacIver, *Leviathan and the People,* p. 150, and the same author's *The Web of Government,* p. 198.

56. The precise relation of democracy to majority rule is a theme that has yet fully to be explored. The denial in absolute terms of democracy as majority rule, as by Dorothy Thompson in her *Essentials of Democracy* (New York, 1938) and Walter Lippmann in his "Why Should the Majority Rule?" is subject to the crucial objection that the only alternative to majority rule is some form of minority rule. On the other hand, the simple equation of democracy with majority rule, as by Edwin Mims, Jr., *The Majority of the People* (New York, 1941), and Max Lerner, "Minority Rule and the Constitutional Tradition," in *The Constitution Reconsidered* (ed. Read, New York, 1938), pp. 199–207, is subject to the equally decisive refutation that majority rule may prevail in even the most dictatorial of governments. A penetrating but somewhat restricted analysis is offered in H. S. Commager, *Majority Rule and Minority Rights* (New York, 1943), and there is a good though brief discussion in MacIver, *Leviathan and the People,* pp. 66–67, 151–53, and *The Web of Government,* pp. 197 ff. See also the comment in Mill, *Representative Government,* chap. vii, pp. 256 ff., and compare the contrasting argument in Hugo Krabbe, *The Modern Idea of the State* (trans. Sabine and Shepard, The Hague, 1922), pp. 72–82.

57. MacIver, *Leviathan and the People,* p. 149.

58. *The Nemesis of Mediocrity,* pp. 23–24.

59. Livingston, in his edition of Mosca, *op. cit.*, p. xxxiv.

60. *The Sins of the Fathers*, pp. 69–70.

61. Raymond Dodge and Eugen Kahn, *The Craving for Superiority* (New Haven, 1931), p. 2.

62. Cf. C. D. Burns, *Democracy* (London, 1935), pp. 244–45 and 76–78.

63. W. R. Inge, *Labels and Libels* (New York, 1929), p. 19.

64. Cf. Dewey, *The Public and Its Problems*, pp. 205–9; L. T. Hobhouse, *Democracy and Reaction* (New York, 1905), pp. 119–21; J. A. Hobson, *Democracy and a Changing Civilisation* (London, 1934), pp. 44–45; Hudson, *op. cit.*, pp. 153–56; and MacIver, *The Modern State*, pp. 208–10.

65. Cf. Arthur Feiler, "Democracy by Class and Occupational Representation," in Ascoli and Lehmann, *op. cit.*, p. 187.

66. M. C. Swabey, *Theory of the Democratic State* (Cambridge, 1937), p. 118.

67. *Towards the Great Peace*, pp. 125-26.

68. Ludwig Bauer, *Leopold the Unloved* (trans. Paul, Boston, 1935), pp. 256, 254. See further E. D. Morel, *The Black Man's Burden* (Manchester, 1920), chap. ix, and other writings by this author.

69. Bernard Moses, *The Spanish Dependencies in South America* (New York, 1914), I, xxv, and *passim;* also Wilhelm Roscher, *The Spanish Colonial System* (ed. Bourne, New York, 1904), especially pp. 22–27, and J. H. Parry, *The Spanish Theory of Empire in the Sixteenth Century* (Cambridge, 1940), especially chap. iv.

70. F. A. Woods, *The Influence of Monarchs* (New York, 1913), pp. 306–403, inadvertently offers a striking evidence that richly sustains the conclusion here.

71. Cf. Cheyney, *op. cit.*, chap. iv.

72. Herbert Spencer, *The Man versus the State* (ed. Beale, New York, 1916). See particularly the commentaries by Butler and Gary.

73. H. S. McKee, *Degenerate Democracy* (New York, 1933), pp. 31 and 77.

74. *The American Individual Enterprise System* (New York, 1946), II, 697.

75. See Munro, *The Invisible Government*, pp. 53–56, and Nock, *Our Enemy, the State*. For the ideas of business leaders and employers' associations, see C. E. Bonnett, *Employers' Associations in the United States* (New York, 1922), and R. A. Brady, *Business as a System of Power* (New York, 1943).

76. Cf. MacIver, *The Modern State*, p. 457.

77. See, for this problem of human costs versus production costs, the work of the welfare school of economists, especially J. A. Hobson, *Work and Wealth* (New York, 1914) and A. C. Pigou, *The Economics of Welfare* (London, 1920); also the latter author's more recent study, *Socialism versus Capitalism* (London, 1939), especially chaps. v and vi.

78. J. M. Clark, "Economics and Modern Psychology," *Journal of Political Economy*, XXVI (1918), 148.

79. Cf. Mannheim, *Diagnosis of Our Time*, pp. 167 and 178.

80. John Thurston, "Government Proprietary Corporations in Great Brit-

ain," in Lippincott, *Government Control of the Economic Order*, pp. 72–73.

81. See, for example, Kemper Simpson, *Big Business, Efficiency and Fascism* (New York, 1941); Miriam Beard, *A History of the Business Man* (New York, 1938), chap. xxvii; and Veblen, *The Engineers and the Price System*, chap. i and pp. 146–50.

82. MacIver, *Leviathan and the People*, p. 150.

83. This recognition alone renders absurd the claim of the dictator that he is above public opinion. At the very moment, indeed, that the totalitarian states assailed the democratic reliance on public opinion, they were themselves most active in attempting to secure public support for their policies. It was no accident that the propaganda function was, as in Nazi Germany, raised to the prominence of a ministry and given a status second, if at all, only to the military or police function. Yet those who were presumed competent to answer through plebiscites the questions put to them were held incompetent to discuss their meaning. See Lindsay Rogers, *Crisis Government* (New York, 1934), p. 44, and Burns, *op. cit.*, pp. 56–57.

84. Cf. Aristotle, *Politics*, Bk. V, chap. ii.

CHAPTER 5

1. Bk. II, 200–201.

2. *Op. cit.*, Bk. III, chap. lxxxi. My italics.

3. See the famous passage on the philosopher-kings in Bk. V, 473.

4. "Aristocracy," *Encyclopaedia of the Social Sciences*, II, 183–90.

5. Max Lerner, *It Is Later Than You Think* (New York, 1943 ed.), p. 247.

6. *The Decline of the West*, II, 342.

7. *Ibid.*, II, chaps. x–xiv.

8. See the citations and discussion in chap. viii below.

9. See, for example, his *Revolt Against Civilization* (New York, 1922), pp. 226 and 229.

10. For Ludovici and More, see the references and discussion in chap. viii below; for Babbitt, see chap. ix. For these and other variations in the definition of the best, see Coker, *Recent Political Thought*, pp. 341–45, and C. E. Merriam, *Systematic Politics* (Chicago, 1945), pp. 188–93.

11. *The Ruling Class*, p. 450.

12. *Ibid.*, p. 333.

13. *The Revolt of the Masses*, p. 127.

14. Salvador de Madariaga, *Anarchy or Hierarchy* (London, 1937), pp. 169–70.

15. This is ably noted by even so extreme a critic of democracy as Lawrence Dennis. See his *Dynamics of War and Revolution*, p. 8.

16. Cf. Hobhouse, *Democracy and Reaction*, chap. iv, and R. E. Coker, "What Are the Fittest?" *Scientific Monthly*, LV (1942), 487–94, LVI (1943), 62–70.

17. Cf. Elton Mayo, *Democracy and Freedom* (Melbourne, 1919), p. 45, and MacIver, *Community*, pp. 392–416.

18. See R. G. Tugwell, *The Industrial Discipline and the Governmental Arts* (New York, 1933), p. 109, and Mosca, *op. cit.*, pp. 406–7.

CHAPTER 6

1. William McDougall, *Is America Safe for Democracy?* (New York, 1921), p. v.

2. Cf. Gunnar Myrdal, *An American Dilemma* (9th ed., New York, 1944), pp. 87–89, 582–83, 597–98. To these considerations should be added the insecurity, fear, and illiteracy that breed prejudice and aggression against minority groups. See John Gunther, *Inside U. S. A.* (New York, 1947), pp. 659, 664–66.

3. *The Inequality of Human Races* (trans. Collins, New York, 1914).

4. *The Foundations of the Nineteenth Century* (trans. Lees, New York, 1910), I, 259–71.

5. *Ibid.*, I, lxvi–lxvii, 324, 577.

6. See F. H. Hankins, "Race as a Factor in Political Theory," in *A History of Political Theories, Recent Times* (ed. Merriam and Barnes, New York, 1924), pp. 508–48, and C. C. Tansill, "Racial Theories in Germany from Herder to Hitler," *Thought*, XV (1940), 453–68.

7. Fitzhugh's *Sociology for the South* (Richmond, 1854) is perhaps the best known of the Southern statements, but hardly less interesting are such works as A. T. Bledsoe, *An Essay on Liberty and Slavery* (Philadelphia, 1856) and F. A. Ross, *Slavery Ordained of God* (Philadelphia, 1859).

8. *Our Country* (New York, 1885), especially p. 174 and chap. xiii.

9. J. W. Burgess, *Political Science and Comparative Constitutional Law* (Boston, 1890), I, 44–45.

10. See his *Reason in Society*, Vol. II of *The Life of Reason* (2d ed., New York, 1936), pp. 165 ff.

11. Note especially his *History of the United States* (New York, 1898 ed.), III, 1058, a page deleted from the later 1910 edition.

12. In LaMonte and Mencken, *op. cit.*, p. 116.

13. As in his *Nemesis of Mediocrity*, pp. 35–37.

14. *Memoirs of a Superfluous Man, passim.*

15. *The Invisible Government*, p. 41.

16. Irving Babbitt, *Democracy and Leadership* (Boston, 1924), p. 210, and Lothrop Stoddard, *The Rising Tide of Color Against White World-Supremacy* (New York, 1920).

17. *Ibid.*, p. 162, and see the discussion of bi-racialism in Stoddard's *Re-Forging America* (New York, 1927), pp. 319–21.

18. *The Passing of the Great Race* (4th ed., New York, 1921) and *The Conquest of a Continent* (rev. ed., New York, 1934).

19. See his prefaces to Grant, *The Passing of the Great Race;* also his crude and vulgar paper on Americanism in *The Alien in Our Midst* (ed. Grant and Davison, New York, 1930), pp. 204–9, and his introduction to Grant, *The Conquest of a Continent.*

20. *The Passing of the Great Race*, pp. 12, 5.

21. *Ibid.*, p. 26.

22. *Ibid.*, pp. xxviii-xxix, 12; introduction to Stoddard, *The Rising Tide of Color*, p. 142.

23. *The Passing of the Great Race*, pp. 197, 19–20, 24–30, 67, 240–42, 228–29; also *The Conquest of a Continent*, pp. 41, 21–22.

24. *The Passing of the Great Race*, pp. 18, xxix, 222, 52–53, 10.

25. Introduction to Stoddard, *The Rising Tide of Color*, pp. xxix-xxxii.

26. See Otto Klineberg, "A Study of Psychological Differences between 'Racial' and National Groups in Europe," *Archives of Psychology*, No. 132 (1931), pp. 8–12, and the same author's *Race Differences* (New York, 1935), pp. 190–91. The interpreter who repudiated his earlier findings as "pretentious" and "without foundation" was C. C. Brigham.

27. Klineberg, "A Study of Psychological Differences between 'Racial' and National Groups in Europe," p. 27.

28. *Ibid.*, pp. 28–29.

29. *Ibid.*, pp. 29–31.

30. *The Foundations of the Nineteenth Century*, I, 540; and see further chap. vi.

31. A. J. Toynbee, *A Study of History* (abr. Somervell, New York, 1947), p. 54. Note, however, the sense in which Toynbee's delineation of "civilization" must be qualified. See Morris Watnick, "Toynbee's Nine Books of History against the Pagans," *Antioch Review*, VII (1947), 589 ff.

32. Cf. Morris Ginsberg, *Sociology* (London, 1934), pp. 74, 88–90.

33. See J. S. Huxley and A. C. Haddon, *We Europeans* (New York, 1936), pp. 72, 226–28.

34. *Politics*, Bk. VII, chap. vii, p. 213. Italics mine.

35. See Ruth Benedict, *Race: Science and Politics* (rev. ed., New York, 1943), pp. 18–19, 127–33; also Klineberg, *Social Psychology*, pp. 292–97.

36. "Closing the Flood-Gates," in Grant and Davison, *op. cit.*, p. 14. See also Grant's *Conquest of a Continent*, p. 349.

37. Aleš Hrdlička, *The Old Americans* (Baltimore, 1925), p. 8 and *passim*.

38. See Jacques Barzun, *Race: A Study in Modern Superstition* (New York, 1937), pp. 162–63.

39. *Contemporary Sociological Theories*, pp. 268–73.

40. Cf. F. H. Hankins, *The Racial Basis of Civilization* (New York, 1926), pp. 189–90, and Sorokin, *op. cit.*, pp. 273–77.

41. *An American Dilemma*, p. 137.

42. *The Passing of the Great Race*, p. 24.

43. *Ibid.*, p. 162.

44. Franz Boas, *The Genetic Basis for Democracy* (New York, 1939), pp. 8–9.

45. Cf. Otto Klineberg, S. E. Asch, and Helen Block, "An Experimental Study of Constitutional Types," *Genetic Psychology Monographs*, XVI, No. 3 (September, 1934), pp. 139–221.

46. Boas, *Aryans and non-Aryans* (New York, 1934), p. 3.

47. *Ibid.*, p. 8.
48. See Klineberg, *Race Differences*, pp. 29–32; Benedict, *Race: Science and Politics*, pp. 54–55; and Huxley and Haddon, *op. cit.*, p. 226.
49. As does Grant, *The Conquest of a Continent*, pp. 9–11. For the invalidity of this view, see Boas, *The Mind of Primitive Man* (New York, 1911), pp. 124–39, and his *Aryans and non-Aryans*.
50. See this confusion in Stoddard, *Clashing Tides of Colour* (New York, 1935), p. 18, and *Re-Forging America*, pp. 255–56. For a criticism see Boas, *Race and Democratic Society* (New York, 1945), pp. 105–12, and MacIver, *Community*, pp. 274–77.
51. E. A. Hooton, *Why Men Behave like Apes and Vice Versa* (Princeton, 1940), p. 184n, reports that Grant classified him as a Nordic despite his cephalic index of eighty-five, brown hair, mixed eyes, and muddy complexion, on the ground that he was of British ancestry!
52. Cf. Klineberg, *Social Psychology*, pp. 303–6, and the same author's "Study of Psychological Differences between 'Racial' and National Groups in Europe," *passim*.
53. Cf. Bentley, *op. cit.*, p. 256.
54. The circular form of the argument is effectively noted in Boas, *The Mind of Primitive Man*, pp. 2–5.
55. *The Myth of the Negro Past* (New York, 1941), pp. 296–97; and see further his *Economic Life of Primitive Peoples* (New York, 1940).
56. See, for example, *The Mind of Primitive Man*, pp. 7–8.
57. See his *Conquest of a Continent*, p. 351.
58. Cf. Benedict, *Race: Science and Politics*, p. 134, and Boas, *The Mind of Primitive Man*, pp. 9, 29.
59. *Ibid.*, pp. 6–7 and chap. vi; Fay-Cooper Cole, "Primitive Societies," in Clark Wissler *et al, Making Mankind* (New York, 1929), pp. 41–69; and Klineberg, *Race Differences*, pp. 255 ff.

The absurd extravagances to which racial theorists will go to establish that race determines culture may be illustrated by the following extract from a Nazi periodical of learning: "The superiority of Nordic races is reflected in race differences among chickens. The Nordic chick is better behaved and more efficient in feeding than the Mediterranean chick, and less apt to over-eat by suggestion. These differences parallel certain typological differences among humans. The Nordic is an inwardly integrated type, the Mediterranean is an outwardly integrated type. The poultry yard confutes the liberal-bolshevik claim that race differences are really cultural differences, because race differences between chicks cannot be accounted for by culture." Quoted in MacIver, *The Web of Government*, p. 469 note 252.

60. *The Conquest of a Continent*, p. 353.
61. *An American Dilemma*, p. 97.
62. See T. R. Garth, *Race Psychology* (New York, 1931), pp. 56–85.
63. See Myrdal, *op. cit.*, p. 97.
64. Klineberg, "An Experimental Study of Speed and other Factors in

'Racial' Differences," *Archives of Psychology,* No. 93 (1928), p. 107 and *passim.*

65. *Negro Intelligence and Selective Migration* (New York, 1935), pp. 59–60 and *passim.*

66. See, for example, Benedict, *Race: Science and Politics,* pp. 120–21, and Boas, *Aryans and non-Aryans,* p. 4.

67. See chap. vii, sec. III, C, below.

68. See Barbara Schieffelin and G. C. Schwesinger, *Mental Tests and Heredity* (New York, 1931), pp. 36–42, and G. C. Schwesinger, *Heredity and Environment* (New York, 1933), pp. 41–42.

69. *An American Dilemma, passim; Inside U. S. A.,* pp. 283–86, 780–83, 869–75, 891–95, and chap. xli; Benjamin Fine, *Our Children Are Cheated* (New York, 1947); Report of the President's Committee on Civil Rights, *To Secure These Rights* (Washington, 1947); and the Report of the President's Commission on Higher Education, *Higher Education for American Democracy* (Washington, 1947), especially Vol. II.

70. Cram, *The Nemesis of Mediocrity,* p. 39.

71. *The Conquest of a Continent,* pp. 269–70.

72. Francis Galton, *Hereditary Genius* (London, 1869), pp. 369, 343; McDougall, *op. cit., passim;* and Sorokin, *op. cit.,* p. 297.

73. *The Negro and the Intelligence Tests,* p. 13 and *passim;* see also the same author's *The American Negro,* pp. 59–66, and Myrdal, *op. cit.,* pp. 695–700.

74. "An Experimental Study of Speed and other Factors in 'Racial' Differences," pp. 70, 107; and see also his *Race Differences,* pp. 211–22.

75. *Race and Civilization* (trans. Levetus and Entz, London, 1928), pp. 129–55. See also Cohen, *The Meaning of Human History,* p. 181.

76. *The Study of Man* (New York, 1945), p. 34.

77. *Anthropology and Modern Life,* p. 86.

78. Cf. Benedict, *Race: Science and Politics,* p. 45.

79. Cf. MacIver, *Community,* pp. 274–75.

80. An effective case could be made against Grant's doctrine on the basis of his own arguments alone, for seldom has there been a book so marred by inconsistencies and contradictions.

Consider, for example, his admission that the Alpines "represented a very great advance in culture," that they not merely "made very large contributions to the civilizations of the world" but were, even more, "the medium through which many advances in culture were introduced from Asia into Europe." (*The Passing of the Great Race,* pp. 138, 146.) And compare with this his dismissal of the Alpines as being "always and everywhere a race of peasants." (*Ibid.,* p. 227.)

Consider too his insistence on Nordic superiority in cultural achievement in the light of his conclusions that the Mediterranean race "is the race that gave the world the great civilizations" of ancient times, that "to it belongs the chief credit of the classic civilization of Europe in the sciences, art, poetry, literature, and philosophy, as well as the major part of the civilization of Greece and a very large share in the Empire of Rome." (*Ibid.*, pp. 153, 165.) Then, bearing in mind Grant's contention that "moral, intellectual and spiritual attributes are as persistent as physical characters and are transmitted substantially unchanged from generation to generation" (*Ibid.*, p. 226), compare further his claim of Nordic intellectual superiority with his statement that the Mediterranean race, "while inferior in bodily stamina to both the Nordic and the Alpine, is probably the superior of both, certainly of the Alpines, in intellectual attainments." (*Ibid.*, p. 299.) Compare, again, his inclusion of Dante, Raphael, Titian, Michelangelo, and Leonardo da Vinci as Nordics with his remark concerning the Mediterraneans that "in the field of art its superiority to both the other Europeans is unquestioned, although in literature and in scientific research and discovery the Nordics far excel it." (*Ibid.*, pp. 215, 229.)

These are but a few of the innumerable contradictions in Grant, yet they may serve to indicate the "logical" and "scientific" nature of his argument.
81. Boas, *Race and Democratic Society*, p. 29.

CHAPTER 7

1. *Theognis Restitus* (Malta, 1842), Verse X, p. 26.
2. Thomas Campanella, *The City of the Sun,* in *Famous Utopias* (New York, Tudor ed.), pp. 291–92. For this type of thought antecedent to Galton, see S. J. Holmes, *Human Genetics and Its Social Import* (New York, 1936), pp. 359–62.
3. *Hereditary Genius,* p. 1.
4. *Inquiries into Human Faculty and Its Development* (London, 1883), pp. 177–78, 181–82.
5. *Hereditary Genius* and *English Men of Science* (London, 1874).
6. *Inquiries into Human Faculty,* pp. 216–41.
7. *Essays in Eugenics* (London, 1909), pp. 11, 24; *Hereditary Genius,* pp. 324–25.
8. *Nature and Nurture* (London, 1910), p. 27.
9. Cf. *The Scope and Importance to the State of the Science of National Eugenics* (2d ed., London, 1909), pp. 33 and 38, and *National Life from the Standpoint of Science* (London, 1901), pp. 29–31.
10. F. A. Woods, *Mental and Moral Heredity in Royalty* (New York, 1906), p. 283.
11. E. M. East, *Heredity and Human Affairs* (New York, 1927), pp. 179, 300–301.
12. Alleyne Ireland, "Democracy and the Accepted Facts of Heredity," *Journal of Heredity,* IX (1918), 339–42.
13. Ireland's position was supported by Madison Grant, "Discussion of Article on Democracy and Heredity," *ibid.,* X (1919), 164–65, and P. F. Hall, "Aristocracy and Politics," *ibid.,* pp. 166–68. The attack on Ireland's thesis was led by E. G. Conklin, "Heredity and Democracy," *ibid.,* p. 161–64, and O. F. Cook and R. C. Cook, "Biology and Government," *ibid.,* pp. 250–

53. Ireland's answer to his critics is contained in his article, "Democracy and Heredity—a Reply," *ibid.*, pp. 360–67. The substance of Ireland's articles was later reproduced in his *Democracy and the Human Equation* (New York, 1921), pp. 119–44.

14. *Applied Eugenics* (New York, 1920), pp. 361, 364.

15. Sait, *Political Institutions: A Preface* (New York, 1938), pp. 445, 437. It is instructive to note that Sait lists among the possessors of this authentic new voice no less a group of spokesmen than Mussolini, Hilaire Belloc, Faguet, Babbitt, and Cram! *Ibid.*, pp. 445–49. And see Lennes, *Whither Democracy?* (New York, 1927).

16. Sait, *op. cit.*, pp. 454–56. There is little need to examine this Spenglerian thesis here. It is sufficient to note that what evidence actually exists on the subject points to the reverse conclusion. See Schwesinger, *Heredity and Environment*, pp. 280–82, 463; MacIver, *Society*, pp. 114–39; and Cohen, *The Meaning of Human History*, pp. 231–35.

17. Sait, *op. cit.*, p. 444. Sait, indeed, regards women as lower than the lowest estate of men, and invokes both the authority of Plato and the words of S. J. Holmes to prove that their exercise of the franchise deteriorates the race and "marks the period of democratic disintegration." No less curious is Sait's argument that "the State rests ultimately on force; and the enfranchisement of women builds a shaky superstructure on the foundation"—this because men and not women are the actual possessors of physical force! *Ibid.*, p. 457 note 2.

Now of all Sait's hypotheses, this postulate of inherent male superiority has the least possible merit to sustain it. If by superiority Sait implies physical force alone, he would have to prove not only that force is the ultimate basis of the state but also that the physical force contained in the individual is the decisive force. If he were to admit the importance of force outside ourselves, as in the weapons and instruments of war and other forms of destruction, the problem would become that of the ability to create and command these tools, in a word, that of intellectual rather than physical superiority. And here, to cite only the evidence of the intelligence tests (on which Sait places so much reliance), there is "no dependable difference in the level of intellectual performance of the two sexes, and it is now customary among psychologists to assume that there is no sex difference in this respect." Klineberg, *Social Psychology*, p. 278.

18. *Political Institutions*, p. 456.

19. *Ibid.*, p. 439.

20. Ireland, *Democracy and the Human Equation*, p. 142.

21. Sait, *op. cit.*, pp. 441–42.

22. The usual citations are the studies of eminent men and families by Galton, Woods, Winship, and Cattell, as compared with the studies of degenerate families such as the Jukes and the Kallikaks by Dugdale, Estabrook, and Goddard. See F. H. Hankins, *An Introduction to the Study of Society* (New York, 1928), pp. 245–47, 256–57; Schwesinger, *op. cit.*, p. 171; and Klineberg, *Social Psychology*, p. 232.

23. L. F. Ward, *Applied Sociology* (Boston, 1906), chap. vii.

24. *The Process of Government*, pp. 108–9; and cf. Hook, *The Hero in History*, chap. iii.

25. *Social Psychology*, p. 232.

26. Cf. MacIver, *Society*, p. 78.

27. See C. B. Davenport, *Heredity in Relation to Eugenics* (New York, 1911), pp. 225–28, and Clarence Darrow, "The Edwardses and the Jukeses," *The American Mercury*, VI (1925), 147 ff. On this and the following illustrations in the text, see Coker, *Recent Political Thought*, pp. 319, 361–62, and the references cited therein.

28. Raymond Pearl, "The Biology of Superiority," *The American Mercury*, XII (1927), 263; Sir John Bowring, *Translations from Alexander Petöfi* (London, 1866), p. 1.

29. See Popenoe and Johnson, *op. cit.*, pp. 333–34.

30. *Encyclopaedia Britannica* (Chicago, 1941), XIX, 611, and III, 317.

31. See the paper by W. F. Giese in *Irving Babbitt: Man and Teacher* (ed. Manchester and Shepard, New York, 1941), p. 24.

32. Pearl, "The Biology of Superiority," pp. 264–65.

33. Schwesinger, *op. cit.*, p. 172.

34. *Mental and Moral Heredity in Royalty*, p. 10.

35. See Schwesinger, *op. cit.*, pp. 175–231, and Klineberg, *Social Psychology*, pp. 233–39.

36. Cf. Schwesinger, *op. cit.*, p. 461.

37. *Social Psychology*, pp. 238–39.

38. "Democracy and Heredity—a Reply," p. 363.

39. Schwesinger, *op. cit.*, chaps. ii and v.

40. Cf. Teggart, *op. cit.*, pp. 139–40, and Raymond Pearl, "Biology and Human Trends," *Journal of the Washington Academy of Sciences*, XXV (1935), pp. 258–59.

41. *The Economics of Welfare*, pp. 98–99.

42. See Lennes, *op. cit.*, pp. 40–45, 173–77.

43. Schwesinger, *op. cit.*, pp. 58–59.

44. *Studies in Sociology* (London, 1932), pp. 162–70; see also pp. 198–99.

45. Quoted in George Catlin, *The Story of the Political Philosophers* (New York, 1939), p. 507.

46. See Myrdal, *op. cit.*, chap. xxxi.

47. H. S. Jennings, *The Biological Basis of Human Nature* (New York, 1930), p. 221. See also *ibid.*, pp. 184–85, 211–13, 220, and Pearl, "The Biology of Superiority," p. 266.

48. MacIver, *Society*, p. 78.

49. Schwesinger, *op. cit.*, pp. 55 and 463. In fact, Schwesinger adds, "a person may differ fifteen or twenty points *from his own I.Q.* under conditions of special advantage or incentive." *Ibid.*, p. 224.

50. Cf. Ginsberg, *Studies in Sociology*, p. 196, and Schwesinger, *op. cit.*, p. 338.

51. Cf. Klineberg, *Social Psychology*, pp. 239–41.

52. No less than sixteen definitions, as well as a variety of generalizations and theories, are listed in Schieffelin and Schwesinger, *op. cit.*, pp. 10–16.
53. *Anthropology and Modern Life*, p. 51.
54. Alexander Goldenweiser, *History, Psychology, and Culture* (New York, 1933), p. 392.
55. *Why Men Behave Like Apes and Vice Versa*, p. 107n.
56. *Social Psychology*, p. 252.
57. *Heredity and Environment*, p. 11.
58. *Ibid.*, pp. 70, 41–42, 277–99.
59. *Introduction to the Study of Society*, pp. 255–56.
60. *Studies in Sociology*, p. 196.
61. See Klineberg, *Social Psychology*, pp. 241–45.
62. *Ibid.*, pp. 252, 247.
63. *Community*, p. 385.
64. MacIver, *Society*, p. 84.
65. *Heredity and Environment*, p. 163.
66. *Ibid.*
67. "Democracy and Heredity—a Reply," p. 365, and *Democracy and the Human Equation*, p. 229.
68. Cf. Conklin, "Heredity and Democracy," p. 163; Ginsberg, *Studies in Sociology*, p. 188; and Klineberg, *Social Psychology*, p. 250.
69. In these terms McDougall's appendix of a picture of his five children to prove he is doing his part becomes patently absurd.
70. Hooton, *Apes, Men, and Morons* (New York, 1937), p. 232, and *Twilight of Man* (New York, 1939), p. 282; R. A. Freeman, *Social Decay and Regeneration* (London, 1921), pp. 309–45.
71. *The Revolt against Civilization*, p. 239. See also the survey in Holmes, *Human Genetics and its Social Import*, pp. 359–85.
72. Cf. Boas, *Anthropology and Modern Life*, pp. 102-19.
73. *Social Psychology*, pp. 230–31.
74. See his *Revolt against Civilization*.

CHAPTER 8

1. The quotations are from the *Republic*, Bk. IV, 423; Bk. II, 374; and Bk. VIII, 555–62.
2. *The Commonwealth of Oceana* (London, 1887 ed.), Part I, pp. 29–30.
3. *Reflections on the Revolution in France*, p. 46.
4. *Reflections on Violence*, p. 5.
5. *Politics*, II, 273.
6. The quotations are from Shakespeare's *Troilus and Cressida*, Act I, sc. iii. See also *Coriolanus*, Act III, sc. i, where the common people, the "curs," are dismissed as "the mutable, rank-scented many." But for a contrary view see *Measure for Measure*, Act II, sc. ii.
Shakespeare's political sympathies have been explored in numerous studies, the evidences of which leave little doubt but that the aristocratic

rather than the democratic element is dominant. For an extreme view of Shakespeare as aristocrat, see Ernest Crosby, *Shakespeare's Attitude Toward the Working Classes* (Syracuse, 1903 [?]). A more temperate study is that of J. A. R. Marriott, "Shakespeare and Politics," *Cornhill Magazine*, New Series LXIII (1927), 678–90. The evidences for both views are considered in C. W. Stearns, *The Shakespeare Treasury of Wisdom and Knowledge* (London, 1869), chap. viii, and A. H. Tolman, "Is Shakespeare Aristocratic?" *Publications of the Modern Language Association of America*, New Series XXII (1914), 277–98.

7. See his *Social Equality* (London, 1882), chap. i, and *Aristocracy and Evolution* (New York, 1898); also *The Limits of Pure Democracy* (4th ed., London, 1918) and *Classes and Masses* (London, 1896).

8. *Aristocracy and Evolution*, pp. 118, 348, 151; *Social Equality*, pp. 4, 100.

9. *A Defence of Aristocracy* (London, 1915), pp. viii-ix.

10. *Ibid.*, pp. 3–5, 15, 241–53. See further Ludovici's *The False Assumptions of "Democracy"* (London, 1921), chaps. iii, iv, and ix.

11. *The Works of John Adams*, IV, 290 and 579. The argument for degree is treated in C. M. Walsh, *The Political Science of John Adams* (New York, 1915), chap. vi.

12. Cf. *ibid.*, chap. xxi, especially pp. 305–10.

13. *The Degradation of the Democratic Dogma* (New York, 1919), pp. 84–86, 108–9, 121.

14. *Democracy and Leadership;* and see below, chap. ix, note 18.

15. More's aristocratic thought is most clearly delineated in his *Shelburne Essays:* VIII, *The Drift of Romanticism* (Boston, 1913); IX, *Aristocracy and Justice;* and in lesser vein XI, *A New England Group and Others* (Boston, 1921).

16. *The Menace of the Herd* (Milwaukee, 1943), especially the introductory chapter and Part I.

17. See particularly his *Freedom Under God* (Milwaukee, 1940) and *Liberty, Equality and Fraternity* (New York, 1938). Of special interest also are his *Philosophies at War* (New York, 1943), *A Declaration of Dependence* (Milwaukee, 1941), and *Old Errors and New Labels* (New York, 1931).

18. For example, his *Platonism* (3d ed., Princeton, 1931), *The Catholic Faith* (Princeton, 1931), and *On Being Human* (Princeton, 1936). For this later deviation of More from the non-theological humanism of Babbitt, see L. J. A. Mercier, *The Challenge of Humanism* (New York, 1933), chap. vii, and Robert Shafer, *Paul Elmer More and American Criticism* (New Haven, 1935), chap. iv.

19. See his *Selected Essays, 1917–1932* (New York, 1932), pp. 383–402, and *Essays Ancient and Modern* (London, 1936), pp. 113–35.

20. *On Being Human*, pp. 154–55.

21. *Aristocracy and Justice*, pp. 215, 120, 122, 7, 31; *A New England Group and Others*, p. 251. See, for More's treatment of dualism, the final chapter in his *Drift of Romanticism*.

22. *Ibid.*, p. 283; *Aristocracy and Justice,* chap. i.

23. *Freedom Under God,* pp. 20, 23, 27, 184 ff.; *A Declaration of Dependence,* p. 127.

24. *Philosophies at War,* pp. 146–47, 58 ff.

25. *Old Errors and New Labels,* pp. 95–116.

26. It is significant to note that Sheen presents himself generally not as a critic but as a defender of democracy, as one who holds to the democratic virtues in opposition to communism, his *bête noir.* But when he departs from his critique of communism and speaks of democracy in a positive vein, highly unorthodox doctrines begin to emerge. We learn that free speech in a democracy is not the right to dissent, but "the right to rational dissent" (*Freedom Under God,* p. 191); that while democracy relies upon freedom, freedom is inseparable from responsibility, which in turn is inseparable from conscience, which itself is inseparable from religion—all of which brings democracy to a concept of freedom as defined by the Church (*Liberty, Equality and Fraternity,* p. 135; also *Freedom Under God,* pp. 181–82); that while democracy is based on a political and economic relative, it is based equally on a theological absolute—"it is intolerant about the foundations of democracy" (*Philosophies at War,* p. 169); and so on.

27. *A Declaration of Dependence,* p. 131; *Freedom Under God,* pp. 216–24; *Liberty, Equality and Fraternity,* chap. iv.

28. *Freedom Under God,* pp. 160, 163.

That there are strands of doctrine in Catholic political theory which lend themselves easily—though by no means necessarily—to employment in the categories of anti-democratic thought becomes apparent when we bear in mind that Catholic philosophy's primary concern is with the purpose rather than with the source of political power. Broadly speaking, the argument is that all forms of government are good and just—whether monarchic, aristocratic or democratic—provided they are directed for the common good; and this, of course, is a matter to be determined not by the people but by the Church. The divisions among Catholic thinkers then follow from differences in such judgments, the controversy being which form is best calculated to produce the best and greatest good.

The extreme form of the conservative Catholic position—so tragically illustrated, for example, by the role of the dominant part of the clergy in the recent history of Spain—has been well stated by Macaulay: "I am in the right, and you are in the wrong. When you are the stronger, you ought to tolerate me, for it is your duty to tolerate truth. But when I am the stronger, I shall persecute you, for it is my duty to persecute error." Quoted in Inge, *Labels and Libels,* p. 5; and see the analysis in Dorothy Fosdick, *What Is Liberty?* (New York, 1939), pp. 109–20.

But for a Catholic argument along democratic (sometimes peculiarly democratic) lines, see the long series of articles (broken off in 1944 and at this date of writing—1948—still unfinished) by M. J. Adler and Walter Farrell, "The Theory of Democracy," *The Thomist,* III (1941), 397–449, 588–652; IV (1942), 121–81, 286–354, 446–522, 692–761; VI (1943), 49–

118, 251–77, 367–407; and VII (1944), 80–131; where the thesis is advanced that other forms of government (i.e., monarchy and aristocracy) may be good and just "if it gives a man the status he deserves and safeguards all the rights and privileges attached thereto" (*ibid.*, VI, 382), but that democracy is best. A less esoteric but at times seriously confused liberal approach is that by Wilfrid Parsons, *Which Way, Democracy?* (New York, 1939) and J. A. Ryan and F. J. Boland, *Catholic Principles of Politics* (New York, 1940), especially chap. vii. Note in connection with this latter work the argument in Niebuhr, *op. cit.*, pp. 126–28.

29. G. W. Howgate, *George Santayana* (Philadelphia, 1938), p. 288.
30. *Essays Ancient and Modern*, pp. 122, 118, 134; *Selected Essays*, p. 387.
31. Aspects of Santayana's anti-democratic thought will be found in nearly all of his many books, even, for example, in such non-political works as *The Sense of Beauty* (New York, 1896), pp. 110–12. The main items, however, are *Reason in Society* (Vol. II of his great achievement, *The Life of Reason*), chaps. iii, iv, and v; *Soliloquies in England and Later Soliloquies* (London, 1922), chaps. xl–xliii; and *Dialogues in Limbo* (New York, 1926), chaps. vi and vii. The two published volumes of his autobiography, *Persons and Places* (New York, 1944) and *The Middle Span* (New York, 1945), give a vivid sense of his aristocratic leanings, as do also the short autobiographical sketches reproduced as "A General Confession," in *The Philosophy of George Santayana* (ed. Schilpp, Evanston, Ill., 1940), pp. 3–30.
32. Bertrand Russell, "The Philosophy of Santayana," in Schilpp, *op. cit.*, p. 455.
33. See his "Apologia Pro Mente Sua," in Schilpp, *op. cit.*, pp. 554–60, and the remark quoted in V. M. Ames, *Proust and Santayana* (Chicago, 1937), p. 72.
34. See his *Persons and Places*, p. 159.
35. *Dialogues in Limbo*, p. 109.
36. *The Sense of Beauty*, p. 112; *Persons and Places*, p. 16; *Dialogues in Limbo*, p. 93; *Winds of Doctrine* (New York, 1913), p. 5.
37. See the concluding statement in M. R. Cohen's chapter on political thought in America, in his forthcoming volume, *American Thought*.
38. *Dialogues in Limbo*, p. 99.
39. *Reason in Society*, pp. 121, 90.
40. *Ibid.*, pp. 83, 78.
41. *Ibid.*, pp. 122, 112, 103, and chap. iv.
42. *Ibid.*, p. 123; *Soliloquies in England and Later Soliloquies*, p. 186.
43. *Reason in Society*, pp. 128–29.
44. *Soliloquies in England and Later Soliloquies*, pp. 166–69.
45. *Dialogues in Limbo*, p. 105; *Reason in Society*, p. 173; *Persons and Places*, pp. 238–39. But see on this last point his *Character and Opinion in the United States* (Norton ed., New York, 1934), chap. vii.
46. *Reason in Society*, chaps. iv and v; *Dialogues in Limbo*, chap. vii.
47. *Reason in Society*, p. 94. In this particular quotation Santayana is primarily stating the theistic rather than his own view, but though not a theist

Santayana's position here is so similar that the quotation fairly expresses his own outlook. See *ibid.*, pp. 112–13.

48. *Ibid.*

49. *Character and Opinion in the United States*, pp. 45–46, 186–87.

50. Cf. *Dialogues in Limbo*, p. 93; and note his stated unfitness "to live under a free government where other people voted as to what I should do." *The Middle Span*, p. 116.

51. *Platonism and the Spiritual Life* (New York, 1927), p. 14; *Dialogues in Limbo*, pp. 101, 106, 115–16. But see his repudiation of absolutism in *The Genteel Tradition at Bay* (New York, 1931), pp. 73–74.

52. *Reason in Society*, p. 136.

53. *Ibid.*, p. 133.

54. In Schilpp, *op. cit.*, p. 557.

55. Toynbee profusely illustrates this point in developing his distinction between a "creative minority" and a "dominant minority." He holds that throughout history the former (which rules by example) has tended to degenerate into the latter (which rules by coercion). See his *Study of History*, pp. 246, 309 ff., 366, 405, 533. But see for a necessary qualification Watnick, *op. cit.*, pp. 597–600.

56. See MacIver, *The Political Roots of Totalitarianism*, (James-Patten-Rowe Pamphlet Series No. 9, 1940), p. 7, and the same writer's *The Web of Government*, pp. 51–58, 415–20.

57. *Ibid.*, p. 415.

58. *Dialogues in Limbo*, p. 133.

59. Cf. Eliseo Vivas, "From *The Life of Reason* to *The Last Puritan*," in Schilpp, *op. cit.*, pp. 329 ff.

60. MacIver, *Community*, pp. 301–2.

61. Cf. H. J. Laski, *A Grammar of Politics* (London, 1925), pp. 290–91.

62. Fosdick, *op. cit.*, p. 119.

63. *Ibid.*, p. 120.

64. Cf. *ibid.*

65. Cf. M. R. Cohen, *Reason and Nature* (New York, 1931), and Dewey, *The Quest for Certainty* (New York, 1929), pp. 210–11.

66. T. N. Carver, *Essays in Social Justice* (Cambridge, 1915), p. vi.

67. Cf. MacIver, *The Web of Government*, pp. 416–19.

68. Cf. C. L. Becker, *Modern Democracy* (New Haven, 1941), pp. 24–27.

69. See MacIver, *Community*, p. 302, and *The Modern State*, pp. 159–60; also Lippincott, *Victorian Critics of Democracy*, p. 53.

70. Cf. Corey, *The Unfinished Task*, pp. 68–69; MacIver, *Community*, p. 327; Mannheim, *Diagnosis of Our Time*, pp. 33, 126; and R. B. Perry, *Puritanism and Democracy* (New York, 1944), pp. 48–50.

CHAPTER 9

1. *Troilus and Cressida*, Act I, sc. iii.

2. It ought perhaps to be observed that there might be a legitimate place

for this position in states where there has been no preparation for genuine national unity or consensus, as in certain Latin American countries, especially in earlier stages of their development. But this is a condition of political backwardness, not of inherent necessity.

3. R. A. Humphreys, *The Evolution of Modern Latin America* (New York, 1946), p. 76 and chap. iv. See also MacIver, *The Web of Government*, pp. 226–28, 233–43, and C. H. Haring, *South American Progress* (Cambridge, 1934).

4. Quoted in Aurel Kolnai, *The War Against the West* (London, 1938), p. 129.

5. Quoted in Melvin Rader, *No Compromise* (New York, 1939), p. 192.

6. Quoted in *ibid.*

7. Quoted in Kolnai, *op. cit.*, p. 29.

8. The literature on the *Führerprinzip* is so voluminous as to defy all but the barest citation. A good note will be found in the unexpurgated Reynal and Hitchcock edition of Hitler's *Mein Kampf* (New York, 1941), I, 116–18, and there are Hitler's own remarks on the subject scattered throughout. For the history of the doctrine, see M. M. Bell, "The Leadership Principle in National Socialism," *Journal of the History of Ideas*, III (1942), 74–93. Kolnai, *op. cit.*, pp. 149–59, treats the mystery of the leader principle, and is invaluable as a bibliographical guide. For Alfred Rosenberg's mystical but highly illuminating work, *The Myth of the Twentieth Century*, see A. R. Chandler, *Rosenberg's Nazi Myth* (Ithaca, N. Y., 1945). For the nature of charismatic authority see *From Max Weber* (ed. Gerth and Mills, New York, 1946), pp. 79–80 and chap. ix, and Weber's *Theory of Social and Economic Organization* (ed. Parsons, New York, 1947), pp. 358–73, 386–92; also Michels, "Some Reflections on the Sociological Character of Political Parties," pp. 753–72. For a broad treatment, Konrad Heiden's two books, *Der Fuehrer* (trans. Manheim, Boston, 1944) and *A History of National Socialism* (Eng. trans. New York, 1935) are indispensable.

9. The quotation from Spengler is from *The Decline of the West*, II, 369. For the class theory see Delbrück, *op. cit.*, pp. 31–32, and MacIver, *The Web of Government*, pp. 116–25, 216–18.

10. See the opening chapters in E. J. Hughes, *Report from Spain* (New York, 1947).

11. *Hegel's Philosophy of Right*, p. 6.

12. Hegel, *Lectures on the Philosophy of History* (trans. Sibree, London, 1881), p. 41.

13. *Ibid.*

14. *Hegel's Philosophy of Right*, secs. 257–58, pp. 155–56.

15. V. L. Parrington, *Main Currents in American Thought* (New York, 1927–30), I, 20.

16. Quoted in *ibid.*, p. 31.

17. *Ibid.*, p. 21.

18. Babbitt's *Democracy and Leadership* is, of course, his central political work, but his antagonism to democracy is given indiscriminate expression

in all his writings. See, for example, the argument against democracy for its alleged denial of distinctions and rank in his first published book, *Literature and the American College* (Boston, 1908), pp. 72–87, and the denunciation of "the cult of the common man" in his posthumous work, *Spanish Character and Other Essays* (ed. Manchester, Giese, and Giese, Boston, 1940), pp. 170–82, and 57–65. The attack on Rousseau, his particular *bête noir* and symbol of democracy, runs like an incessant stream throughout all his utterances—e.g., *The New Laokoon* (Boston, 1910), chap. v, and *The Masters of Modern French Criticism* (Boston, 1912), *passim*, especially chap. xi—but is most vigorously pressed in his *Rousseau and Romanticism* (Boston, 1919). A short and adequate statement of his humanist philosophy is offered in the introduction to his *On Being Creative and Other Essays* (Boston, 1932). For his immersion in Buddhism, see particularly his translation of *The Dhammapada* (New York, 1936) and the essay on Buddha therein.

A sympathetic treatment of Babbitt's humanist thought will be found in Mercier, *The Challenge of Humanism*, chaps. ii and iii. More critical evaluations are F. E. McMahon, *The Humanism of Irving Babbitt* (Washington, 1931), though the restricted approach of the author renders this work of limited value, and Folke Leander, *Humanism and Naturalism* (Göteborg, 1937). Highly critical assessments will be found in the *Critique of Humanism* (ed. Grattan, New York, 1930), and Walter Lippmann, "Humanism as Dogma," *Saturday Review of Literature*, VI (1930), 817–19. For some illuminating portraits of Babbitt, see *Irving Babbitt: Man and Teacher* (ed. Manchester and Shepard).

19. See Babbitt, "Humanism: An Essay at Definition," in *Humanism and America* (ed. Foerster, New York, 1930), p. 39; also More, *On Being Human*, pp. 16–18, 36–38. For the full extent of Babbitt's belief in the supernatural, see the comment by W. F. Giese (in Manchester and Shepard, *op. cit.*, p. 8) that Babbitt "would talk in the most matter-of-fact manner of having seen tables, nay, even pianos, float in the air, and used to laugh away my doubts of Madame Blavatsky's power of levitating herself piano-fashion into space."

20. *Democracy and Leadership*, p. 252.
21. *The New Laokoon*, p. 190.
22. *Democracy and Leadership*, pp. 24–26, 97, 84.
23. *Rousseau and Romanticism*, p. 16; *Democracy and Leadership*, pp. 254, 17, 225.
24. *The Dhammapada*, p. 26.
25. *Democracy and Leadership*, p. 108.
26. *Ibid.*, p. 238; *Spanish Character and Other Essays*, p. 174.
27. *Democracy and Leadership*, pp. 205, 127; *Literature and the American College*, p. 8.
28. *Democracy and Leadership*, p. 243.
29. *Ibid.*, pp. 43, 16.
30. *Ibid.*, p. 246.
31. *Ibid.*, pp. 308, 110, 96, 246–50.

32. *Rousseau and Romanticism,* p. 399; *Literature and the American College,* p. 22.

33. *Democracy and Leadership,* p. 261.

34. *Ibid.,* pp. 278, 259–60.

35. *Literature and the American College,* p. 105; "Humanism: An Essay at Definition," in Foerster, *Humanism and America,* p. 40.

36. *Democracy and Leadership,* pp. 304, 246–47.

37. *Ibid.,* pp. 273, 307.

38. *Ibid.,* pp. 136–37, 221–23, 207.

39. *Ibid.,* pp. 294, 298, 306, 201–2, 293.

40. *Ibid.,* pp. 295–96, 61; *Spanish Character and Other Essays,* pp. 58, 64–65.

41. *Puritanism and Democracy,* p. 628.

42. But see Randolph Bourne, *History of a Literary Radical* (ed. Brooks, New York, 1920), pp. 176–87, who interprets the Puritan's denial of joy as itself a joy.

43. Cf. MacIver, *The Web of Government,* pp. 84–85, and the same author's *Leviathan and the People,* p. 166; also Hobson, *Democracy and a Changing Civilisation,* p. 77.

44. *Literature and the American College,* p. 184; italics mine.

45. For the totalitarian element in Rousseau's thought, see his *Social Contract,* Bk. I, chaps. vi-viii, Bk. II, chaps. i-iii, and Bk. IV, chap. viii; also the introduction by G. D. H. Cole to the Everyman edition, pp. xxix ff. See further E. H. Wright, *The Meaning of Rousseau* (London, 1929), chap. iii, especially pp. 94 ff., and MacIver, *The Web of Government,* pp. 405–9.

46. Quoted in Perry, *op. cit.,* p. 251.

47. See his *Democracy and Leadership,* p. 299.

48. *Ibid.,* pp. 264, 152, 209, 312, 206.

49. *Literature and the American College,* p. 167; and see further *Democracy and Leadership,* pp. 16, 265, 281, and *Rousseau and Romanticism,* pp. 378–79, 389.

50. *Democracy and Leadership,* p. 310.

51. Cf. Gerth and Mills, *From Max Weber,* pp. 246–47, and P. F. Drucker, *The End of Economic Man* (New York, 1939), pp. 231–32.

52. Cf. Santayana, *Egotism in German Philosophy* (2d ed., London, 1939), p. 7.

53. *Representative Government,* chap. vi, p. 252–53.

54. See, for example, *Democracy and Leadership,* pp. 207 ff.

55. Cohen, *Reason and Nature,* p. 386.

56. *The Theory of the State* (Eng. trans., 3d ed., Oxford, 1895), Bk. I, chap. i, p. 23.

57. For a survey of such organismic doctrines, see F. W. Coker, *Organismic Theories of the State* (New York, 1910) and Sorokin, *op. cit.,* pp. 196–206.

58. Cf. MacIver, *The Modern State,* pp. 448–53, and *Community,* pp. 28–38, 72–88, 207–16, 421–29; also Cohen, *Reason and Nature,* pp. 386 ff.

59. R. E. Desvernine, *Democratic Despotism* (New York, 1936), p. 44.

60. For the contradictions in the Court see E. S. Corwin, *Court Over Con-*

stitution (Princeton, 1938) and *The Twilight of the Supreme Court* (New Haven, 1934); also Conyers Read (ed.), *The Constitution Reconsidered*, Part II, and C. P. Curtis, *Lions Under the Throne* (Boston, 1947). For an analysis of the way in which the Court has re-written a particular constitutional provision, see R. L. Mott, *Due Process of Law* (Indianapolis, 1926). For a philosophical analysis see B. N. Cardozo, *The Nature of the Judicial Process* (New Haven, 1921) and M. R. Cohen, *Law and the Social Order* (New York, 1933), especially Parts II and III. For a broad historical treatment see A. C. McLaughlin, *A Constitutional History of the United States* (New York, 1936).

61. *Essays Ancient and Modern*, p. 85.

62. As Babbitt argues in his *Democracy and Leadership*, pp. 68 and 226, and his article in Foerster, *Humanism and America*, p. 27.

63. Leander, *op. cit.*, p. 222.

64. Norman Foerster, *Toward Standards* (New York, 1930), pp. 157–59, 166–67.

65. Cf. Hudson, *op. cit.*, pp. 132–34; Lippincott, *Victorian Critics of Democracy*, pp. 48–50 and 198; and MacIver, *The Web of Government*, pp. 72–81 and *The Modern State*, pp. 212–13, 340–41. See also the suggestive experiments of Ronald Lippitt, particularly "An Experimental Study of the Effect of Democratic and Authoritarian Group Atmospheres," *Studies in Topological and Vector Psychology*, I (1940), 43–195, and Pigors, *op. cit.*, chaps. iv and viii.

66. *Democracy and Leadership*, p. 299.

67. Cf. Lippincott, *Victorian Critics of Democracy*, p. 90.

68. Benedetto Croce, "The Future of Democracy," *New Republic*, LXXXX (1937), p. 255.

69. *Studies in the Problem of Sovereignty* (New Haven, 1917), p. 25.

70. The quotation is from Corey, *The Unfinished Task*, p. 88.

71. MacIver, *The Modern State*, p. 219.

72. See F. E. Johnson (ed.), *Foundations of Democracy* (New York, 1947), p. 202.

73. Cf. MacIver, *Leviathan and the People*, pp. 19, 165–66, and *The Web of Government*, pp. 198–205; Lippincott, *Victorian Critics of Democracy*, p. 264, and Niebuhr, *op. cit.*, pp. 46–47.